New York City For Dummies®, 2nd Edition

Cheat Sheet

Manhattan Subways

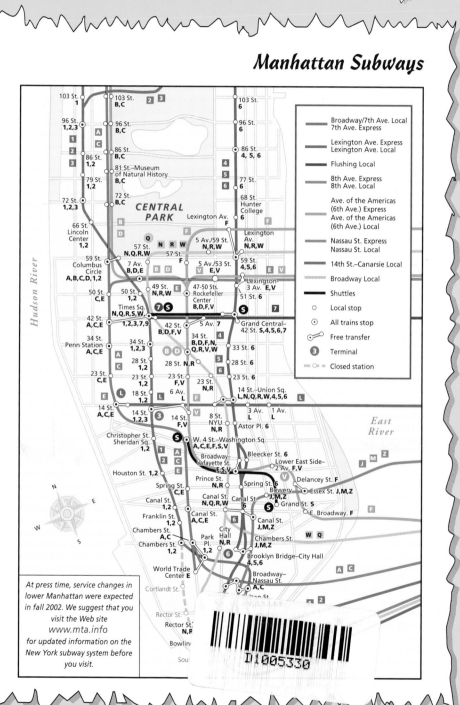

Legend:

- Broadway/7th Ave. Local / 7th Ave. Express
- Lexington Ave. Express / Lexington Ave. Local
- Flushing Local
- 8th Ave. Express / 8th Ave. Local
- Ave. of the Americas (6th Ave.) Express / Ave. of the Americas (6th Ave.) Local
- Nassau St. Express / Nassau St. Local
- 14th St.–Canarsie Local
- Broadway Local
- Shuttles
- ○ Local stop
- ⊙ All trains stop
- Free transfer
- Terminal
- Closed station

At press time, service changes in lower Manhattan were expected in fall 2002. We suggest that you visit the Web site *www.mta.info* for updated information on the New York subway system before you visit.

D1005330

New York City For Dummies, 2nd Edition

Cheat Sheet

Subway Stops for New York's Top Attractions

ATTRACTION	SUBWAY STOP
MUSEUMS	
American Museum of Natural History	**B C** to 81st St.–Museum of Natural History
The Cloisters	**A** to 190th St.
Ellis Island	**4 5** to Bowling Green or **N R** to Whitehall St.-South Ferry (for ferry)
Guggenheim Museum	**4 5 6** to 86th St.
Intrepid Sea-Air-Space Museum	**A C E** to 42nd St.–Port Authority
Metropolitan Museum of Art	**4 5 6** to 86th St.
Museum of Modern Art QNS	**E V** to 23rd St./Ely Ave. in Queens or **7** to 33rd St. in Queens
South Street Seaport and Museum	**1 2 4 5 A C J M Z** to Fulton St.–Broadway/Nassau St.
PARKS	
Central Park	**1 2 A C B D** to 59th St.–Columbus Circle or **N R W** to Fifth Ave./59th St.
HISTORIC BUILDINGS & ARCHITECTURE	
Brooklyn Bridge	**4 5 6** to Brooklyn Bridge–City Hall
Chrysler Building	**4 5 6 7 S** to Grand Central–42nd St.
Empire State Building	**B D F V N R Q W** to 34th St./Herald Sq.
Grand Central Terminal	**4 5 6 7 S** to Grand Central–42nd St.
Guggenheim Museum	**4 5 6** to 86th St.
Rockefeller Center	**B D F V** to 47-50th Sts.–Rockefeller Ctr.
Statue of Liberty	**4 5** to Bowling Green or **N R** to Whitehall St.–South Ferry (for ferry)
United Nations	**4 5 6 7 S** to Grand Central–42nd St.
NEIGHBORHOODS	
Chinatown	**6 J M Z N R Q W** to Canal St.
Greenwich Village	**A C E F V S** to West 4th St.
Times Square	**1 2 3 7 N R Q W S** to 42nd St.–Times Square
Wall Street	**4 5** to Wall St. or **N R** to Rector St.
CHURCHES	
Cathedral of St. John the Divine	**1** to Cathedral Parkway (110th St.)
St. Patrick's Cathedral	**B D F V** to 47-50th Sts.–Rockefeller Ctr. or **E V** to Fifth Ave./53rd St.

Copyright © 2002 Wiley Publishing, Inc.
All rights reserved.
Item 5451-4.
For more information about Wiley Publishing, call 1-800-762-2974.

For Dummies: Bestselling Book Series for Beginners

X-MAS 2002

New York City
FOR
DUMMIES®
2ND EDITION

by Bruce Murphy and Alessandra de Rosa

Daddy ~♡   12/2002

I know that someday you want to go to New York so heres a little something to help you get started. (There are maps inside)!!

I ♡ u,

Sara

Ⓦ

Wiley Publishing, Inc.

& Bisquito

New York City For Dummies® **2nd Edition**

Published by
Wiley Publishing, Inc.
909 Third Avenue
New York, NY 10022
www.wiley.com

About the Authors

Bruce Murphy was born in New York City, where he now works as a freelance writer. **Alessandra de Rosa** is a world traveler and professional tourist who has worked for the United Nations. Together they have been traveling and collaborating for several years. Among their other books is *Italy For Dummies,* also published by Wiley.

Dedication

This book is dedicated to all those who died in the terrorist attacks on the World Trade Center — workers, visitors, and rescuers — as well as to those who lost someone dear to them in the disaster and are struggling to go on. The courage of all New Yorkers is the true spirit of the city, and what makes New York City a unique place on Earth. Manhattan is and remains a wonderful place to visit thanks to the millions of New Yorkers who make it alive with energy, hope, and enthusiasm — and thanks also to the millions who don't live in Manhattan.

Authors' Acknowledgments

Many people have played a part in the creation of this book. We would like to thank all those who contributed to the first and second editions: Kathy Iwasaki, who started us on this path by helping along the publication of our previous New York guide; Mike Spring, whose idea it was in the first place; Suzanne Jannetta, who gave us support and shepherded *New York City For Dummies,* 1st Edition, along its circuitous path to publication; our editors of the first edition, Claudia Kirschhoch, Alexis Lipsitz, and the editor of the current edition, Kelly Regan. Last but not least, we would like to give special thanks to all the other members of the staff who have helped to bring the project to fruition.

Most of all, we would like to thank the dozens of friends and hundreds of strangers who contributed ideas and inspirations to this book, whether they knew it or not — the New Yorkers whose creativity, humor, and enterprise make the city an almost absurdly varied and constantly surprising place.

Publisher's Acknowledgments

We're proud of this book; please send us your comments through our Online Registration Form located at www.dummies.com.

Some of the people who helped bring this book to market include the following:

Editorial

Development Editor: Kelly Regan

Project Editor: Pam Mourouzis

Cartographers: Roberta Stockwell, Nicholas Trotter

Editorial Supervisor: Michelle Hacker

Editorial Assistant: Stephen Bassman

Senior Photo Editor: Richard Fox

Cover Photos: Front Cover: Bob Handelman/Tony Stone Images; Back Cover: Harald Sund/Image Bank

Production

Project Coordinator: Regina Snyder

Layout and Graphics: Carrie Foster, Joyce Haughey, Heather Pope

Proofreaders: Laura Albert, TECHBOOKS Production Services

Indexer: TECHBOOKS Production Services

Publishing and Editorial for Consumer Dummies

Diane Graves Steele, Vice President and Publisher, Consumer Dummies

Joyce Pepple, Acquisitions Director, Consumer Dummies

Kristin A. Cocks, Product Development Director, Consumer Dummies

Michael Spring, Vice President and Publisher, Travel

Brice Gosnell, Publishing Director, Travel

Suzanne Jannetta, Editorial Director, Travel

Publishing for Technology Dummies

Andy Cummings, Vice President and Publisher

Composition Services

Gerry Fahey, Vice President of Production Services

Debbie Stailey, Director of Composition Services

Contents at a Glance

Cartoons at a Glance

By Rich Tennant

"Hey! Stop that running and put that cigarette out! This is the Statue of Liberty. You can't run around here doing anything you want."

page 177

"Unfortunately, on me, Giorgio Armani clothes take on a certain Lou Costello quality."

page 279

"Ooo—look at this—we've got a perfect view of the Chrysler Building, the Buick Building, and the Chevy Building."

page 93

"The closest hotel room I could get you to Times Square for that amount of money is in Cleveland."

page 7

"You know, getting us to the front door of the Empire State Building would have been quite sufficient, driver."

page 37

"...and for our entree special, we're offering New York's famous foot-long Veal Oscar."

page 125

"It's a play in 2 Acts. The middle Act is about to start now."

page 251

Cartoon Information:
Fax: 978-546-7747
E-Mail: richtennant@the5thwave.com
World Wide Web: www.the5thwave.com

Maps at a Glance

Table of Contents

Introduction

● ●

*N*ew York is back: The city that never sleeps couldn't lie low for long. On the surface, everything has returned to normal, although the scars of September 11, 2001, are slow to heal, as they are for all Americans. Within two hours of those horrific terrorist attacks, the Twin Towers of the World Trade Center had collapsed, leaving a gaping wound in Lower Manhattan and in the heart of the city. But in the hours and days following the tragedy, New Yorkers pulled together. Thousands of volunteers offered their services to the rescue efforts, and many, many more donated supplies, blood, and money to aid the victims and their families. The city suffered a devastating blow, but the recovery has been swift and the healing process is ongoing. The area of the destruction, now referred to as Ground Zero, has become not an attraction, but a destination of pilgrimage.

Life goes on, and New York is as interesting as ever. In today's New York, you find the usual merry-go-round of artistic and cultural events, commercial ferment, music, lights, entertainment, and business. If some people have left the city and the economy perhaps isn't booming, the many who stayed — and have come since — continue to create the energy that's unique to New York. All in all, the city is now at its best as far as tourists are concerned. Things are happening, but prices are lower and crowds are a little smaller — a combination that should add to your experience.

About This Book

This book is designed to help you take a bite out of the Big Apple without getting the worm. Maybe this is your first trip to New York, or maybe you're a repeat visitor; in either case, we assume that you want to find out what you need to know, but *only* what you need to know. You probably don't have the time or the patience for those monstrous travel tomes in which you need 11 or 12 fingers to keep track of all the information about a single topic, books in which the salient details are buried under pages of filler. Neither do we.

This book is a guidebook and also a reference book. You can read it cover to cover, or you can jump in anywhere to find the information you want about a specific task, such as finding a hotel or working out your budget. Whether you're sitting in your living room trying to make a reservation or standing on the corner of 42nd Street and Fifth Avenue wondering where to eat, *New York City For Dummies,* 2nd Edition, is set up so that you can get the facts, analysis, and recommendations you want, quickly.

Please be advised that travel information is subject to change at any time — this is especially true of prices. We therefore suggest that you write or call ahead to confirm prices and details when making your travel plans. The authors, editors, and publisher cannot be held responsible for readers' experiences while traveling. Your safety is important to us, however, so we encourage you to stay alert and be aware of your surroundings. Keep a close eye on cameras, purses, and wallets, all favorite targets of thieves and pickpockets.

Conventions Used in This Book

The structure of this book is nonlinear: You can dig in anywhere to get information about a specific issue. We list hotels and restaurants alphabetically with prices and frank evaluations. In addition, we use some abbreviations to let you know which credit cards an establishment accepts:

- **AE:** American Express
- **CB:** Carte Blanche
- **DC:** Diners Club
- **DISC:** Discover
- **JCB:** Japan Credit Bank
- **MC:** MasterCard
- **V:** Visa

Because hotels do fill up, we decided to add a short list of "runner-up" hotels that still get our hearty seal of approval. Don't be shy about considering these accommodations if you're unable to get a room at one of our favorites or if your preferences differ from ours — the amenities and services that the runners-up offer make them excellent choices to consider as you determine where to rest your head at night.

We also include some general pricing information to help you as you decide where to stay or dine. We use a system of dollar signs to show a range of costs for one night in a hotel or a meal at a restaurant (including appetizer, entree, dessert, one drink, taxes, and tip — per person). The following table tells you how to decipher the dollar signs:

Cost	*Hotel*	*Restaurant*
$	$85–$150	Less than $25
$$	$150–$225	$25–$35
$$$	$225–$325	$35–$45
$$$$	$325–$425	$45–$60
$$$$$	$425 and up	$60 and up

Foolish Assumptions

As we wrote this book, we made some assumptions about you and what your needs as a traveler might be. Here's what we assumed about you:

- ✔ You may be an inexperienced traveler looking for guidance in determining whether to take a trip to New York and how to plan for it.

- ✔ You may be an experienced traveler, but you don't have a lot of time to devote to trip planning, or you don't have a lot of time to spend in New York City once you get here. You want expert advice on how to make the most of your time and enjoy a hassle-free trip.

- ✔ You're not looking for a book that provides *all* the information available about New York or that lists *every* hotel, restaurant, or attraction. Instead, you're looking for a book that focuses on the places that will give you the best or most unique New York experiences.

If you fit any of these criteria, then *New York City For Dummies,* 2nd Edition, will give you the information you're looking for!

How This Book Is Organized

This book is divided into seven parts covering the major aspects of your trip. Each part is further broken down into specific components so that you can go right to the subtopic you want (you don't have to read all about nightlife if you're just looking for a jazz club, for example). Following are brief summaries of the parts.

Part 1: Getting Started

In this part, we give you the big picture — New York in a nutshell. Then we address the major questions you have to answer right off the bat: when to go, how to get there, and how much it's all going to cost.

Part II: Ironing Out the Details

This part takes you from the general to the particular: how to make your travel arrangements, whether through an agent, on the Web, or on your own; whether to take an escorted or a guided tour; how to choose the neighborhood where you'd like to stay and a hotel within that neighborhood, and how to make your booking; and last-minute details like what to pack for a stay in New York.

Part III: Settling into New York

This part is all about getting around, from the moment your plane lands or you step off the train or land your balloon. We cover ground transportation into the city, the public transit system, and sites to see on foot. We also discuss that other element of getting along: money, and where to get it.

Part IV: Dining in New York

This part is about dining, but in the broadest sense. We give you a feeling for the culinary culture of New York, its typical foods and food habits. We include reviews of restaurants and indexes by location and price, and we describe places to grab a quick bite, breakfast, cup of coffee, ice cream, or treat.

Part V: Exploring New York

This part describes what to see and do, from touring famous buildings to attending a taping of a TV show. To help you fit in all that you want to see without getting worn out, we provide some sample itineraries to help you organize your time in the city.

Part VI: Living It Up after the Sun Goes Down: New York Nightlife

This part covers New York's major arts attractions, from Broadway shows to clubs, and gives you an idea of what each activity costs and how to get discount tickets. We also include a chapter on nightclubs, places to have a drink, and other more or less civilized forms of relaxation.

Part VII: The Part of Tens

The Part of Tens gives you the top tens of New York and answers your burning questions. It also serves as a handy reference and trouble-shooting section.

You'll find two other elements near the back of this book as well. We include an appendix — your Quick Concierge — containing lots of handy information that you may need when traveling in New York, like phone numbers and addresses of emergency personnel, area hospitals, and pharmacies; contact information for baby-sitters; lists of local newspapers and magazines; and the protocol for finding taxis. Check out this appendix when you're searching for answers to little questions that may come up as you travel.

We also include worksheets to make your travel planning easier. Among other things, you can determine your travel budget, create specific itineraries, and keep a log of your favorite restaurants so that you can visit them again the next time you're in town. You can find these worksheets easily because they're printed on yellow paper.

Icons Used in This Book

Keep your eyes peeled for icons, which appear in the margins throughout the book. These little pictures serve as a kind of shorthand or code to alert you to special information. Here's the decryption key:

Find useful advice on things to do and ways to schedule your time where you see the Tip icon.

The Heads Up icon identifies annoying or potentially dangerous situations to beware, such as tourist traps, unsafe neighborhoods, and budget-spoiling rip-offs.

Look to the Kid Friendly icon for attractions, hotels, restaurants, and activities that are particularly hospitable to children or people traveling with kids.

Keep an eye out for the Bargain Alert icon if you seek money-saving tips and great deals.

A great hotel, restaurant, or attraction may require a bit of effort to locate or get to. When we let you in on one of these finds, we mark it with the Worth the Search icon — and rest assured, we won't include any spots that aren't worth the energy. We also use this icon to highlight resources that are particularly useful and worth the time to seek out.

Where to Go from Here

Guess what? New York doesn't have to be a rat race. It doesn't have to be overwhelming. It doesn't even have to be frighteningly costly. You can do pretty much what you want here — that's what makes it so exciting. By reading this book, paying attention to the details, and getting your ducks (and your bucks) in a row beforehand, you can set yourself up for a top-notch vacation.

Part I
Getting Started

The 5th Wave
By Rich Tennant

"The closest hotel room I could get
you to Times Square for that amount
of money is in Cleveland."

In this part . . .

*I*n this part, we guide you through the important steps of preparing for your trip to New York. Whatever you like to call it — The Big Apple, The City That Never Sleeps — New York is a real handful, for better or worse. The best way to maximize your fun is to know before you go and plan ahead.

Chapter 1 gives you the highlights of the long list of things to see and do in New York — the attractions not to miss and the best activities. Chapter 2 helps you decide when to go based on weather considerations and the scheduling of special events. In Chapter 3, you can find budgeting advice. Chapter 4 covers special needs — advice for families with kids, gay travelers, and travelers with disabilities, for example.

Chapter 1

Discovering the Best of New York

In This Chapter

▶ The most eye-catching edifices

▶ The most intriguing cuisines

▶ The most exciting things to see and do

▶ The best shopping

*N*ew York has always been about traffic — traffic in money, in ideas, in trends, in commerce (and in the streets, of course). Visiting New York gives you a chance to participate in this long and rich history. Every group that has visited New York has brought something here and left its mark; even if all you leave behind is your vacation money, you're playing a part in keeping the merry-go-round spinning (and enjoying a pleasant ride yourself).

Of course, the terrorist attacks of September 11, 2001, continue to resonate with local residents and visitors alike. Life bustles along as before (the only difference being a more obvious security presence) despite a sense of loss as profound and far-reaching as the Twin Towers themselves.

In this chapter, we give you a sampling of the sights, sounds, and flavors that draw people to New York. Think of this chapter as an appetizer or a teaser — something else is always coming along, whether it's a new museum or a different way to cook a potato.

To help you understand the layout of this vast city, we include on the next few pages a series of maps. The maps — which we call "Downtown Orientation," "Midtown Orientation," and "Uptown Orientation" — show you the important streets, neighborhoods, and sights in those three main areas of town. As you read the rest of this chapter and the rest of this book, feel free to refer to these maps and really get to know New York.

Downtown Orientation

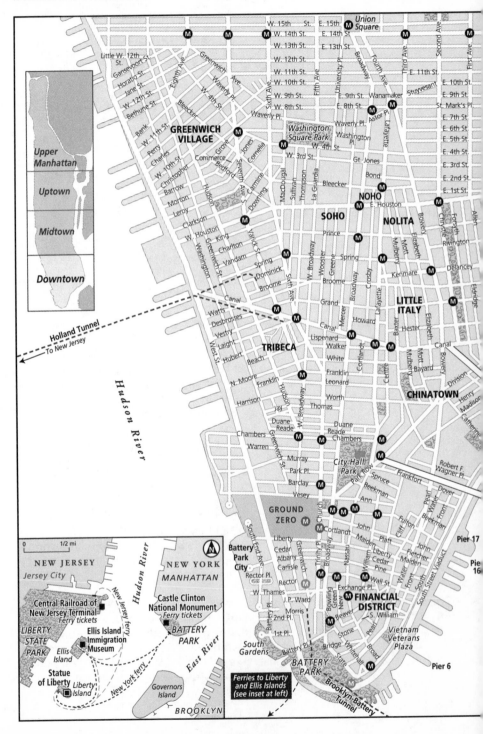

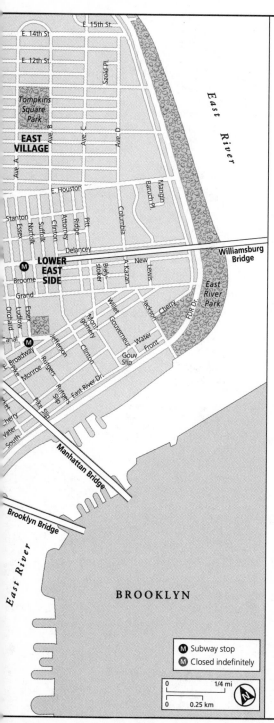

GREENWICH VILLAGE
This quintessential bohemian neighborhood is one of the city's prettiest walking areas, with vintage small-scale architecture and cozy little cafes and jazz clubs. Stroll the newly refurbished park along the Hudson River.

NOHO
A relative newcomer, tiny NoHo (the name stands for *No*rth of *Ho*uston Street) embodies old and new; here families and singles have converted old manufacturing businesses into homes, state-of-the-art restaurants, and a mini cluster of furniture stores.

EAST VILLAGE
The neighborhood's ornery, anarchic soul is wearing a glossy fresh patina, as cool new restaurants and bars open almost daily.

NOLITA
This neighborhood (the name is an acronym for *No*rth of *Li*ttle *Ita*ly) boasts the architecture of Little Italy and an artsy bohemian vibe that recalls the SoHo of old—affordable restaurants and relaxed cafes abound, as do small boutiques by up-and-coming designers.

SOHO
The epicenter of New York hip and Euro transplantation, SoHo ("*So*uth of *Ho*uston") offers the ultimate in Manhattan shopping, dining, and people-watching. This trendy, pricey area has a fabulous collection of historic cast-iron buildings.

LOWER EAST SIDE
Long a bastion of Manhattan's Jewish community, the sprawling Lower East Side still has a sprinkling of kosher delis and Jewish businesses. It also has a hipster scene around Stanton and Rivington streets, as well as a famous discount shopping district around Orchard Street.

TRIBECA
With its expansive streets, Hudson River breezes, and wealth of fine restaurants, TriBeCa has perhaps become the most desirable neighborhood in New York to live. It's certainly one of the priciest: giant, airy loft spaces carved out of old manufacturing buildings command mega-million prices.

LITTLE ITALY
If you're looking for a big plate of old-fashioned spaghetti and meatballs, this is the neighborhood. It's one Italian restaurant after another, many with outdoor tables under umbrellas, red checkered cloth linens, and waiters urging you to step inside.

CHINATOWN
Twisting little streets lead past Chinese herb shops, tea shops, and food stands selling live seafood, exotic vegetables, and dumplings. But most of all, Chinatown is Chinese restaurants and exciting new eateries selling specialties from Vietnam, Thailand, Malaysia, and Korea.

FINANCIAL DISTRICT
The canyonlike corridors of Wall Street are impressive indeed, even to the businessmen and women who toil in the shadow of the Stock Exchange. Narrow streets are lined with skyscrapers standing shoulder to shoulder, some structures dating to the 1920s.

Midtown Orientation

MIDTOWN EAST
This tony neighborhood of luxury apartment houses holds many of the big department stores, including Saks Fifth Avenue, Bloomingdale's, and Bergdorf-Goodman. Here, too, is St. Patrick's Cathedral, the Art Deco splendor of Rockefeller Center, the United Nations, and the gloriously refurbished Grand Central Station.

MIDTOWN WEST
This largely residential area holds some of the best eating in New York: the stretch along 9th Avenue from 57th Street to 34th Street has a wealth of ethnic restaurants, seafood retailers, and spice shops. It's also home to the glass-and-steel Javits Convention Center.

TIMES SQUARE/THEATER DISTRICT
Only 10 years ago, Times Square had as many seedy businesses as it had theaters. Today, the district has been spiffed up, the seedy element sent on its way, and restaurants and businesses given a no-holds-barred green light to be as big and brassy as they please. The result is eye-popping, to say the least.

MURRAY HILL
Quiet side streets are lined with shined-to-the-nines brownstones with flower-filled window boxes. This little neighborhood has been one of the city's smartest addresses for years. It's the kind of place where you can't turn a corner without seeing another charming café or restaurant.

GRAMERCY PARK
Perhaps the prettiest little park in the city is surrounded by perhaps the handsomest residential architecture, some structures dating back to the 1800s. It's a jewel of a neighborhood, home of the National Arts Club, which holds forth in a dandy 19th-century salon. Exclusive, yes–the only people who hold a key to the gated park are neighborhood residents–but fascinating nonetheless.

FLATIRON DISTRICT & UNION SQUARE
This neighborhood has become one of New York's hot spots in just a few short years. Its emblem is the historic Flatiron Building, a singular work of architecture that comes to a point on 23rd Street. Side streets are filled with trendy restaurants and clubs.

CHELSEA
Chelsea has been reborn of late. Holding some of the prettiest streets in New York, with sun-dappled brownstones and lacy ironwork, Chelsea is now the arts center of the city. Art galleries and cool restaurants are the name of the game, and the city's gay population continues to make this neighborhood its center.

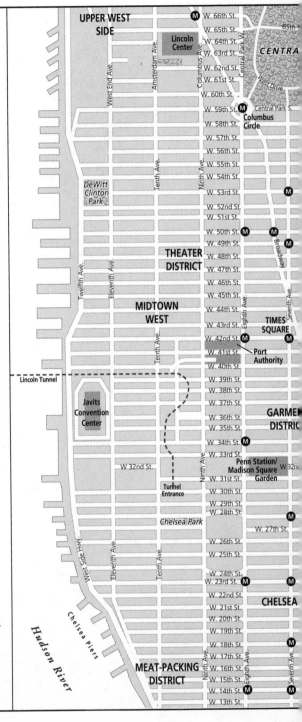

Uptown Orientation

CENTRAL PARK

Uptown Manhattan is bisected by Central Park, a mammoth swath of green some four blocks wide. For many active New Yorkers, the park is a salvation, an 843-acre oasis of recreational pursuits. Wollman Rink, on the park's southeast edge, hosts ice skating in the winter and various entertainments in the summer. The Central Park Zoo is a miniature gem, where polar bears, seals, and penguins play year-round. Just north is the Sheep Meadow, where sheep indeed once grazed; the large green with the stunning city skyline views is now a haven for sunbathers and frisbee throwers. The Loeb Boathouse and Café face the Lake, filled with ducks and turtles. The Great Lawn, recently reseeded, abuts the Metropolitan Museum of Art, whose Roof Garden opens up in the warm seasons with a splendid treetop view. Just north is the Reservoir, a favorite among joggers, and the Central Park Tennis Center. A flower garden lies at the park's northernmost edge.

THE UPPER WEST SIDE

This largely residential neighborhood attracts families with its imposing prewar apartment houses, charming brownstones along side streets, and proximity to two world-class parks (Central Park and Riverside Park). Streets are big and wide. Speaking of big, check out St. John the Divine Cathedral, the largest cathedral in the world. Even the fossils are huge at the American Museum of Natural History, which enraptures kids and adults alike (don't miss the revamped planetarium). It's also a neighborhood of thespians, drawn by the opera, ballet, and theater at Lincoln Center.

THE UPPER EAST SIDE

The traditional home of Manhattan's upper crust and some of the most exclusive shops in the world, the Upper East Side has some substantial attractions. Museum Mile, along Fifth Avenue, is a sparkling necklace of museums, from the Frick to the Metropolitan to the Guggenheim. A good number of hospitals and research institutions are here too, as are some of the city's most elegant hotels. Peer through the gates at homey Gracie Mansion and you might get a glimpse of the mayor (although "Mayor Mike" Bloomberg chose not to live there, he uses the mansion for social engagements). And don't worry, you won't go hungry: the neighborhood holds one of the city's thickest concentrations of restaurants and cafes.

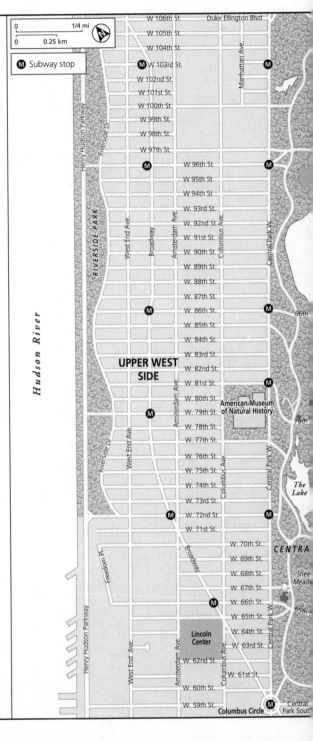

A Feast for the Senses

Manhattan is a city to enjoy in the streets. The city offers a global assortment of people, outrageous outfits and personalities, street musicians, sidewalk artists, and hipsters. This abundant street life makes New York a great city for walking. Don't shortchange yourself on these pedestrian pleasures. (But to really enjoy yourself, you must bring comfortable shoes!)

Classic New York experiences include crossing the **Brooklyn Bridge** at sunset, walking through **Central Park** on a summer day, making your way — slowly — up **Fifth Avenue** with the Christmas crowds, and inline skating or walking along the **Hudson River** on the new riverfront promenade.

Because of its unique internationalism, New York has an incredible depth and breadth when it comes to cuisine. How many places do you know that can easily support a Belgian cuisine craze or an Indian food renaissance? A city with somewhere around 10,000 restaurants is not likely to be exhausted of possibilities in one, or even many, visits. Whether you're having exquisite continental fare at **Chanterelle** or stopping for takeout *takoyaki* (chopped octopus-filled balls) in **Little Tokyo** on East 9th Street, you take home with you great memories from the frontiers of taste. Visiting New York is a perfect chance to try Ethiopian, Tibetan, Turkish, Senegalese, or other cuisines you may not find at home. Italian is still the reigning ethnic cuisine, outnumbering all the others; and, of course, pizza is ubiquitous and available in many diverse styles.

Broadway and Times Square: The Great White Way

For many visitors, seeing a Broadway show is the quintessential New York experience. Although the long-running musical *Cats* has closed, having finally used up all nine of its lives, *The Lion King* is still roaring, *Rent* is still being collected, and there will be no shortage of future blockbusters.

The area where most shows are located, along **Broadway** and **Times Square,** is more squeaky clean than ever. The porn shops and peep shows have been swept away, the theaters gutted and renovated. Disney's presence has helped make Times Square as nonthreatening as a theme park — and about as crowded. You won't find the romantic-criminal charm that Damon Runyon immortalized in his stories (the basis for the musical *Guys and Dolls*); that charm has long since disappeared, unless you count the slippery pickpockets who continue to operate on the city's crowded streets. Stay alert!

Off-Broadway and **off-off-Broadway** continue to produce experimental, challenging, and exciting shows. New York is in no danger of losing its primacy in American theater.

Cultural Revolutions

New York's cultural offerings have no end. We devote a number of chapters in this book to helping you find out what's going on and getting tickets to events that interest you.

If you enjoy art, New York's museums (the **Metropolitan Museum of Art,** the **Museum of Modern Art,** and the **Guggenheim,** to name the big three) rank among the best in the world. Beyond theater, you have opera; beyond opera, ballet; beyond these, you find modern dance, performance art, poetry readings, and various new forms of exhibitionism. The premier institutions in these fields are in New York. Take music, for example: New York is the home of **Carnegie Hall, Lincoln Center,** famous jazz clubs like **Blue Note** and **Birdland,** worldrenowned rock music clubs like **CBGB,** and newer clubs where the next phenomenon may be discovered.

Don't forget film, either. The Big Apple is seriously challenging Hollywood as the seat of the film and TV industry. Some 60 to 90 new productions are filmed in New York every day! In recent years, a couple hundred feature films or more have been filmed in the city each year, not to mention countless documentaries and smaller independent films. That number will surely rise in the near future, when the new, huge sound stage complex of the **New York Studios** at the Brooklyn Navy Yard is completed. In addition to movie-making, New York is also the center of important film festivals, and you can catch films you may not see in other cities at art houses and on plenty of screens.

Shopping 'til You Drop

From high-fashion houses to designer sample sales, New York is the place for clothing, whether from known fashion superdesigners or from ambitious recent graduates of the Fashion Institute of Technology. Shopping can encompass visits to a few of the most famous department stores in the world, such as **Bloomingdale's** and **Macy's,** and some of the most high-end, such as **Bergdorf Goodman.** You can get everything in New York, from homemade goods to high-end imported Italian shoes and Persian carpets.

New York also has a thriving discount electronics business, huge CD and record stores, gigantic bookstores, a diamond district . . . the list goes on. At various times, the city has had entire stores devoted to fossils or maps. If you want it, believe us — it's here.

Chapter 2

Deciding When to Go

- -

In This Chapter

▶ Choosing the best time to go

▶ Flipping through a calendar of events

- -

*B*ecause New York offers such a wide variety of attractions and
sights, people visit the city year-round, regardless of the weather.
In addition to giving you the lowdown on New York life during each of
the four seasons, this chapter includes a calendar of events in case
you'd like to plan your visit around a particular activity.

Unlocking the Secrets of the Seasons

To catch New York at its best and brightest, consider visiting during
the fall or the spring. In the spring (April to June), temperatures are
usually mild and pleasant; in the fall (September to early November),
the sun almost always shines through crisp, chilly days. In mid-
October, the city sometimes experiences an unseasonably mild spell
known as Indian summer.

The word is out on the pleasures of New York in the fall and spring, so
if you travel during these peak times, be prepared to book in advance
for everything — hotels, theater and cultural events, and even restaurants. We've heard of people booking a table five months in advance
from back home.

During two short periods of the year, only the bravest really want to be
here:

> ✔ **The dog days of summer:** Sometime between mid-July and mid-
> August, the city usually suffers through a period when tempera-
> tures soar to around 100°F (38°C), with 70% to 80% humidity.
> During this time, it's hard to be anywhere except an air-
> conditioned hotel room — the city literally stinks and people
> are often in a bad mood. However, the city often puts on free
> events, such as plays and concerts. Also, you'll have more elbow
> room as you sample the city's offerings.

✔ **The depths of winter:** In January and February, temperatures can drop to 20°F (–6°C) or lower. This post-holiday part of the winter is also a somewhat less busy time in New York. The cold seems to create a general chill-out effect, and as a result, the city sees fewer visitors and fewer cultural events — at least outdoor ones!

Anxious hoteliers and merchants court tourists and their dollars during the winter slow season. If you travel in January or February, getting tickets for a show or a discounted room in a hotel will be easier.

To get an idea of the kind of temperatures and weather you may experience during a particular month in New York, take a look at Table 2-1.

Table 2-1	**Average Temperature and Rainfall**											
	Jan	**Feb**	**Mar**	**Apr**	**May**	**Jun**	**Jul**	**Aug**	**Sep**	**Oct**	**Nov**	**Dec**
Daily temp. (°F)	38	40	48	61	71	80	85	84	77	67	54	42
Days of rain	11	10	11	11	11	10	11	10	8	8	9	10

New York City's Calendar of Events

Regardless of when you plan to visit New York, you'll find several events that draw people to the Big Apple by the millions. This section lists the highlights.

January

In January, you can enjoy the following festivities:

✔ **National Black Fine Art Show.** Organized by Wainwright/Smith Associates, this show focuses on works by black artists from around the world. Call ☎ **212-777-5218** (Fax: 212-477-6490; Internet: www.nationalblackfineartshow.com) for information. Late January.

✔ **Winter Antiques Show at the Seventh Regiment Armory,** 643 Park Ave. at 66th Street. Call ☎ **212-879-9713** for information. Antiques, antiques, and more antiques in a historic building. Third week in January.

✔ **Winter Restaurant Week.** Participating fine-dining restaurants offer two- or three-course fixed-price lunches for a price that corresponds to the year ($20.02 in 2002, $20.03 in 2003, and so on). This winter edition of the traditional summer event was created for the new millennium. For a list of participating restaurants and exact dates, go to www.restaurantweek.com. Second week in January.

February

In February, you can look forward to the following events:

✔ **Chinese New Year,** Chinatown. Call ☎ 212-484-1222 for information. The famous dragon parade and fireworks highlight this two-week celebration. Late January/early February.

✔ **Westminster Kennel Club Dog Show,** Madison Square Garden. Call ☎ 212-465-6741 for information. More than 2,500 dogs and their owners compete for the top prize in mid-February.

March

March offers the following events for your enjoyment:

✔ **International Cat Show,** Madison Square Garden. Call ☎ 212-465-6741 for information. Now that *Cats* has closed, here's your chance to see felines — 800 of them, and their fur isn't glued on. Early March.

✔ **Ringling Brothers and Barnum & Bailey Circus,** Madison Square Garden. Call ☎ 212-465-6741 for information. Don't miss the parade from Twelfth Avenue and 34th Street to the Garden the morning before the show opens. March through April.

✔ **St. Patrick's Day Parade,** Fifth Avenue between 44th and 86th streets. Call ☎ 212-484-1222 for information. Make sure to wear green to this parade of 150,000 marchers showing their love of all things Irish. March 17.

April

April in New York is abloom with the following events:

✔ **Greater New York International Auto Show,** Javits Convention Center. Call ☎ 800-282-3336 or 212-216-2000 for information. This car show, featuring classics, futuristic models, and everything in between, is the largest in the U.S. First week in April.

✔ **The Easter Parade,** Fifth Avenue from 49th to 57th streets. Call ☎ 212-484-1222 for information. Silly hats abound; the *New York Times* recently featured a picture of a ferret attending the parade in an Easter bonnet. Easter Sunday.

May

May boasts these events, among others:

- ✔ **Fleet Week,** Intrepid Sea-Air-Space Museum. Call ☎ 212-245-0072 for information (Internet: www.fleetweek.navy.mil). A plethora of ships and thousands of crew members visit New York during Fleet Week; activities include flyovers, ship tours, 21-gun salutes, and more. Last week in May.

- ✔ **Ninth Avenue International Food Festival,** 37th to 57th streets. Call ☎ 212-581-7029 for information. Food, entertainment, and music combine to make this 20-block fair a must-see. Third weekend in May.

June

June wouldn't be June in New York without the following:

- ✔ **Hudson River Festival,** parks and public spaces of Battery Park City. Call ☎ 212-945-0505 for information. Free concerts along the river. June through August.

- ✔ **Lesbian and Gay Pride Week and March,** Fifth Avenue from 52nd Street to the West Village. Call ☎ 212-807-7433 for information. A week of events and a lively parade celebrate gay rights. The week including June 27.

- ✔ **Museum Mile Festival.** Call ☎ 212-606-2296 for information. Free admission to the nine museums of the famous mile-long stretch of Fifth Avenue (from 82nd to 104th streets), plus live music and street performers make this a mile of fun. June 11.

- ✔ **Restaurant Week.** Participating fine-dining restaurants around the city offer two- or three-course lunches for $20.00. Third week in June. See also the entry for "Winter Restaurant Week" under January events.

- ✔ **Summer Stage,** Central Park at 72nd Street. Call ☎ 212-360-2777. Free afternoon concerts including a wide range of contemporary groups and often some big-name performers.

July

Don't miss the following events if you're in the city in July:

- ✔ **Fourth of July fireworks.** Get as high a vantage point as you can to watch any of the several fireworks shows that light up the skyline. Usually, the fireworks are set off from barges in the East River. Call ☎ 212-695-4400. July 4.

✔ **Rockefeller Center Flower and Garden Show,** Rockefeller Plaza, between 48th and 51st streets. Call ☎ **212-632-4000** or 212-632-3975 for information. A premier horticultural event. Mid-July.

✔ **Midsummer Night's Swing,** Lincoln Center Fountain. Call ☎ **212-546-2656** for information. Dancing under the summer skies to a live band. Throughout July.

✔ **Mostly Mozart,** Avery Fisher Hall, and **Lincoln Center Festival,** Lincoln Center. Call ☎ **212-875-5030** and 212-546-2656, respectively, for information. The former is an important appointment for classic music fans, while enthusiasts of dance, opera, ballet, and theater enjoy the latter. July and August.

✔ **Shakespeare in the Park.** The Public Theater stages one or two free plays (one is usually by Shakespeare) every summer at the Delacorte Theater in Central Park. Call ☎ **212-861-2777** or 212-539-8750 (Internet: www.publictheater.org). Throughout July and August.

August

August in New York may be hot, but you can still enjoy the following events:

✔ **Harlem Week,** Harlem and other public areas around the city, including City Hall, Gracie Mansion, Columbia University, and the Schomburg center. Call ☎ **212-283-3315** or visit www.discover harlem.com for information. Theater, symposia, art, sport, and the famous Harlem Jazz and Music Festival. August.

✔ **Lincoln Center Out-of-Doors,** Damrosch Park, Lincoln Center. Call ☎ **212-546-2656** for information. Free concerts and dance performances. August.

✔ **U.S. Open Tennis Championships,** Flushing Meadows, Queens. Call ☎ **718-760-6200** or visit www.usopen.org for information. The world's best tennis players gather for the final Grand Slam tournament of the year. The two weeks before and after Labor Day.

September

September heralds the arrival of fall in New York with the following events:

✔ **New York Film Festival,** sponsored by the Film Society of Lincoln Center. Call ☎ **212-875-5610** for information. This two-week festival has seen many important premieres over the years. Get your tickets in advance. September through October.

✔ **Wigstock,** 11th Street Pier. Call ☎ **212-213-2438** for information. Drag queens don full regalia during this party, whose location varies from year to year. Labor Day weekend.

October

October features the following events to keep you entertained:

- ✔ **Greenwich Village Halloween Parade,** West Village/Chelsea. Call ☎ 212-484-1222 for information. Not your average group of trick-or-treaters, this parade — the nation's largest public Halloween parade — features outrageous costumes and people (soon to be outnumbered by boring floats advertising radio stations and the like). October 31.

- ✔ **Next Wave Festival,** Brooklyn Academy of Music. Call ☎ 718-636-4100 for information. Enjoy experimental dance, theater, and music. October through December.

November

We can recommend the following events held in November:

- ✔ **Big Apple Circus,** Lincoln Center. Call ☎ 212-268-2500 for information. You don't have to be a kid to enjoy this fabulous spectacle. November through January.

- ✔ **Macy's Thanksgiving Day Parade,** Central Park West/Broadway. Call ☎ 212-494-5432 or 212-494-4495 for information. The night before the parade, you can watch the workers inflate the world-famous balloons. Thanksgiving Day (late November).

- ✔ **New York City Marathon.** Ends in Central Park. Call ☎ 212-860-4455 for the exact route and more information. Join this race, which runs through all five boroughs, or stand at the sidelines to cheer on the thousands of competitors. First Sunday in November.

December

December in New York is magical, in part because of the following events:

- ✔ **Rockefeller Center Christmas Tree Lighting,** Rockefeller Center. Call ☎ 212-632-3975 or 212-632-4000 for information. Prepare to join thousands of others to watch the lighting of the huge tree. Early December.

- ✔ **New Year's Eve,** Times Square. Call ☎ 212-768-1560 or 212-354-0003 (the hotline) for information. The vast number of people who flood Times Square to watch the ball drop make this event an all-day, and sometimes unpleasant, way to celebrate the New Year. If you don't mind the crowds, arrive early and be ready to deal with literally hundreds of thousands of people in various stages of intoxication. December 31.

Chapter 3

Planning Your Budget

● ●

In This Chapter

▶ Watching out for hidden expenses

▶ Cutting corners with great money-saving tips

● ●

*N*ew York has a way of devouring your cash. With almost as many ATMs as there are things to spend money on (a dangerous combination), the Big Apple can be a big budget-buster. But as long as you have your wits about you and plan ahead, you won't have to worry about having to take out a second mortgage to finance your trip — not even close. We include plenty of money-saving ideas in this chapter to make sure of that.

Adding Up the Elements: What to Expect

This section helps you figure out what the various elements of your trip will cost in relation to one another. Turn to the worksheet "Making Dollars and Sense of It" at the back of this book for help keeping track of your expenses.

Hotel

We tackle the toughest expense first: your hotel room. As we discuss in Chapter 8, a decent hotel room in New York generally runs at least $150 per night, including a hotel tax of 13.25%. Just resign yourself to this expense and be done with it — you'll wear yourself out trying to locate cheaper accommodations, and what you get for less money may not turn out to be such a bargain.

Transportation

Manhattan is a small island. You can walk to many of the sights you want to visit, getting a free tour of the city as you go, or you can take the subway or bus. You may have heard horror stories about New York transportation, but in reality, as long as you avoid rush hour (from 8 to 9 a.m. and 5 to 6 p.m.), it's quite efficient, relatively inexpensive, and only occasionally smelly. With $1.50 (or less if you invest in a multiple-ride MetroCard), you can take the subway, bus, or both and get anywhere you want to go. See Chapter 11 for more information about getting around New York.

Yellow cabs are the city's other great resource. They're usually plentiful (except on rainy days and at the pre-theater hour) and relatively affordable. You pay $2 just to step into a taxi, plus 30¢ per ⅕ mile or 20¢ per minute when stuck in traffic, plus a 50¢ nighttime surcharge. The average fare in Manhattan is $5.25.

If you're thinking about renting a car in New York, think again. (See the discussion of this subject in Chapter 9.)

Food

You can get every conceivable kind of food in New York at just about any price. If you favor the kind of dining that requires a suit and large cash outlays, you'll have no problem finding menus to satisfy your epicurean dreams. However, if dining is an area in which you prefer to economize, you can find breakfasts and lunches for about $3 to $5 and early-bird dinners from $10 to $15. Burritos, pizza, bagels, and New York's famous hot dogs also can stop the hunger pangs and help you save money. Chapters 14 and 15 offer tips on selecting food that fits both your appetite and your budget.

Don't shortchange yourself! Make sure to sample some of the ethnic specialties that you would have to travel far and wide to taste otherwise. Plus, eating ethnic is a great way to save money; ethnic restaurants often offer quite affordable menus.

Sights

Entrance fees vary from attraction to attraction. Unfortunately, the admission at one museum is not good at another as is the case in some other cities, but you can buy a CityPass, which for $38 gets you half-price admission to seven of the city's top attractions (a savings of more than 50%). See Chapter 16 for more information about places and things to see.

Some attractions request a suggested contribution for admission, which means that you can pay whatever you want. But be reasonable — if you offer up a couple of dollars to get a family of six into the Metropolitan Museum, you're likely to get a sneer with your tickets. Some museums also offer a free admission night, which, for obvious reasons, is usually the busiest night of the week. See the individual museum listings in Chapters 16 and 17 for details.

Shopping

When it comes to shopping, only you know how much you want to spend. New York is a great place to buy shoes (homegrown, Italian, French, whatever) that you won't find back home, funky clothes that you don't see on Main Street, and discount couture.

New York recently abolished its odious sales tax for clothing purchases of less than $110, making it easier than ever to pick up a little something for yourself. Think of it as an automatic 8.25% discount.

Nightlife

Unless your tastes run to pitchers of beer in Hell's Kitchen dives, your evening entertainment is going to be your biggest expense in the nightlife category. A good ticket to a Broadway show costs about $75. A ticket to an off-Broadway show runs around $50. Nightclubs usually have a cover charge of about $15 to $20, but it may be higher depending on who's playing that night (see Chapter 23 for details).

Typical day-to-day purchases

Table 3-1 gives you an idea of what you can expect to pay for typical purchases in New York.

Table 3-1	What Things Cost in New York City
Item	*Price*
Subway or city bus ride	$1.50
Can of soda	$1.00
Pay-phone call	25¢
Movie ticket	$10 or more
Coffee (your standard cuppa joe)	60¢–$1
Decaf macchiato with yak milk (or something similarly complicated)	$2–$4
Ticket to top of the Empire State Building	$9
Cover charge at a Village jazz club (excluding 1- or 2-drink minimum)	$15–$30
Boat ride around Manhattan on the Circle Line, adult	$25
Boat ride on the Circle Line, child	$12.50

(continued)

Table 3-1 *(continued)*

Item	Price
Admission to the Guggenheim Museum, adult	$12
Sidecar at a hotel bar	$10–$12
Bar-brand martini at the Rainbow Grill	$17

Keeping a Lid on Hidden Expenses

The price you see is not always the price you pay, for two reasons: tips and taxes. You have to keep these two things in mind when looking at prices, as both can put you over budget. A 20% tip on a $100 dinner would buy a lot of subway rides.

Taxes

Regular sales taxes are 8.25% — not a small amount, especially if you buy some expensive article. Remember that advertised prices, from restaurants to hotels to most shops, almost always exclude sales tax. The prices in this book also do not include sales tax.

The good news is that in March 2000, the city of New York abolished sales taxes on purchases of clothes and shoes under $110 — to the joy of both merchants and customers. Despite tough economic times, there's been no word of rescinding this boon.

Hotel taxes run 13.25%. If you think this seems ridiculous, be glad that you didn't plan your trip a few years ago, when the hotel tax was 19.25%! (Occasionally, things in New York get cheaper.) There's also a room charge of $2 per night. Remember to ask whether the price quoted to you includes these additional amounts, both for packages and hotel rooms; they can make quite a difference.

Tips

Bottom line: Expect to tip for every service you get in New York. Use the following guidelines when tipping:

- ✔ **Waiters:** Simply double the tax on your bill and round up to the nearest dollar. Often, restaurants add the tip (15% to 20%) to the bill automatically for parties of six or more.

- ✔ **Bartenders:** If you're just drinking at a bar, 10% to 15% will take care of it.

- ✔ **Taxi drivers:** No matter how bumpy the ride, tip 15%.

- ✔ **Everybody else:** Bellhops get $1 or $2 per bag, maids get $1 per day, coat-check people get $1 per garment, and automobile valets get $1.

Cutting Costs

You can cut down on costs in plenty of ways — some little and some big. Note the Bargain Alert icons scattered throughout this book, which offer hints on ways to trim the fat from your budget. While you're planning a trip, here are a few things to keep in mind:

- ✔ **Travel at off-peak times.** Although New York doesn't have a real off-season, the prices at some hotels at nonpeak times are half of what they are during the peak seasons. See Chapter 2 for a discussion of the New York travel seasons.

- ✔ **Travel on "cheap" days.** The price of your airplane ticket can vary significantly, depending on which days you fly. If you can be flexible with your travel days, you may be able to knock down the price of your ticket. For more ways to save on airfare, turn to Chapter 5.

- ✔ **Check out a package tour.** A package deal may get you your airfare and hotel, as well as other aspects of your trip, for a good price. See the section on package tours in Chapter 5 for suggestions of specific companies to call.

- ✔ **Have some meals in your room.** Some hotel rooms come with kitchenettes, making eating in a comfortable and cheap option.

- ✔ **Always ask for discount rates.** You won't get them if you don't ask for them. Don't forget to mention your membership in any clubs that may earn you a discount.

- ✔ **Ask if your kids can stay in your room with you.** You may have to pay a few extra dollars to have them stay with you, but it sure beats paying for a second room.

- ✔ **Try expensive restaurants at lunch instead of dinner.** Lunch tabs are usually a fraction of what dinner costs at most restaurants, and the menu often offers many of the same specialties, only sometimes in smaller portions. Many of New York's best restaurants participate in Restaurant Week in January and June — $20 nets you a two- or three-course lunch — and some extend this fixed-price bargain throughout the summer or even year-round.

- ✔ **Ask about hotel telephone charges up front.** Many of the hotels in the moderate-to-expensive range now offer free local calls from rooms, but don't count on it. Ask when you reserve your room, or you may wind up with a whopping service charge for those 30 restaurants you called on Saturday night, trying to get a reservation for six at the last minute.

✔ **Avoid the minibar.** Hotel-room minibars are a potential rude sur-
prise: Just because it's stocked doesn't mean that it's free. Prices
are often two or three times higher than in a local store ($5 for an
airline-sized bag of peanuts!). The cost-conscious will want to
follow the golden rule of BYO snacks and beverages.

✔ **Use the buses and subways.** Taxis get expensive quickly, especially in gridlock traffic. See Chapter 11 for hints on navigating the
public transit system.

✔ **Buy a daily or weekly MetroCard pass.** See Chapter 11 for more
info about the MetroCard and its budget-saving powers.

✔ **Seek out small local restaurants,** not just big, famous tourist-
gougers. Turn to Chapters 14 and 15 for suggestions.

✔ **Visit museums that only suggest an admission fee, or on the
nights that are free.** See Chapters 16 and 17 to find out which
days and nights are free at our favorite museums.

✔ **Don't order movie tickets over the phone.** Dying to see a movie
that's been sold out for weeks? Don't give in to the temptation to
order tickets in advance on the phone — you'll pay an extra $1.50
per ticket, which can raise your total ticket price to a ridiculous
$11 or more. Instead, visit the theater a few hours early so that
you can purchase tickets in person.

Chapter 4

Planning Ahead for Special Travel Needs

● ●

In This Chapter

▶ Traveling with your kids

▶ Traveling for the senior set

▶ Traveling with disabilities

▶ Traveling for gays and lesbians

● ●

*I*f you're feeling a bit intimidated by the Big Apple, you may be surprised to discover that things are easier here for people with special needs than in other cities. There are so many things to see and do that anybody can find something suitable, and specialized services are available for just about everything and everyone.

Tips for Families

The question we hear most from parents about New York is, "Is it a safe place to take the kids?" Absolutely! New York can be one of the world's best destinations for families — just as long as parents and children prepare appropriately for the trip.

Parents should research all the places the family plans to visit; see Chapter 10 for descriptions of New York's neighborhoods. Parents and children should go over safety issues before leaving (see the Quick Concierge appendix); make sure to create a plan so that children know what to do if they get lost.

Finding a family-friendly hotel

Finding a hotel that caters to children may be your biggest concern when traveling to New York. You're in luck — some New York hotels market special services just for families, including play areas and programs. Make sure to ask about these services when you call for a reservation.

If watching your wallet is a concern, look for a hotel that lets children stay for free. You may also want to consider getting a room with a kitchenette; eating some meals in your room will help defray food costs. In Chapter 8, we put Kid Friendly icons next to hotels that offer family-friendly options.

Getting around

If you and your children don't want to tangle with public transportation from the airport or around the city, you can always take taxis. But if your children are patient enough, you can get almost anywhere on the bus or subway. Make sure to review the safety tips we give in Chapter 11 and in the Quick Concierge appendix before hitting the road.

Children under 3 feet, 8 inches tall ride New York's subways for free.

Finding baby-sitting services

Many hotels have baby-sitting services or can provide lists of reliable sitters. If your hotel can't make a recommendation, try the **Baby Sitters Guild** (☎ 212-682-0227) or the **Frances Stewart Agency** (☎ 212-439-9222). These sitters are licensed, insured, and bonded and will take your children on an outing.

Touring the town

To help you plan outings with your children, look for the Kid Friendly icons throughout this book, which point out places of particular interest to children. You'll find this icon next to such sights as the Empire State Building, the Bronx Zoo, Central Park Zoo, the Statue of Liberty, the Museum of Natural History, and Central Park. For more information about planning activities for children, pick up a copy of Frommer's *New York City with Kids.*

Time Out New York, a magazine that comes out every Wednesday, is an excellent source for finding out about child-friendly activities and events. Look for the "Kids" listings near the back of the magazine.

For teenagers, some neighborhoods may be more interesting than others. Downtown neighborhoods such as Chelsea, the East and West Village, SoHo, NoHo, and NoLiTa have younger crowds, lots of alternative music stores, coffee shops, funky clothing stores, and such. (For more detailed descriptions of these neighborhoods, see Chapter 10.) Fans of MTV's *Total Request Live* may want to check out the Times Square studios.

Tips for Seniors

A variety of specialized agencies offer travel discounts to seniors. Two of the best are

- ✔ **AARP (American Association of Retired Persons),** 601 E St. NW, Washington, DC 20049 (☎ **202-434-AARP;** Internet: www.aarp. org). Membership gets you discounts on car rentals and hotel rooms.

- ✔ **Mature Outlook,** P.O. Box 9390, Des Moines, IA 50306-9519 (☎ **800-336-6330;** Fax: 847-286-5024). This organization offers discounts on car rentals and hotel stays, as well as a bimonthly magazine and other benefits. Membership is open to all Sears customers 18 and over, but the organization's primary focus is on the 50-and-over market.

In addition, most of the major domestic airlines offer discount programs for senior travelers — be sure to ask whenever you book a flight.

If you're looking for an organized tour, here are two good choices among the literally hundreds of travel agencies specializing in vacations for seniors:

- ✔ **Grand Circle Travel** (☎ **800-221-2610** or 617-350-7500; Internet: www.gct.com) offers a range of options; however, many of its organized vacations are of the tour-bus variety, with free trips thrown in for those who organize groups of 20 or more. Seniors seeking more independent travel should probably consult a regular travel agent.

- ✔ **SAGA International Holidays,** 222 Berkeley St., Boston, MA 02116 (☎ **800-343-0273**) offers tours and cruises for people 50 and older.

 Seniors get a 50% discount on bus and subway fares in New York (see the following section for more info). Certain theaters, museums, and other attractions give senior discounts as well — always inquire when buying your tickets. Be sure to carry identification with proof of age.

Tips for Travelers with Disabilities

In general, New York is progressive in its efforts to make the city accessible for the disabled. Equal access is now mandated by law, but implementation has been gradual and is not complete. The city makes progress every day, though; you may want to check on the latest changes.

Hotels

Some older, smaller, and budget hotels have not been updated to current access regulations. However, other hotels, including chains such as Hilton, offer features that accommodate wheelchairs, like roll-in showers, lower sinks, and extra space for maneuverability. Simply ask for one of these accessible rooms when you reserve. For more information, you can call one of the associations listed in the "Accessible buildings" section later in this chapter.

Transportation

Taxis are required by law to take disabled persons, wheelchairs, and guide dogs. For getting into the city from one of the airports, the **Gray Line Shuttle** (☎ 800-451-0455 or 212-315-3006) has minibuses with lifts. The vans go only to Midtown hotels, and you must make a reservation.

All buses in Manhattan and 95% of New York City buses are equipped with wheelchair lifts and special areas where the bus seats fold up to make extra room. The buses also "kneel," scrunching down so that the first step is more accessible. Wheelchair passengers don't have to request these bus services in advance; just show up at the bus stop. The driver usually will help put a wheelchair on the ramp and secure the chair inside the bus.

Subway access for travelers with disabilities is still limited, but the MTA New York City Transit keeps working at increasing accessibility. You can certainly experience the thrill of a New York subway ride by boarding and getting off at the accessible stations, but the bus is a much more flexible option. The following are wheelchair-accessible stations and lines in Manhattan:

- ✔ Brooklyn Bridge/City Hall (4/5/6)
- ✔ 14th Street/Union Square (4/5/6/N/Q/R/W)
- ✔ 34th Street/Herald Square (B/D/F/Q/N/R/V/W)
- ✔ 42nd Street/Port Authority Bus Terminal (A/C/E)
- ✔ Grand Central/42nd Street (4/5/6)
- ✔ 50th Street (southbound only, C/E)
- ✔ 51st Street (6)
- ✔ Lexington/63rd Street (F)
- ✔ 66th Street/Lincoln Center (1/2)
- ✔ 125th Street (4/5/6)
- ✔ 175th Street (A)
- ✔ Roosevelt Island (F)

Accessible stations are marked with an icon on the free subway map distributed in the subway. You also can get a free brochure, *Accessible Transfer Points,* from MTA Customer Assistance, 370 Jay St., Room 702, Brooklyn, NY 11201 (☎ **718-330-3322;** TTY 718-596-8273). Braille subway maps are available from **The Lighthouse, Inc.,** 111 E. 59th St., New York, NY 10022 (☎ **800-334-5497** or 212-821-9200), which also produces concerts and exhibitions by the vision impaired.

Seniors and disabled persons get a 50% discount with the MTA. Getting a discount MetroCard takes a little planning, however. You need to get an application by writing to Customer Assistance Division, MTA, 370 Jay St., 7th Floor, Brooklyn, NY 11201. Or you can download the application from the MTA Web site (www.mta.info) or call ☎ **718-243-4999.**

Accessible buildings

Many restaurants, most cultural institutions, and all the major sights are accessible to travelers with disabilities. Call in advance of your visit to ensure that you get all the care you need. A number of small restaurants are not wheelchair accessible; you may want to call ahead to make absolutely sure. Another possibility is to get listings from the following organizations:

- ✔ **Hospital Audiences, Inc.,** 220 W. 42nd St., 13th Floor, New York, NY 10036 (hotline ☎ **888-424-4685,** local 212-575-7676, TTY 212-575-7673). You also can order *Access for All,* the accessibility guidebook on city cultural institutions, for $5.

- ✔ **The American Foundation for the Blind,** 11 Penn Plaza, Suite 300, New York, NY 10001 (☎ **800-232-5463** or 212-502-7600), offers information about traveling with a seeing-eye dog.

- ✔ **The New York Society for the Deaf,** 817 Broadway, 7th Floor, New York, NY 10003 (☎ TTY **212-777-3900**). Contact this organization for travel tips for the hearing impaired.

- ✔ **The Society for Accessible Travel and Hospitality,** 347 Fifth Ave., Suite 610, New York, NY 10016 (☎ **212-447-7284;** Internet: www.sath.org), offers a wealth of travel resources for people with all types of disabilities and recommends access guides, travel agents, tour operators, companion services, and more. Annual membership costs $45 for adults and $30 for seniors and students.

Guided tours

Try these companies that feature tours for travelers with disabilities:

- ✔ **Big Apple Greeter** (☎ **212-669-2896,** TTY 212-669-8273; Internet: www.bigapplegreeter.org). This organization offers tours for the disabled free of charge. As with its other tours (see Chapter 18), advance reservations are necessary.

✔ **FEDCAP Rehabilitation Services,** 211 W. 14th St., New York, NY 10011 (☎ 212-727-4200). Contact this group for information about membership and summer tours.

✔ **Flying Wheels Travel,** 143 West Bridge, P.O. Box 382, Owatonna, MN 55060 (☎ 800-533-0363). The company offers various escorted tours and cruises, as well as private tours in minivans with lifts.

Tips for Gay and Lesbian Travelers

New York ranks with San Francisco as one of the most gay-friendly cities in the United States. Greenwich Village and Chelsea have large gay populations, and the West Village and Chelsea areas offer abundant nightlife.

For help in planning your trip to New York, try the **International Gay & Lesbian Travel Association** (IGLTA) (☎ 800-448-8550 or 954-776-2626; Fax: 954-776-3303; Internet: www.iglta.org). This group provides information about gay-friendly hoteliers, tour operators, and airline representatives. It offers monthly newsletters and a membership directory that's updated once a year. Annual membership is $200, plus a $100 fee for new members.

Another excellent trip-planning source is **Now, Voyager** (☎ 800-255-6951; Internet: www.nowvoyager.com), a San Francisco–based gay-owned and -operated travel service.

The following are a few of the major gay organizations in the city:

✔ **The Lesbian and Gay Community Services Center,** 208 W. 13th St. between Seventh and Eighth avenues (☎ 212-620-7310; Internet: www.gaycenter.org). Call or visit the Center's excellent Web site to get information about the programs it sponsors. The Center also offers a list of gay-friendly accommodations and a calendar of local cultural events.

✔ **The Organization of Lesbian and Gay Architects and Designers** (☎ 212-475-7652) offers a free map of lesbian and gay historical landmarks.

✔ **Gay Men's Health Crisis (GMHC),** 119 W. 24th St., has an AIDS hotline (☎ 212-807-6655), serves anyone with HIV, and offers a wide variety of programs.

For the most up-to-date information about events and entertainment, try any of the city's gay-friendly publications. The weekly *Time Out New York* (Internet: www.timeoutny.com) includes a comprehensive gay and lesbian section. *Homo Xtra* (Internet: www.hx.com), a free publication available in restaurants, clubs, and bars, lists events around town. *Gay City News* (Internet: www.lgny.com) appears every other Tuesday, and *The New York Blade News,* a weekly newspaper, is published on Fridays.

Part II
Ironing Out the Details

The 5th Wave   By Rich Tennant

You know, getting us to the front door of the Empire State Building would have been quite sufficient, driver.

In this part . . .

Now that you've decided to go to New York, you need to get down to the work of planning. Planning a trip to a new destination can be tedious and complicated, but our step-by-step strategy will take you from your front door to your accommodation in New York quickly and easily. We've got it all covered: the best ways to get to New York, choosing a hotel that meets your needs, and ways to get the best price on both. We even throw in tips on how to deal with all those pesky last-minute things, from packing your bag to remembering your toothbrush.

Chapter 5

Getting to New York City

· ·

In This Chapter

▶ Working with travel agents

▶ Taking a package tour

▶ Deciding which airline to fly

▶ Getting a great deal on a flight

▶ Discovering other ways to get to New York

· ·

*Y*ou can get to New York in a variety of ways, and choosing the best mode of transit may seem overwhelming. The most basic questions are: What's more important to you, convenience or cost? Are you willing to arrange your transportation on your own, or would you prefer to get a travel agent to help you? When you arrive, do you want to explore the city by yourself, or do you want the company of a group tour? We give you the pros and cons of every option in this chapter.

Travel Agents: Help or Hindrance?

Travel agents can be really helpful when you're arranging a trip to New York — if you work with one who can search out true flight and hotel bargains that don't trade convenience for money. When selecting a travel agent, get recommendations from friends and relatives. Agents with good track records are invaluable resources.

Before you approach a travel agent, use the information in this book to form tentative plans for your trip — have some ideas about the area of town you want to stay in and the things you want to do and see. Doing so will help your travel agent make the best possible plans for you.

To make sure that your travel agent is getting you a good price on your airfare, do some checking on the fares yourself beforehand (see "Getting the Best Airfare" later in this chapter). Agents have access to more resources than you can find on the Web or elsewhere, and they should be able to get you a better price than you could get by yourself.

After you and the agent agree to a flight itinerary and price, the agent can issue your tickets. If the agent can't get you into the hotel of your choice, he or she should be able to recommend an alternative.

The Ins and Outs of Package Tours

Tour packages are sold in bulk to tour operators who then resell them to travelers like you. In many cases, a package that includes airfare, hotel, and transportation to and from the airport can cost you less than the hotel alone if you booked it yourself.

Tour operators offer a variety of packages to fit the needs of any traveler. Some packages let you choose between escorted vacations and independent vacations; others allow you to add on just a few excursions or escorted day trips (also at prices lower than if you booked them yourself) without booking an entirely escorted tour. Some packages offer a better class of hotels than others. Some offer the same hotels for lower prices. Some offer flights on scheduled airlines, while others book charters. With some packages, your choice of accommodations and travel days may be limited. To select the package that's best for you, you need to spend time with a tour operator going over all the options.

Deciding whether to hire an escort

The decision whether to take an escorted tour or an independent vacation depends on your tastes. On an escorted tour, everything is planned for you; you just sit back and take it all in. You know your costs up front, and there aren't many surprises. Escorted tours can take you to the maximum number of sights in the minimum amount of time with the least amount of hassle. However, an escorted tour may reduce spontaneity and freedom during your trip because you have to stick to an established schedule.

Escorted tours can be more expensive because the cost of the tour reflects all that personalized attention. However, New York offers a wealth of local tour operators (see Chapter 18 for our choices). So if you prefer organized excursions, we recommend purchasing a package tour (see "Shopping for package tours," later in this chapter), with which you can reap substantial savings, and then scheduling your guided tours once you arrive in town.

Shopping for an escorted tour

When researching an escorted tour, ask about the following details:

- ✔ **Cancellation policy:** Do you have to put down a deposit? Can the tour operator cancel the trip if not enough people sign up? How late can you cancel if you're unable to go? When do you pay? Do you get a refund if you cancel? If the tour operator cancels?

- ✔ **Schedule:** Make sure that the pace of the tour matches your idea of a vacation. If you want to relax, check that your tour's schedule isn't as hectic as a road race.

- ✔ **Group size:** Generally, you want to be in as small a group as possible to minimize the time you spend waiting for the group to get coordinated. Even if the tour operator can't give you an exact number at the time of your inquiry, he or she should be able to give you a rough idea. Some tours have a minimum group size and may cancel if they don't book enough people.

- ✔ **Hidden costs:** Make the tour operator list any and all costs that are not included in the quoted price. You may have to pay to get yourself to and from the airport, for example.

- ✔ **Flexibility:** Find out whether you are required to attend all events and whether you will have any choices during planned meals.

Prices vary, particularly for airlines and hotels. Before you book a package, price the individual components yourself by contacting the airline and hotel directly to make sure that you're getting a good deal.

When shopping for an escorted tour, try checking with the following companies:

- ✔ **Globus,** 5301 South Federal Circle, Littleton, CO 80123 (☎ **800-221-0090** or 303-797-2800; Internet: www.globusandcosmos.com), sometimes runs first-class independent tours of New York (often as part of a larger, multi-city itinerary). A "host" is available to answer questions but doesn't take you around the city, except on a designated day. The package includes everything — hotel, local transportation, and even tips. Check the Web site for the most up-to-date tour offerings.

- ✔ **Maupintour,** Box 807, 1421 Research Park Dr., Lawrence, KS 66044 (☎ **800-255-4266** or 913-843-1211; Internet: www.maupintour.com), specializes in lavish "grand tours." These escorted tours often feature Broadway shows and an excursion to the Hudson Valley. The cost of a tour may run about $2,000 per person depending on the options you select, plus airfare.

Consider getting travel insurance if you choose to go on an escorted tour, especially if the tour operator asks you to pay up front. That way, if the tour company reneges on its obligations, you won't lose your vacation money. Get travel insurance through an independent agency — not from the tour company itself. See Chapter 9 for more information about travel insurance.

Shopping for package tours

Airlines often package their flights with accommodations. The variety among airline packages is vast. At its most basic, the package is just hotel-plus-airfare; other packages give you dinners, tours, and ground transportation or car rental (hint: take the ground transport) — the whole nine yards.

To find a bargain, you may need to be flexible. Prices vary significantly depending on the time you travel and the hotel you pick. For example, a six-night stay at the Marriott Marquis, including airfare from Los Angeles but with no extras, costs about $1,400. If you choose the Holiday Inn, however, the price drops to about $1,000. The same packages from Chicago are priced slightly lower, at about $1,300 and $975, respectively.

Try the following resources to research package tours:

- ✔ **Liberty Travel** (check your local telephone directory because there isn't a central 800 number; Internet: www.libertytravel. com) is one of the biggest packagers in the business.

- ✔ **New York City Vacation Packages** offers a wide variety of packages year-round, some of them at unbeatable prices. Call ☎ **888-692-8701,** check www.nycvp.com, or send an e-mail to info@nycvp.com.

- ✔ **NYC & Company,** the city's Convention and Visitors Bureau, offers special packages, usually during the slower first months of the year. Call ☎ **800-NYC-GUIDE** or 800-NYC-VISIT or check www.nycvisit.com for information about these packages. At press time, NYC & Company was offering the NYC Freedom Package starting at $157 per person for a one-night stay, including hotel, a Broadway show, and one dinner gift certificate.

- ✔ The **travel section** of your local Sunday newspaper.

- ✔ The ads in the back of **national travel magazines.**

- ✔ Through the Web site www.vacationpackager.com. There you can link up with many different operators — about 150! — and design your own package.

Getting the Best Airfare

Fares for the same flight vary from day to day according to availability. Read this section to find out how to get the best fare. To help you with your comparison shopping, we added a worksheet at the end of this book called "Fare Game: Choosing an Airline."

Timing your trip

When it comes to airfares, you pay for flexibility. If you buy a ticket at the last minute or choose to fly on a premium day, such as Friday, you will probably have to pay full fare. However, if you book your ticket far in advance, stay over Saturday night, or travel on a Tuesday, Wednesday, or Thursday, you may pay only a fraction of the full fare.

The airlines sometimes reduce the price of tickets to New York during the off-season, which is in late summer (July and August) and in the heart of winter, after the holidays. These sales are usually advertised in the travel section of your local newspaper.

Buying your ticket from a consolidator

Consolidators, also known as bucket shops, often offer lower prices than you can get from a travel agent or by yourself. Consolidators buy seats in bulk from the airlines and then sell them back to the public at prices usually below even the airlines' discounted rates. Check the travel section of your local newspaper for their ads.

Here is a list of reliable consolidators:

- **1-800-FLY-CHEAP** (Internet: www.1800flycheap.com) offers fares on all the major U.S. airlines but does not list flights on budget carriers.

- **Council Travel** (☎ 800-226-8624; Internet: www.counciltravel.com) and **STA Travel** (☎ 800-781-4040; Internet: www.sta.travel.com) cater to young travelers, but their bargain-basement prices are available to people of all ages.

- **TFI Tours International** (☎ 800-745-8000 or 212-736-1140; Internet: www.lowestprice.com) serves as a clearinghouse for unused seats.

- **The TravelHub** (☎ 888-AIRFARE; Internet: www.travelhub.com) represents nearly 1,000 travel agencies, many of which offer consolidator and discount fares.

Before you pay a consolidator, request a confirmation number and then call the airline to confirm your seat. Be aware that consolidator tickets are usually nonrefundable or rigged with stiff cancellation penalties, often as high as 50% to 75% of the ticket price. Protect yourself by paying with a credit card rather than cash. And keep in mind that if an airline sale is going on, or if it's high season, you often can get the same or better rates from the airlines directly.

Buying your ticket on the Internet

What could be easier than shopping for airfares from the convenience of your own computer anytime day or night? Scores of travel agents populate the Web. Most sites allow you to enter your dates of travel and destination; then they produce a list of flights and fares from which you can choose.

Using an online travel agent

Two of the better-respected online travel agents are **Travelocity** (www.travelocity.com) and **Expedia** (www.expedia.com). Each site offers an excellent range of options for booking flights and package tours as well as reserving hotels and car rentals. **Orbitz** (www.orbitz.com) is a popular site launched by United, Delta, Northwest, American, and Continental airlines that often offers special deals that are unavailable on other sites. **Qixo** (www.qixo.com) is another powerful search engine that enables you to search for flights and accommodations from some 20 airline and travel-planning sites (such as Travelocity) at once. Qixo sorts results by price.

Keep in mind that because several airlines are no longer willing to pay commissions on tickets sold by online travel agencies, these Web sites may add a $5 or $10 surcharge to your bill if you book on one of those carriers — or neglect to tell you about those carriers' flights.

Using an "opaque fare" service

Another category of online travel agent is the "opaque fare" service, so called because some details of your flight remain hidden until you purchase your ticket. When you book an opaque fare, you give up control of your flight times and your choice of airline (although you're guaranteed to fly a full-service, large-scale carrier). You give up frequent flier miles and lock yourself into a nonchangeable, nonrefundable ticket. You *can* specify your days of travel, whether you're willing to take off-peak flights (those that leave before 6 a.m. or after 10 p.m.), and how many connections you will accept (with a minimum of one). You also get to pick the airports you fly into and out of. Only after you pay for your ticket do you get the full details of your flight.

The most popular opaque-fare sites are Priceline (www.priceline.com) and Hotwire (www.hotwire.com), although Expedia and Travelocity now offer similar services too. Priceline allows you to "name your price" for airline tickets, hotel rooms, and rental cars, while Hotwire, Expedia, and Travelocity offer fixed-price deals on unnamed airlines (at least, unnamed until you purchase the ticket).

Opaque-fare sites are undoubtedly the source of the cheapest domestic fares around. But you need to be flexible. Opaque fares are a *bad choice* for these types of people:

- ✔ Those who can't stomach 6 a.m. departures.
- ✔ Those who may need to change their tickets.
- ✔ Those who demand nonstop flights.
- ✔ Those who are planning a quick two-day trip — you might land in town at 10 p.m. on Saturday and be forced to leave at 6 a.m. on Sunday, eight hours later!

Finding last-minute specials online

Airlines regularly offer last-minute specials, such as weekend deals or Internet-only fares, to fill empty seats. Most of these specials are announced on Tuesday or Wednesday and must be purchased online. They're often valid for travel only that coming weekend, but some can be booked weeks or even months in advance. Check one of the sites that compile comprehensive lists of last-minute specials, such as **Smarter Living** (www.smarterliving.com) and **WebFlyer** (www.webflyer.com), or sign up for weekly e-mail alerts at individual airline Web sites (refer to the Quick Concierge appendix at the back of this book for a complete list).

Almost every travel-booking Web site will send you an e-mail notification when a cheap fare becomes available to your favorite destination. (Deals to New York, a major destination city, pop up all the time.) Register at as many of these sites as you can so that you can keep on top of all the fare sales.

Choosing the Airport

Three major airports serve New York City: LaGuardia, JFK, and Newark. The city is easily accessible from all three (see Chapter 10 for details on transportation between airport and city), although choosing to arrive at one or another may influence the price of your ticket. Flying into Newark used to be the cheapest, but not anymore. If you're looking for the best price, be flexible and accept a flight to any of these three airports. However, you may want to consider these differences:

- ✔ **LaGuardia Airport,** in northern Queens, is the closest airport to Manhattan (and therefore the cheapest and fastest to come from and go to). It's also the smallest. Although the number of flights that are allowed to arrive there has increased in recent years, the choices are more limited than at the other two airports. Also, the increase in number of flights has led to an increase in delays.

✔ **John F. Kennedy Airport,** in southern Queens, is the official international airport for New York. That makes it the largest and busiest (although Newark may have overtaken it). Also, of the three major airports, it's the farthest from the city center.

✔ **Newark International Airport** is in New Jersey but is somewhat closer to Manhattan than JFK, especially if your accommodations are on the west side or downtown. The newest and (we think) most pleasant airport to fly into, Newark is also the airport with the most convenient direct public-transportation link to Manhattan; in 2001, the airport monorail was extended to connect with a commuter rail station that offers service to Penn Station in Manhattan for less than $15.

Two other airports in outlying areas service New York City: Westchester Airport in White Plains, New York (25 miles north of the city), and MacArthur Airport in Islip, Long Island (50 miles east of the city). MacArthur is the closest airport that budget carrier Southwest Airlines services. However, we feel strongly that the inconvenience and high cost of getting into the city from these out-of-the-way airports far outweigh the money you would save by using them.

Understanding the New Air Travel Security Measures

In the wake of the terrorist attacks of September 11, 2001, the airline industry began implementing stricter security measures in airports. Expect a lengthy check-in process and extensive delays. Although regulations vary from airline to airline, you can make the process of traveling smoother by taking the following steps:

✔ **Arrive early.** Arrive at the airport at least two hours before your flight is scheduled to depart.

✔ **Try not to drive your car to the airport.** Parking and curbside access to the terminal may be limited. Call ahead and check.

✔ **Don't count on curbside check-in.** Some airlines and airports have stopped curbside check-in altogether, while others offer it on a limited basis. For up-to-date information about specific regulations and implementations, check with the individual airline.

✔ **Be sure to carry plenty of documentation.** A government-issued photo ID (federal, state, or local) is now required. You will need to show your ID at various checkpoints. With an electronic ticket, you also may be required to have with you printed confirmation of purchase, and perhaps even the credit card with which you bought your ticket. This policy varies from airline to airline, so call ahead to make sure that you have the proper documentation.

And *be sure that your ID is up-to-date:* An expired driver's license, for example, may keep you from boarding the plane.

✔ **Know what you can carry on and what you can't.** Travelers in the United States are now limited to one carry-on bag plus one personal item (such as a purse or briefcase). The Transportation Security Administration (TSA) also has issued a list of newly restricted carry-on items, but the list changes frequently. Consult the TSA Web site at www.tsa.gov for the latest information.

✔ **Prepare to be searched.** Expect spot-checks. Remove electronic items, such as laptops and cell phones, from your carry-on bags and hand them over for additional screening. Limit the metal items you wear on your person so that you're less likely to set off the metal detector.

✔ **Don't joke around.** When a check-in agent asks if someone other than you packed your bag, don't decide that this is the time to be funny. The agent will not hesitate to sound an alarm.

✔ **Don't try to get to the gate unless you have a ticket.** Only ticketed passengers are allowed beyond the screener checkpoints, except for those people with specific medical or parental needs.

Other Ways to Get There

Although the most common way for tourists to arrive in New York is by air, the city can easily be reached by land-based transportation.

By train

New York is well served by **Amtrak** (☎ **800-USA-RAIL;** Internet: www.amtrak.com). The most convenient is the Northeast Corridor line, which runs between Washington, D.C., and Boston. If you're coming from anywhere on this line, taking the train is a lot smarter than taking a plane. The ride is likely to be shorter: no commute in traffic to and from the airport, no need to be there two hours in advance to check in and pass through security, and no waiting on the other end to collect your luggage. The train is also more comfortable — no dry airplane air, more freedom to stroll along the aisle, more room to work or sleep, and so on. Be sure to book in advance.

The train isn't necessarily cheaper, though. Prices on Amtrak remain high, but it offers specials and package tours that are worth looking into. Call ☎ **800-250-4989** for information about special rates, or check the Web site.

Amtrak trains arrive at Penn Station on the west side, a hub for land transportation in the heart of the city. The average round-trip fare to New York on regular trains is around $126 from Boston (a 4½-hour journey);

$168 and up from Chicago (a 16- to 18-hour trip, usually overnight); and $142 from Washington, D.C. (about 3½ hours). Note that these are coach fares, which means (except for Chicago) that seats are unreserved and not guaranteed (that is, if all the seats are full, you have to stand). You can reserve a seat in the pricier business-class and first-class wagons.

Amtrak has instituted new security measures: To buy a ticket, you must show a photo ID such as a driver's license or passport.

The recently introduced **Acela** (Internet: www.acela.com) express train cuts down the travel time, although you pay for that privilege. For example, the New York–Boston run costs about $220 round-trip. Travel between Washington, D.C., and New York takes about 2 hours and 45 minutes; between Boston and New York about 3 hours.

By car

In Chapter 9, we give you a number of compelling reasons *not* to drive in New York City. If you insist on driving into the city (see Chapter 10 for directions), plan on paying up to $45 per day for indoor parking.

Some long-term outdoor lots charge less than $35 a day for parking. You can find these lots along the West Side Highway and in the 50s west of Eighth Avenue.

You also can park near a commuter train station in New York, New Jersey, or Connecticut and take the commuter rail into the city. You still have to find parking near the station, but it will be somewhat cheaper than parking in Manhattan. For information about PATH train stations in New Jersey, contact the Port Authority of New York & New Jersey (☎ 800-234-PATH; Internet: www.panynj.gov). The MTA New York City Transit (Internet: www.mta.info) operates not only the city's subways and buses but also the Long Island Rail Road (☎ 718-217-LIRR), which serves Long Island (no kidding!), and the Metro-North Railroad (☎ 212-532-4900), which serves upstate New York and Connecticut.

In all cases, plan your arrival to avoid rush hours. Traffic jams in New York can be dreadful at the points of connection between the island of Manhattan and the surrounding metropolitan area (where all the airports are located). At rush hour, tunnels and bridges completely clog up. And don't think that you can get around the traffic by "reverse commuting" — coming into the city when everybody is leaving — because it doesn't work that way. Even if most of the traffic is outbound at around 5:00 p.m., a significant number of people commute back to Manhattan and the number of inbound lanes is reduced.

Try to arrive well outside the peak hours of 8:00 a.m. to 10:00 a.m. and 4:30 p.m. to 7:00 p.m. The weekend rush is the worst. In summer, outbound traffic starts as early as 2:00 p.m. on Fridays, and inbound traffic on Sunday evenings is absolutely nightmarish.

Chapter 6

Deciding Where to Stay

* *

In This Chapter

▶ Selecting the type of hotel that's right for you

▶ Picking the right neighborhood

▶ Choosing the right price range

* *

*W*ith more than 230 hotels — not counting bed-and-breakfasts (B&Bs) and other alternatives — and something like 63,000 hotel rooms, New York can make the task of selecting the best place to stay for your needs seem daunting. But it needn't be. Your decision depends on four factors: location, price, amenities, and space.

 Hotel rooms in New York average about $250 a night. Accommodations may take up a much larger portion of your total travel budget than they would in another city (see Chapter 3 for more information about budgeting); that's why you need to do a bit of planning.

Determining Which Kind of Place Is Right for You

The variety of accommodations in New York can set you back on your heels. There are small hotels with a few rooms and big ones with a thousand, trendy boutique hotels, national and worldwide chains, B&Bs, and a variety of apartments available for short-term stays. Choosing between one type of accommodation and another is only a matter of personal taste: Do you prefer cozy surroundings or a corporate business atmosphere? A trendsetter or a no-frills failsafe?

Independent hotels

Most of the hotels we list in Chapter 8 fall in the class of independent hotels (versus hotel chains) because we feel that such hotels give you more of a flavor of the city. Don't be misled, though; in New York, independent hotels include everything from huge business hotels run by large corporations — or by the ubiquitous Donald Trump — to small boutique hotels that are family run.

Chain hotels

A few of the hotels we list in Chapter 8 are major national chains. Far from the kind of cookie-cutter sameness you may find elsewhere, the chains we chose hold up in comparison to similarly located independent hotels. (See the Quick Concierge appendix for the toll-free numbers and Web sites of New York's major chain hotels.)

B&Bs and inns

A few very nice homes in Manhattan — for example, some historic houses in the West Village — have been turned into inns, but they have only a few rooms and are off the beaten path. Also, they're usually quite expensive, and you can find equivalent amenities (but minus the homey atmosphere) for less money in one of the city's many hotels.

Another kind of accommodation that you can get through a B&B association is a room in someone's apartment. The quality and price of these rooms vary considerably. If you'd like to check out some B&B options, try these associations and reservation agencies:

- ✔ **A Hospitality Company,** 247 W. 35th St., 4th Floor, New York, NY 10001 (☎ **800-987-1235** or 212-965-1102; Internet: www. hospitalityco.com).

- ✔ **At Home In New York Inc.,** P.O. Box 407, New York, NY 10185 (☎ **212-956-3125;** Fax: 212-247-3294; Internet: www.athomeny.com).

- ✔ **City Lights Bed & Breakfast,** 308 E. 79th St., New York, NY 10021 (☎ **212-737-7049;** Fax: 212-288-6972).

- ✔ **Manhattan Lodgings,** 70 E. 10th St., Suite 18C, New York, NY 10003 (☎ **212-475-2090;** Fax: 212-477-0420; Internet: www.manhattan lodgings.com).

- ✔ **New York Bed and Breakfast Reservation Center,** 331 W. 57th St., Suite 221, New York, NY 10019 (☎ **212-977-3512;** E-mail: smartsleep@aol.com).

Speaking of breakfast, don't be too enticed by the free continental breakfast that some hotels offer. It usually consists of coffee, juice, and some type of bread — a far cry from the hearty bacon-and-eggs with home fries and corned-beef hash that you may be craving to jump-start your day. Pricewise, you're usually better off going out for a bagel and coffee.

Short-term apartment rentals

If you want to look into renting a furnished apartment or subletting someone's place as an alternative to staying in a hotel, try the following companies:

- **Manhattan Getaways** (☎ **212-956-2010**; Fax: 212-265-3561; Internet: www.manhattangetaways.com)

- **New York Habitat** (☎ **212-255-8018**; Fax: 212-627-1416; Internet: www.nyhabitat.com)

- **NYC Residence** (☎ **212-226-2700**; Fax: 212-226-7555; Internet: www.nycresidence.com)

Choosing Your Location

The neighborhood in which your hotel is located is the springboard for your whole New York experience. It pays to be aware of a hotel's surroundings before booking a room. In the following sections, we run through all the major Manhattan neighborhoods you have to choose from, giving you the highlights. See Chapter 10 for more detailed neighborhood descriptions.

The Upper West Side

The **Upper West Side** (see Chapter 10 to pinpoint this neighborhood on a map) is a great neighborhood for people who like to walk around and explore — the area features quiet brownstone-lined streets and tons of upscale shops. Attractions include Lincoln Center and the American Museum of Natural History at the southern end, Central Park to the east, and Riverside Park to the west.

The paucity of restaurants on the Upper West Side has long been a source of regret for residents (and ridicule for those who live elsewhere), but recently some newcomers have improved the offerings. The hotels are cheaper here, although the selection is slimmer and there aren't as many high-end hotels as there are on the Upper East Side. At the same time, the atmosphere is livelier. Also, you face quite a trek if you want to go downtown, and you'll have to hop in a cab or on the subway to get to any theater shows.

The Upper East Side

The **Upper East Side** (see Chapter 10 to pinpoint this neighborhood on a map) is home to some of the most luxurious and expensive hotels in the city, with a few lower-priced options also available. Museum Mile is here, which makes it a convenient neighborhood if you plan to visit the Met, the Frick, or the Guggenheim Museum. This quiet area also offers easy access to Central Park, which runs along most of the neighborhood's western border.

On the downside, only the Lexington Avenue subway line (the 4/5/6) runs through the neighborhood, and that line is often congested. (Buses are usually a better choice for getting around.) Because of that, the Upper East Side is a little cut off and less convenient to the Theater District and certain downtown sights than Midtown and the Upper West Side are. Plus, night owls may be disappointed that the neighborhood pretty much shuts down after dark, although the area east of Third Avenue remains lively.

Midtown

Bordered by 59th Street to the north (the lower limit of Central Park), **Midtown** (see Chapter 10 to pinpoint this neighborhood on a map) is New York's other major business area after Wall Street. It's a large and varied neighborhood, including such landmarks as the Empire State Building, the Chrysler Building, Grand Central Terminal, Rockefeller Center, Radio City Music Hall, Times Square, and the United Nations, as well as the Theater District, the Garment District, and the major shopping areas of Fifth and Madison avenues and 57th Street. Many of Manhattan's major hotels and famous stores are also in Midtown. You're close to Central Park, and the trip downtown is easy.

Of course, all this convenience adds up to people. Lots and lots of people, especially in Times Square and on Fifth Avenue. The crowds can be intolerable (particularly on matinee Wednesdays and during rush hour), and finding good deals on dining is difficult unless you head east of Third Avenue or west of Eighth Avenue.

Toward the south, at about 26th street, Midtown merges into the neighborhoods of **Chelsea, Gramercy Park,** and the **Flatiron District,** which are currently the sites of much activity and growth. Quieter than Midtown proper, this part of town is still very central, offering a great starting point for most destinations in Manhattan. The recent development of this area as the new hip scene of the city has brought about the opening of a few very nice hotels and many excellent restaurants — the only drawbacks being that the number of hotels is still quite small and that you run across drab blocks that haven't yet been spruced up.

Downtown

Downtown is a general term covering a large area that loosely encompasses the **Financial District, SoHo, Greenwich Village,** the **East Village, NoLiTa, Little Italy, TriBeCa,** and **Chinatown** (see Chapter 10 to pinpoint these neighborhoods on a map). Most of the big downtown hotels are at this end of the island, close to major attractions like Wall Street, the Brooklyn Bridge, South Street Seaport, and Battery Park, but a few have opened in trendy SoHo and TriBeCa.

If you stay at the southern tip of the island, you're far from the main nightlife, and you'll need to take relatively long rides by taxi or subway to most theaters and museums in town. The area of the Financial District is fairly deserted at night, but you have access to beautiful views over New York Harbor and quiet nights — a real luxury in New York. The busy South Street Seaport area stays lively all day and night and is home to an increasing number of interesting restaurants.

If you choose to stay farther north, in TriBeCa, SoHo, or Greenwich Village, you'll be in the heart of one of New York's most beautiful historic areas and a center for alternative culture, nightlife (especially jazz), and fine dining. TriBeCa is the quietest of these three areas, home to many *very* expensive residential lofts but also to some undeveloped blocks that feel a little forlorn. (This area did sustain some damage in the September 11 attacks, and in the immediate aftermath many residents relocated; however, TriBeCa's restaurants and nightspots have hung tough, and people have begun to return in droves.) At the other end of the spectrum, you'll never be completely alone (and never experience complete quiet) in Greenwich Village, where the whole population of New York City seems to converge in the evenings and at night. SoHo is somewhere in between.

Although the terrorist attacks on the World Trade Center on September 11, 2001, changed the city's landscape horrifically, the affected area is relatively small. A few blocks away from the site, you really can't tell that something awful has happened. The only area that's off-limits to the public is the actual site of the World Trade Center — now referred to as Ground Zero — and the adjacent streets where some machines and construction equipment are still parked. Excavation has been completed, and hearings have begun to determine the future of the site. Meanwhile, the restoration of the World Financial Center (the building complex adjacent to Ground Zero) is well under way, and the beautiful Winter Garden should have reopened by the time this book is released (see Chapter 16 for more information).

Hotel dining

Most hotels in the moderate and upper brackets offer room service, but it's not always of the 24-hour variety. If room service is important to you, be sure to inquire when you call to reserve a room. But don't sweat it — you're not staying on the lonesome prairie where the coyotes howl. New York really is open all night, and if you choose to stay in a high-traffic neighborhood, you're likely to find all-night bars and restaurants close to your hotel. Many places will deliver right to your room, too.

You Get What You Pay For: Picking a Price Range

In Chapter 8, we preface each hotel listing with a number of dollar signs ranging from one ($) to five ($$$$$), corresponding to price. Here's a glance at what you can expect in terms of room size and standard amenities in each of these price categories:

- ✔ **$ ($85–$150):** These hotels are true bargains, but services are spare. Your room will probably be small, and don't expect room service, fitness equipment, movie or cable channels, or bellhops.

- ✔ **$$ ($150–$250):** Expect the rooms to be a little larger and of better quality and comfort. You may have access to a fitness center and business facilities, and the hotel may throw in a complimentary continental breakfast.

- ✔ **$$$ ($250–$350):** Typically, you get room service, a phone with a dataport, probably a refrigerator and perhaps some kind of minimal cooking facility, cable TV and/or VCR, free access to a health club, complimentary breakfast or beverages (and possibly afternoon wine and cheese), and an on-site restaurant.

- ✔ **$$$$ ($350–$450):** On top of the amenities listed for the preceding category, you can expect plenty of space, fine furnishings, a variety of dining and drinking options in the hotel, and excellent service. Because these hotels often cater to businesspeople, they sometimes offer special amenities like complimentary car service to the Financial District.

- ✔ **$$$$$ ($450 and up):** In this range, you get more than a place to stay: You get an experience. These hotels have style, elegance, and a reputation for impeccable service.

Chapter 7

Booking Your Room

. . . .

In This Chapter

▶ Understanding why rack rates aren't as painful as they sound

▶ Getting a good room at a reasonable price

▶ Finding a room at the last minute

. . . .

The word is out: New York is safer, better, and busier than ever. It's always been a hectic city, and even now, when the economy has slowed down a bit, tourism is soaring. On some days — especially in Times Square — it seems that everyone in the world wants a piece of the Apple. As a result, finding a hotel room, especially on short notice, is not always easy; finding something in your price range is even harder. In this chapter, we give you some tips for getting the best room at the best price — even if you need a room at the last minute.

Avoiding Rack Rates

Even though the term *rack rate* sounds like something that dates back to the Spanish Inquisition, the only place it'll hurt you is your wallet. The rack rate is the maximum rate that a hotel charges for a room, a rate that you can easily avoid paying. Just ask for a cheaper room or a discounted rate. If a hotel can't offer you anything better than its rack rate, consider going elsewhere.

Getting the best room and rate

You don't have to sit back and take the room and rate that a hotel offers you. With a little know-how, you can get the room you want at a price you can afford. We tell you how in this section.

As you proceed with the selection process, don't forget that the basic rate a hotel charges you isn't what you'll end up paying. The hotel tax in New York City is 13.25%, and there's also a room charge of $2 per night. When you reserve a room, make sure to find out whether the price you're being quoted includes taxes. Ditto for packages (see Chapter 5).

Saving money in the "off-season"

Remember that New York really has no off-season (see Chapter 2 for more information). For that reason, hotel rooms are always hotly contested. High demand means that you may or may not be able to get a discounted room. All you can do is try and hope for low volume at the hotel you plan to visit.

Trying a travel agent

Travel agents sometimes can get good deals on rooms at selected hotels. Hotels sometimes have discount rates that they offer only to travel agents; business is business, and a travel agent represents more business and more dollars than little old you. A good side of this equation is that, when the city is full, no rooms are available, and you're pulling your hair out, your travel agent may have the juice to get you a room even when you've been told, "Sorry, we're full up."

On the other hand, your travel agent could end up making you spend *more* money, depending on how well he or she knows the New York market. If the agent just calls a wholesaler or a tour operator and doesn't dig around for the best deals, you might spend more than you would if you did a lot of legwork yourself (see Chapter 5 for more on the pros and cons of using a travel agent). Making some calls for comparison never hurts, even if you plan to use an agent.

Using the do-it-yourself approach

The following tips can help you save money on your room if you decide to go it alone without a travel agent:

- ✔ **Shop for packages.** Check the travel section of the *New York Times* for advertised weekend and all-in-one/inclusive packages, or use one of the packagers whose addresses we list in Chapter 5.

- ✔ **Ask for the best rate.** Sometimes the easiest approach is a straightforward one. A hotel typically won't extend its discount room rates unless you ask for them.

- ✔ **Be aware of special rates.** Different rates may apply to your reservation depending on who you are and when you travel. For example, many hotels have special rates that may apply if you're traveling over a holiday; others offer special weekend rates. If you think that you may be eligible, ask about corporate, senior-citizen, and family rates when you reserve as well. (See Chapter 4 for more information about discounts for families and seniors.)

- ✔ **Mention your memberships.** When you reserve, mention your membership in AAA, AARP, frequent-flyer programs, and any other corporate rewards programs you belong to. These memberships may mean a few dollars off your room rate.

✔ **Call all available numbers.** Most hotels have both a local number and an 800 central reservation number. Sometimes these numbers have different rate information. Call both numbers and compare the rates that each one gives you.

Selecting the best room

Rooms within a hotel vary quite a bit. Asking about the following will pay off with increased comfort:

✔ **Smoking:** Declare your smoking preference when you reserve your room. If you want to smoke in your room, ask for "a smoker."

✔ **Noise:** Ask to be placed away from any renovations, restaurants, bars, or discos in the hotel. If the hotel is located on a busy street, ask for an inside room to insulate yourself from the street noise.

✔ **Corner rooms:** Always ask for a corner room, which is usually larger and quieter, has more windows and light, and doesn't always cost more than a standard room.

If you aren't happy with your room when you arrive, talk to the attendant at the front desk. Usually, the attendant will work with you to resolve the problem.

Surfing the Web for hotel deals

The major travel-booking sites — Travelocity, Expedia, Orbitz, and so on — offer hotel-booking services and often feature amazing specials on weekend or three-day stays. But when you're searching the Web for hotel deals, consulting sites devoted primarily to lodging is a good idea; you may find properties that more general online travel agencies don't list.

Depending on the time of year you visit New York, a booking site that can yield fabulous hotel room deals is Priceline (Internet: `www.price line.com`). As with plane tickets, you "name your own price" for a hotel room; you may choose a particular neighborhood and specify a luxury level, but you won't see the name of the hotel until your bid is accepted. If you're making last-minute reservations, it's possible to get a $275 hotel room for as low as $99. (Most hotels would rather book an empty room at a rock-bottom rate than let it go empty.)

Some lodging sites specialize in a particular type of accommodations, such as bed-and-breakfasts, which you won't find on the more mainstream booking services. Others, such as TravelWeb, offer weekend deals on major chain properties, which cater to business travelers and have more empty rooms on weekends.

Whatever route you choose, do a little homework before jumping on the Web. Call some hotels directly to see what kind of rates (rack rates and otherwise) they're offering. That way, you'll know whether these bargain-hunter Web sites are truly saving you money.

We recommend the following sites for information about hotels and discount room rates:

✔ **Accommodations Express** (Internet: www.accommodations express.com) books hotel rooms for trade shows and conventions, but it makes its volume discounts on room rates available to individual leisure travelers as well.

✔ **Hotel ConXions** (Internet: www.hotelconxions.com) is another consolidator that offers up to 60% discounts on hotel rack rates. Like others in this list, because it reserves blocks of rooms, Hotel ConXions is often able to get you into a certain hotel even if you know that it's already sold out.

✔ **hoteldiscount!com** (Internet: www.180096hotel.com) lists bargain room rates at hotels in more than 50 U.S. and international cities. Even cooler, hoteldiscount!com prebooks blocks of rooms, so it sometimes has discount rooms at hotels that are "sold out." Select a city, type in your travel dates, and you get a list of the best prices for a selection of hotels. This site is notable for delivering deep discounts in cities where hotel rooms are expensive, including New York.

✔ **TravelWeb** (Internet: www.travelweb.com) lists more than 26,000 hotels in 170 countries, focusing on chains such as Hyatt and Hilton. You can book rooms at almost 90% of these hotels online. TravelWeb's Click-It Weekends feature, updated each Monday, offers weekend deals at many leading hotel chains.

In addition, you can read descriptions of some hotels online through **NYC & Company,** the New York City Convention & Visitors Bureau (☎ **212-484-1222;** Internet: www.nycvisit.com). Some of the descriptions offer links to individual hotel Web sites, allowing you to book your room online. **Hotelguide.com** (Internet: www.hotelguide.com) is another source of information about New York hotels. **Citysearch** (Internet: newyork.citysearch.com) has a hotel guide as well.

Also, check out the sites of airline packagers, some of which we list in Chapter 5. Several of them have hotel guides attached, and you can browse their pictures of rooms and descriptions of amenities whether or not you book a package.

Arriving without a Reservation (Not Recommended)

Your options may be limited if you arrive without a reservation. However, making a few phone calls can get you a room most of the time.

As with airline travel, services that call themselves consolidators or wholesalers purchase lots of rooms at a big discount and then pass some of the savings on to you. The hotel stays full, the consolidator makes money, and you may save a lot (or only a little) in the bargain. Money aside, consolidator and reservation services often can get you a room when you can't find one anywhere else. The service usually makes you pay for your stay up front and in full; however, you've gotta pay sometime, and this way the figure may be more like what you had in mind.

In addition to Accommodations Express, Hotel ConXions, and hotel-discount!com, which we described earlier in the chapter, try the following bureaus if you arrive in New York without a reservation and have trouble booking directly with the hotels:

- ✔ **1800 New York Hotels.com** (☎ 212-267-5500; Internet: www.1800newyorkhotels.com). More than 80 hotels discounted up to 65%. In addition, at press time the service was offering 1,000 frequent flyer miles for each online reservation made at www.1800nyhotels.com.

- ✔ **Quikbook** (☎ 800-789-9887; Internet: www.quikbook.com). Covers 50 hotels; discounts can reach 60%.

- ✔ **Turbotrip.com** (☎ 800-473-7829; Internet: www.turbotrip.com). Provides comprehensive lodging and travel information for destinations throughout the United States and worldwide.

Chapter 8

New York City's Best Hotels

● ●

In This Chapter

▶ Getting the details on New York's best hotels

▶ Knowing where to go if your favorites are full

▶ Seeing at-a-glance listings of hotels by location and price

● ●

*I*n this chapter, we review all our favorite New York hotels, giving you the information you need to decide where to stay. At the end of the chapter, you can find some runner-up options, in case our top choices are unavailable, and some handy lists that break down our favorite hotels by price and neighborhood.

Turn to Chapter 10 to acquaint yourself with the city's various neighborhoods, and use the lists at the end of this chapter to quickly select the best hotel for your needs. If you want to be near the theaters, for example, Midtown West is your part of town. If you want to be near Central Park, you want either the Upper West Side or the Upper East Side. For a young, funky scene, try the Village or Chelsea; for Museum Mile, the Upper East Side; and for Lincoln Center, the Upper West Side.

Throughout this chapter, we place Kid Friendly icons next to the hotels that are especially good for families.

As you read this chapter, keep track of the reviews that appeal to you by checking them off in the margin. Use the "Sweet Dreams: Choosing Your Hotel" worksheet at the back of this book to help you keep track of the hotels you like best.

The Best New York City Hotels from A to Z

We use the following dollar-sign icons in each listing to denote the rack rate range for the hotel (refer to Chapter 7 for more information about rack rates). Prices quoted are for a double room with private bath unless otherwise noted.

$	=	$85–$150
$$	=	$150–$225
$$$	=	$225–$325
$$$$	=	$325–$425
$$$$$	=	$425 and up

If a hotel's rack rate is within $10 of the upper end of a range (say, $335), we give it the lower of the dollar-sign designations (in this case, we'd give it a $$$) rather than jumping all the way up to the next price range. Also note that some hotels — like the Chelsea Savoy — have a broad range of rack rates, and the room you get could be a real bargain or just average.

This list of our favorite hotels is based on the following criteria:

- ✔ **Capacity:** All the listed hotels are reasonably large (for their neighborhood), minimizing the chance of their being booked up.

- ✔ **Value for price:** We looked for hotels that are good values for their price category.

- ✔ **Amenities:** Unless otherwise noted, the hotels we've chosen include, at the very least, basic in-room amenities such as telephones, cable TV, and air conditioning. Most hotels have irons, ironing boards, and hairdryers either in the room or upon request at the front desk.

- ✔ **Condition:** We checked that the hotels we recommend are recently renovated or well maintained. These hotels are decent and reputable; we screened out those in dire need of renovation. All the hotels that we selected, unless otherwise noted, offer smoke-free rooms (and usually smoke-free floors).

- ✔ **Location:** All the hotels we chose are within walking distance of major attractions, public transportation, restaurants, and shops, and they're all in safe areas.

As you read the listings in this chapter, refer to the maps "Downtown Hotels," "Midtown Hotels," and "Uptown Hotels" to see where a particular hotel is located.

Downtown Hotels

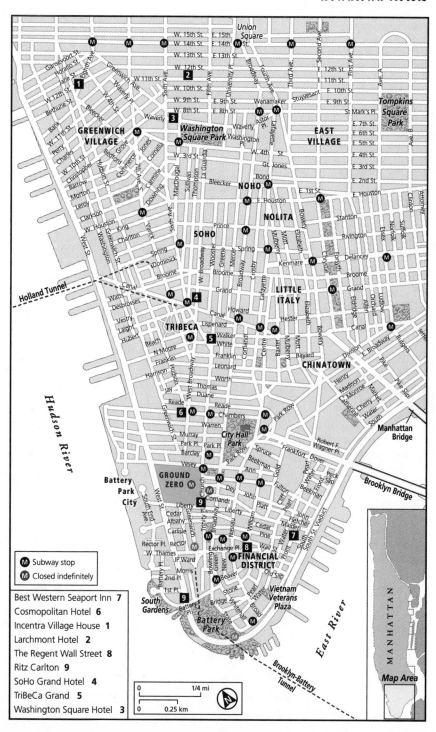

- Subway stop
- Closed indefinitely

Best Western Seaport Inn **7**
Cosmopolitan Hotel **6**
Incentra Village House **1**
Larchmont Hotel **2**
The Regent Wall Street **8**
Ritz Carlton **9**
SoHo Grand Hotel **4**
TriBeCa Grand **5**
Washington Square Hotel **3**

Midtown Hotels

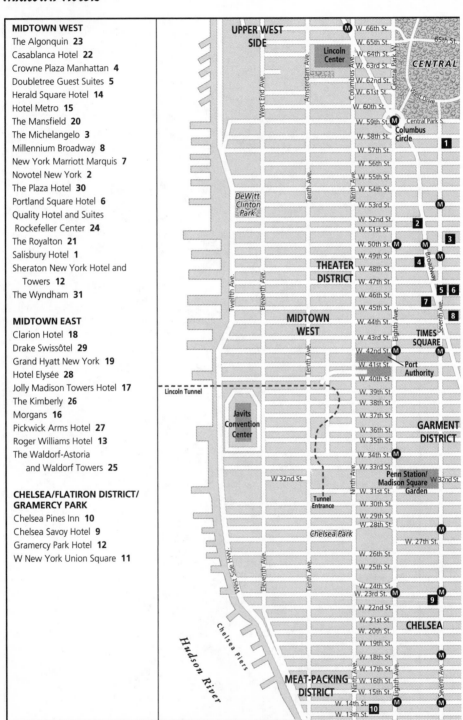

MIDTOWN WEST
The Algonquin **23**
Casablanca Hotel **22**
Crowne Plaza Manhattan **4**
Doubletree Guest Suites **5**
Herald Square Hotel **14**
Hotel Metro **15**
The Mansfield **20**
The Michelangelo **3**
Millennium Broadway **8**
New York Marriott Marquis **7**
Novotel New York **2**
The Plaza Hotel **30**
Portland Square Hotel **6**
Quality Hotel and Suites
 Rockefeller Center **24**
The Royalton **21**
Salisbury Hotel **1**
Sheraton New York Hotel and
 Towers **12**
The Wyndham **31**

MIDTOWN EAST
Clarion Hotel **18**
Drake Swissôtel **29**
Grand Hyatt New York **19**
Hotel Elysée **28**
Jolly Madison Towers Hotel **17**
The Kimberly **26**
Morgans **16**
Pickwick Arms Hotel **27**
Roger Williams Hotel **13**
The Waldorf-Astoria
 and Waldorf Towers **25**

**CHELSEA/FLATIRON DISTRICT/
GRAMERCY PARK**
Chelsea Pines Inn **10**
Chelsea Savoy Hotel **9**
Gramercy Park Hotel **12**
W New York Union Square **11**

UPPER EAST SIDE
MIDTOWN EAST
MURRAY HILL
FLATIRON DISTRICT
GRAMERCY PARK
QUEENS
East River
PARK
Transverse
East Drive
Center Drive
The Pond
Central Park S.
Fifth Ave.
Madison Ave.
Park Ave.
Lexington Ave.
Third Ave.
Second Ave.
First Ave.
York Ave.
Sutton Pl.
Sutton Pl. South
Beekman Place
Mitchell Place
Sixth Ave. (Ave. of the Americas)
Vanderbilt Ave.
Park Ave. S.
Broadway
Union Sq. W.
Union Sq. E.
Irving Pl.
N.D. Perlman Pl.
Asser Levy Pl.
Ave. C
FDR Drive
E. 66th St.
E. 65th St.
E. 64th St.
E. 63rd St.
E. 62nd St.
E. 61st St.
E. 60th St.
E. 59th St.
E. 58th St.
E. 57th St.
E. 56th St.
E. 55th St.
E. 54th St.
E. 53rd St.
E. 52nd St.
E. 51st St.
E. 50th St.
E. 49th St.
E. 48th St
E. 47th St.
E. 46th St.
E. 45th St.
E. 44th St.
E. 43rd St.
E. 42nd St.
E. 41st St.
E. 40th St.
E. 39th St.
E. 38th St.
E 37th St.
E 36th St.
E. 35th St.
E. 34th St.
E. 33rd St.
E. 32nd St.
E. 31st St.
E. 30th St.
E. 29th St.
E. 28th St.
E. 27th St.
E. 26th St.
E. 25th St.
E. 24th St.
E. 23rd St.
E. 22nd St.
E. 21st St.
E. 20th St.
E. 19th St.
E. 18th St.
E. 17th St.
E. 16th St.
E. 15th St.
E. 14th St.
E. 13th St.
From Lower Level
To Upper Level
Roosevelt Island Tram
Queensboro Bridge
Rockefeller Center
Grand Central Terminal
Bryant Park
New York Public Library
United Nations
Queens-Midtown Tunnel
Tunnel Exit
Tunnel Entrance
Empire State Bldg.
Madison Square Park
Gramercy Park
Union Square
Peter Cooper Village
Stuyvesant Town
0
1/4 mi
0.25 km
Subway stop
Upper Manhattan
Uptown
Midtown
Downtown
11
12
13
14
15
16
17
18
19
20
21
22
23
24
25
26
27
28
29
30
31

Best Western Seaport Inn
$$ Downtown

Here's a modern Best Western hotel wrapped inside an Old New York package. The hotel is situated in an 1852 structure in the heart of the South Street Seaport historic waterfront area, convenient to all downtown attractions. Standard rooms have many conveniences, including safe, refrigerator, dataport, and coffeemaker, and the rooms on the top floor have terraces with sweeping views of downtown and the harbor. The best rooms come with a whirlpool tub. The hotel does not offer room service, but you do get a complimentary continental breakfast. The hotel has a fitness room that's open 24 hours. Your kids, if under 18, stay free in your room; a rollaway bed is available for a $25 charge. Each floor has one room equipped for people with disabilities.

23 Peck Slip between Front and Water streets (2 blocks north of South Street Seaport). ☎ *800-HOTELNY, 212-766-6600. Fax: 212-766-6615. Internet:* www.bestwestern.com/seaportinn. *Subway: 1/2/4/5/A/C train to Fulton Street/Broadway Nassau stop. Walk east on Fulton about 5 blocks, turn left on Water Street, walk 3 blocks, and turn right on Peck Slip. Parking: $20. Rack rates: $149–$209. AE, CB, DC, DISC, MC, V.*

The Carlyle
$$$$$ Upper East Side

This prestigious hotel is known for its luxury and excellent service (the hotel's ratio of staff to guests is better than one to one). A top choice with stars and dignitaries as well as regular folks, the Carlyle boasts world-class amenities: marble baths with whirlpool tubs, Givenchy toiletries, plush towels and terrycloth robes, baby-sitting service, and a top-quality fitness center. Of course, you pay through the nose for this level of service and amenities, but for many people, the price is worth it. Rooms on the upper floors afford a great view of Central Park, and the hotel is convenient to Museum Mile. A variety of celebrities play regularly in the Cafe Carlyle downstairs (pianist Bobby Short appears twice a week, and filmmaker Woody Allen plays clarinet in a Dixieland band most Monday nights). The excellent restaurant is a destination in its own right, serving classic French food and a renowned Sunday brunch. The hotel's Bemelmans Bar, named for the man who wrote the *Madeline* children's books (he painted the mural in the bar), is a lovely spot for cocktails.

35 E. 76th St. at Madison Avenue (1 block north of the Whitney Museum). ☎ *800-227-5737, 212-744-1600. Fax: 212-717-4682. Subway: 6 train to 77th Street stop, and then walk 1 block west on 76th Street to Madison Avenue. Parking: Valet, $44 per day. Rack rates: $495–$795 double. AE, DC, MC, V.*

Casablanca Hotel
$$$ Midtown West

This hotel offers good value with a Moroccan theme. The room decoration is inspired by the famous movie, with ceiling fans overhead and

Uptown Hotels

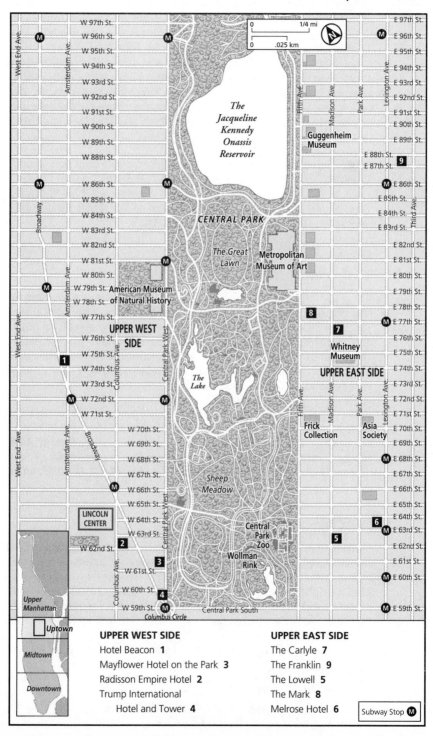

UPPER WEST SIDE

Hotel Beacon **1**

Mayflower Hotel on the Park **3**

Radisson Empire Hotel **2**

Trump International
    Hotel and Tower **4**

UPPER EAST SIDE

The Carlyle **7**

The Franklin **9**

The Lowell **5**

The Mark **8**

Melrose Hotel **6**

Subway Stop Ⓜ

carved wooden headboards on the beds. You also get great service and nice amenities, including fine chocolates in the room, Caswell-Massey toiletries, complimentary continental breakfast, tea and cookies throughout the day, and complimentary wine and cheese on weekday evenings. The hotel also offers free access to the New York Sports Club in the nearby Crowne Plaza Hotel, with pool and sauna. Two children under 13 stay free in their parents' room. The guests-only restaurant, called — you guessed it — Rick's Cafe, serves both breakfast and a steady stream of coffee, tea, and cookies, with wine, beer, and cheese in the evenings. Soak up the atmosphere provided by the piano and fireplace and take advantage of the cafe's free Internet access.

147 W. 43rd St. between Sixth Avenue and Broadway (½ block from Times Square). ☎ *888-922-7225, 212-869-1212. Fax: 212-391-7585. E-mail:* casahotel@aol.com. *Internet:* www.casablancahotel.com. *Subway: 1/2/3/7/W/Q/N/R/S train to Times Square stop, and then walk ½ block east on 43rd Street. Parking: $25 per day. Rack rates: $235–$295 double. AE, DC, JCB, MC, V.*

Chelsea Pines Inn
$ **Greenwich Village**

Close to Chelsea and the West Village, this hotel has a location and welcoming staff that make it ideal for gay travelers. The inn, housed in an 1850 row house, was recently renovated and is graced by a greenhouse and a seasonal backyard garden. Most rooms have private baths; a few share a bath but have showers and sinks in the rooms. The room price includes breakfast with homemade breads and Krispy Kreme doughnuts. Free Internet access is available to guests.

317 W. 14th St. between Eighth and Ninth avenues (on the border between Greenwich Village and Chelsea). ☎ *888-546-2700, 212-929-1023. Fax: 212-620-5646. E-mail:* CPINY@aol.com. *Internet:* www.chelseapinesinn.com. *Subway: A/C/E/L train to 14th Street/Eighth Avenue stop, and then walk ½ block west on 14th Street. Parking: On the street. Rack rates: $89–$139 double. AE, CB, DC, DISC, MC, V.*

Chelsea Savoy Hotel
$$ **Chelsea**

Good prices and clean, bright spaces — you can't go wrong with the Chelsea Savoy. In addition, you'll be in trendy Chelsea, which has virtually displaced SoHo as the focus of the New York art gallery scene; it's also a neighborhood with many new, interesting restaurants. The decor of the rooms is modern and pleasant, with lots of wood and tasteful furnishings. Among the in-room amenities are refrigerators, irons, and hairdryers. Children under 13 stay for free in their parents' room. The hotel offers specially designed rooms for disabled travelers.

204 W. 23rd St. at Seventh Avenue (2 blocks west of the Flatiron Building). ☎ *866-929-9353, 212-929-9353. Fax: 212-741-6309. Internet:* www.chelseasavoynyc.com. *Subway: 1/2 train to 23rd Street stop; the hotel is at the corner. Parking: On the street. Rack rates: $99–$195. AE, JCB, MC, V.*

Clarion Hotel

$$ Midtown East

Built in 1990 and formerly a Quality Inn, this hotel is at the foot of the most elegant stretch of Fifth Avenue. It's convenient to most Midtown sights yet remains relatively inexpensive (it's also a mere block away from Lord & Taylor department store). It offers discounts and specials; the cheaper rooms are simple but tidy. You get free coffee and newspapers in the morning, as well as free local calls. Some of the rooms on the upper stories have views of Manhattan. Access to a nearby health club with a pool is available for a $15 fee, and the hotel has a business center on the mezzanine level with computers, fax machines, and photocopiers. Children under 19 stay free in their parents' room; an extra person costs $15. Ten of the rooms are wheelchair accessible.

3 E. 40th St. at Fifth Avenue (south of the New York Public Library). ☎ *800-CLARION, 212-447-1500. Fax: 212-213-0972. Internet:* www.clarionfifthavenue.com. *Subway: 7 train to Fifth Avenue stop, walk 2 blocks south on Fifth Avenue, and turn right on 40th Street; or 4/5/6/S train to Grand Central stop, exit at 42nd Street, walk 2 blocks south on Park Avenue, turn right on 40th Street, and walk 2 blocks west. Parking: $18 per day. Rack rates: $175–$355 double. AE, DC, DISC, JCB, MC, V.*

Cosmopolitan Hotel

$ TriBeCa

The Cosmopolitan is a real find — simple, clean accomodations with a modernist touch at one of the most affordable prices in Manhattan. All rooms come with a private bath and the basic amenities; the addition of in-room ceiling fans and dataports is a big plus. The furnishings are streamlined and pleasant in color. Don't expect luxury, but do expect quiet and basic comforts. Although this hotel is not far from the World Trade Center site, it was not adversely affected by the attacks, and business continues to thrive.

95 W. Broadway at Chambers Street (in the heart of TriBeCa, steps from Little Italy and Chinatown). ☎ *888-895-9400, 212-566-1900. Fax: 212-566-6909. Internet:* www.cosmohotel.com. *Subway: 1/2 train to Chambers Street stop; or A/C train to Chambers Street stop, and then walk west on Chambers. Parking: $20 per day. Rack rates: $119–$149 double. AE, CB, DC, JCB, MC, V.*

Doubletree Guest Suites

$$$ Midtown West

Many features of this Times Square hotel make it one of the best choices for families. First of all, it's located in the heart of the Theater District, and Central Park is a short walk up Broadway. Two floors of the hotel offer child-proofed suites, and the Doubletree provides a playroom and an arts-and-crafts center. All rooms are suites with a bedroom and a living room, which includes a sofa bed. A microwave, coffeemaker, and refrigerator in each suite make it easy to prepare light meals in your room.

Children under 12 stay free in their parents' suite (an extra person costs $20), and cribs are available at no extra charge. The hotel is well adapted to the needs of travelers with disabilities.

1568 Broadway at 47th Street and Seventh Avenue (in the Theater District just north of Times Square). ☎ *800-222-TREE, 212-719-1600. Fax: 212-521-9212. Internet:* www.nyc.doubletreehotels.com. *Subway: N/R train to 49th Street stop, and then walk 2 blocks south on Seventh Avenue; or 1/2/3/7/W/Q/S train to Times Square stop, and then walk 4 blocks north on Seventh Avenue. Parking: $28 for self-parking and $35 for valet per day. Rack rates: $225–$325 suite. AE, DC, DISC, JCB, MC, V.*

Drake Swissôtel
$$$ Midtown East

The spacious rooms in this hotel, in a quiet neighborhood, have big closets with safes and refrigerators. Business travelers flock to the Drake for its business center (two hours of meeting-room use per stay is complimentary) and for its free car service to Wall Street on weekday mornings. The hotel also offers a brand-new fitness center. Children under 15 stay free in their parents' room; an extra person costs $30.

440 Park Ave. at 56th Street (just east of Central Park). ☎ *800-DRAKENY, 212-421-0900. Fax: 212-372-4190. Internet:* www.swissotel.com. *Subway: E/V train to Lexington Avenue/53rd Street stop, walk 1 block west on 53rd, turn right, and walk 3 blocks north on Park Avenue; or 6 train to 51st Street stop, walk 1 block west to Park Avenue, turn right, and walk 5 blocks north. Parking: Valet, $30 per day. Rack rates: $235–$395 double. AE, CB, DC, DISC, JCB, MC, V.*

The Franklin
$$$ Upper East Side

The Franklin's appeal is that it's a moderately priced choice in an expensive area of the city. The rooms, recently renovated, are small, but the furnishings are tasteful and in a style that Franklin would approve of, with canopied beds and modern amenities (including VCRs and CD players and the hotel's complimentary CD and video library). The room price includes breakfast, complimentary soft drinks in the evenings, and coffee and tea 24 hours a day. The service is top-notch; you'd have to pay far more at the nearby Pierre or the Mark to get more attention.

164 E. 87th St. between Lexington and Third avenues (just east of Museum Mile and Central Park). ☎ *800-600-8787, 212-369-1000. Fax: 212-369-8000. Internet:* www.franklinhotel.com. *Subway: 4/5/6 train to 86th Street stop, walk 1 block north on Lexington, and turn right. Parking: $20–$30 per day. Rack rates: $210–$295 double. AE, MC, V.*

Grand Hyatt New York
$$$ Midtown East

A Donald Trump hotel, the Grand Hyatt is next door to Grand Central Terminal and offers several levels of accommodation from standard to

Regency Club. The standard rooms are small, but all rooms are equipped with fax machines and dataports, and you get access to the hotel's new fitness center. Regency Club rooms have a private concierge. Regency Deluxe and Business Plan rooms give you access to a private business center with photocopiers and printers at all hours. Both Business Plan and Regency Club guests receive a complimentary continental breakfast. Two children under 18 can stay for free in their parents' room.

109 E. 42nd St. at Park Avenue (next to Grand Central Terminal). ☎ *800-233-1234, 212-883-1234. Fax: 212-687-3772. Internet:* www.newyork.hyatt.com. *Subway: 4/5/6/7/S train to Grand Central stop; exit at 42nd Street and turn left. Parking: Valet, $37 per day. Rack rates: $209–$429 double. Special discounts available for senior citizens and weekend guests. AE, CB, DC, DISC, JCB, MC, V.*

Herald Square Hotel
$ Midtown West

You can't beat the price of the rooms here; a tiny double goes for less than $100. But this is no fleabag — all the hotel's rooms are comfortable and feature the usual basic amenities. A major expansion with the addition of 54 rooms was recently completed, and all the rooms have been renovated. On top of all that, you'll be in the heart of the city.

19 W. 31st St. between Fifth Avenue and Broadway (2 blocks south of the Empire State Building). ☎ *800-727-1888, 212-279-4017. Fax: 212-643-9208. E-mail:* info@heraldsquarehotel.com. *Internet:* www.heraldsquarehotel.com. *Subway: B/D/F/V/Q/N/R/W train to 34th Street/Herald Square stop, walk south 2 blocks on Broadway to 31st Street, and turn left. Parking: $21 per day with hotel discount at a nearby lot. Rack rates: $85–$120 double. AE, DISC, JCB, MC, V.*

Hotel Beacon
$$ Upper West Side

This recently renovated hotel is a good deal for everybody but especially for those traveling with children. The prices are reasonable, the rooms are good-sized and have kitchenettes with new microwave ovens and marble baths, and a coin-op laundry and valet service are available. The hotel's suites have an additional room with a pull-out couch. The Beacon offers easy access to many family-oriented attractions, such as Central Park, the Museum of Natural History, and the Children's Museum. Coffee at the 24-hour coffee shop helps make up for the lack of room service, and in-room movies are complimentary. Children under 17 stay free in their parents' room (an extra person costs $15). Make sure to check the Beacon's Internet specials.

2130 Broadway at 75th Street (3 blocks west of the Museum of Natural History). ☎ *800-572-4969, 212-787-1100. Fax: 212-724-0839. E-mail:* info@beaconhotel. com. *Internet:* www.beaconhotel.com. *Subway: 1/2/3 train to 72nd Street stop, and then walk 3 blocks north on Broadway. Parking: $15 per day. Rack rates: $195–$225 double. AE, CB, DISC, MC, V.*

Hotel Elysée
$$$$ Midtown East

The Elysée is a chic "boutique" hotel with European flair, both in the clientele and the furnishings. It has long been popular with writers and artists (Tennessee Williams lived there for 15 years). The hotel is known for understated elegance: marble baths, good-sized rooms, complimentary continental breakfast, afternoon tea, and weekday evening wine and cheese served in the second-floor clubroom. The Monkey Bar is a popular nightspot from which you can order room service during the lunch and dinner hours. Guests enjoy free access to the nearby New York Sports Club.

60 E. 54th St. between Madison and Park avenues (near Rockefeller Center and Central Park). ☎ *800-535-9733, 212-753-1066. Fax: 212-980-9278. Internet:* www.members.aol.com/elysee99. *Subway: E/F train to Fifth Avenue stop, walk 1 block north to 54th Street, and then walk 1½ blocks east. Parking: Valet, $24 per day. Rack rates: $325–$400 double. AE, DC, JCB, MC, V.*

Hotel Metro
$$ Midtown West

Bargain-minded travelers should be satisfied at the Hotel Metro. For a relatively low rate, you get complimentary continental breakfast, room service available from the highly rated Metro Grill, marble baths, and access to a fitness room. In addition, the roof terrace of this Art Deco hotel offers a great view of the Empire State Building. The location is excellent for sightseeing.

45 W. 35th St. between Fifth and Sixth avenues (just east of Herald Square, 1 block from the Empire State Building). ☎ *800-356-3870, 212-947-2500. Fax: 212-279-1310. Internet:* www.hotelmetronyc.com. *Subway: B/D/F/V/Q/N/R/W train to 34th Street/Herald Square stop, and then walk north on Sixth Avenue to 35th Street and turn right. Parking: $18 per day. Rack rates: $160–$250 double. AE, DC, MC, V.*

Incentra Village House
$$ Greenwich Village

What's not to like about the Incentra? This gay-friendly hotel is within walking distance of West Village and Chelsea nightlife, and the M20 bus that stops right across the street offers easy access to the Theater District and uptown. The rooms are attractively decorated with antiques and other nice furniture, and many offer kitchenettes and functioning fireplaces. Constructed out of two historic 19th-century red brick townhouses, the Incentra is certainly distinct from most Manhattan hotels. The only detracting feature is its size. With only 12 rooms, the Incentra books up quickly, so reserve well in advance.

32 Eighth Ave. between 12th and Jane streets, just north of Abingdon Square (in Greenwich Village). ☎ *212-206-0007. Fax: 212-604-0625. Subway: A/C/E/L train to 14th Street/Eighth Avenue stop, and then walk 2 blocks south on Eighth Avenue. Parking: On the street. Rack rates: $149–$169 double. AE, MC, V.*

Jolly Madison Towers Hotel
$$$ Midtown East

This beautiful building, done in Southern European Renaissance style, opened in 1923 as Midston House, a fashionable "club" hotel. One of its attractions, the Whaler Bar — a replica of a New Bedford whaling ship — still exists. The lobby is also striking with its marble staircase and Venetian glass light fixtures. Now owned by an Italian hotel group, the Jolly Madison was completely renovated in the 1990s. The rooms feature marble baths, rosewood furniture, and touches of European elegance, as well as modern conveniences like personal computer connections in every room. The spa located on the third floor will pamper you with shiatsu massage and a sauna and Jacuzzi for an additional charge of $60 per hour. You can eat at the on-site cafe as well as the Cinque Terre restaurant (Italian, of course). One child under 13 can stay for free in the parents' room.

22 E. 38th St. at Madison Avenue (1 block north of the Pierpont Morgan Library, just south of Grand Central Terminal and the New York Public Library). ☎ *800-221-2626 in the U.S., 800-237-0319 in Canada, 212-802-0600. Fax: 212-447-0747. Internet:* www.jolly hotels.it/Default_eng.asp. *Subway: 4/5/6/7/S train to Grand Central stop, exit at 42nd Street, walk west to Madison Avenue, turn left, and walk 4 blocks south. Parking: $25 per day. Rack rates: $250–$380 double. AE, DC, JCB, MC, V.*

The Kimberly
$$$ Midtown East

This hotel offers attractive, comfortable standard rooms as well as huge suites that include dining and living rooms, kitchens, marble baths, and balconies. Its ornate neoclassical and French-style lobby and public spaces aspire to the manner of a grand hotel, but the Kimberly also bills itself as a boutique hotel and spa. One of the main attractions is its connection to the New York Health & Racket Club: Guests receive a free three-hour cruise on the club's boat (May through October only) and can use the club's pools, tennis courts, gyms, and indoor golf facility free of charge. The rooms feature fax machines and safes in which you can stow your laptop computer and other valuables. Children under 17 stay free in their parents' room; an extra person costs $25. The hotel's upscale French restaurant, L'Actuel, provides room service.

145 E. 50th St. between Lexington and Third avenues (3 blocks east of Rockefeller Center). ☎ *800-683-0400, 212-755-0400. Fax: 212-750-0113. Internet:* www. kimberlyhotel.com. *Subway: 6 train to 51st Street stop, walk 1 block south on Lexington, and turn left on 50th Street; or E/V train to Lexington/53rd street stop, walk 3 blocks south on Third Avenue, and turn right on 50th Street. Parking: $23 per day. Rack rates: $259–$385 double. AE, DC, DISC, JCB, MC, V.*

Larchmont Hotel
$ Greenwich Village

A harbor of peace in a beautiful block of the West Village, this small hotel (55 rooms) is nicely appointed and clean. The rooms are small but brightly furnished and quiet, as is the breakfast room. The drawback? None of the rooms has a private bathroom; there's a bath on each floor, and each room has a wash basin. The advantage? Each floor is equipped with a small kitchen, and the price is a steal given the location and exemplary service. The rooms feature rattan furniture, writing desks, and small collections of books. The price includes continental breakfast with juice, coffee, and tea. The hotel fills up fast, so book in advance.

27 W. 11th St. between Fifth and Sixth avenues (near Washington Square, in the heart of the Village). ☎ *212-989-9333. Fax: 212-989-9496. Internet:* www. larchmonthotel.com. *Subway: 4/5/6/L/N/Q/R/W train to 14th Street/Union Square stop, walk 3 blocks south on University Place, turn right on 11th Street, and walk 1½ blocks west. Parking: $18 per day. Rack rates: $90–$135 double. AE, MC, V.*

The Lowell

$$$$ **Upper East Side**

Located in a historic Art Deco building close to Museum Mile, the medium-sized Lowell has elegant and individually appointed rooms and suites — for example, one has a private gym, and another has a huge bathtub. All the bathrooms are done in marble and brass. To top off the luxury, the hotel's fitness center offers spa treatments. The hotel's restaurant is the Post House, an acclaimed steakhouse. The charge for an extra person is $40.

28 E. 63rd St. between Park and Madison avenues (just east of Central Park). ☎ *800-221-4444, 212-838-1400. Fax: 212-319-4230. Internet:* www.lhw.com. *Subway: F train to Lexington Avenue/63rd Street stop, and then walk west 1½ blocks on 63rd Street; or 4/5/6/N/R/W train to Lexington Avenue/59th Street stop, walk 4 blocks north, turn left on 63rd Street, and walk 1½ blocks. Parking: Valet, $45 per day. Rack rates: $415 double. AE, DC, DISC, JCB, MC, V.*

The Mark

$$$$$ **Upper East Side**

The Mark is a big name in luxury, and a list of the hotel's amenities helps you understand why. The bathrooms feature oversized tubs and heated towel racks, and each room is decorated with fresh flowers. The hotel offers free car service to Wall Street on weekdays and to the Theater District on Friday and Saturday evenings. You also get access to a small health club and to the amazing food at Mark's, the hotel's restaurant and stylish bar. Among recent additions are computer terminals with Web access in every room and "free" cellular phones (you pay $1.75 per minute for calls). Families can ask for one of the connecting doubles or for an executive suite, which includes a queen-size bed and a sofa bed. Children under 16 stay free in their parents' room. An extra person costs $30.

25 E. 77th St. between Fifth and Madison avenues (just off Central Park, 2 blocks north of the Whitney Museum). ☎ *800-THEMARK, 212-744-4300. Fax: 212-744-2749. E-mail:* reservations@themarknyc.com. *Internet:* www.themarkhotel.

com. *Subway: 6 train to 77th Street stop, and then walk west 2½ blocks on 77th to Madison. Parking: Valet, $35 per day. Rack rates: $525–$605 double. AE, CB, DC, DISC, JCB, MC, V.*

Mayflower Hotel on the Park
$$$ Upper West Side

It's not fancy, but you get quite a bit for your money at the Mayflower — for example, a great view of Central Park. (The hotel's location makes it a wonderful place to watch the Macy's Thanksgiving Day Parade; reserve a room well in advance if you want to stay at the Mayflower at that time.) This well-maintained hotel has large rooms with refrigerators and sinks; the bathrooms, however, tend to be small (all the bathrooms are gradually being modernized). Connecting doubles and suites are available for families. There's an exercise room as well as a restaurant (the Conservatory) that serves three meals a day. Children 16 and under stay free in their parents' room. An additional bed is $20.

15 Central Park West between 61st and 62nd streets (on Central Park, between Columbus Circle and Lincoln Center). ☎ ***800-223-4164,*** *212-265-0060. Fax: 212-265-0227. E-mail:* resinfo@mayflowerny.com. *Internet:* www.mayflowerhotel.com. *Subway: A/C/1/2/B/D train to Columbus Circle stop, and then walk north 2 blocks on Central Park West. Parking: Valet, $28 per day. Rack rates: $225–$265 double. AE, CB, DISC, JCB, MC, V.*

Melrose Hotel
$$$ Upper East Side

With its Spanish Gothic front and Art Deco lobby, the Melrose (formerly the Barbizon) speaks of elegance but also whispers of economy. Once a residential hotel for women only (guests included Grace Kelly), the Melrose has been renovated and offers nicely appointed rooms with all-new furnishings and good stereo systems (the hotel has a CD library available to guests). For a small fee, guests receive access to the sizeable Equinox Fitness Club located in the building, with pool and spa. Children under 12 stay free in their parents' room with existing bedding.

140 E. 63rd St. at Lexington Avenue (north of Bloomingdale's). ☎ ***800-223-1020,*** *212-838-5700. Fax: 212-888-4271. Internet:* www.melrosehotel.com. *Subway: F train to Lexington Avenue/63rd Street stop; N/R/W to Lexington Avenue/59th Street stop; or 4/5/6 to 59th Street stop, and then walk 3 blocks north on Lexington. Parking: $29 per day. Rack rates: $250–$350 double. AE, DC, DISC, MC, V.*

The Michelangelo
$$$$ Midtown West

Near the top of the price scale, the Michelangelo delivers luxury commensurate with its high room rates. You can look forward to spacious rooms with king-size beds, terrycloth robes, Baci chocolates on your pillow, complimentary continental breakfast, and marble baths with large tubs. The hotel offers complimentary car service to Wall Street on week-days, and you can request a room with computer, fax, and modem. For those who don't get enough exercise pacing the streets of Manhattan during their visit, the hotel offers access to a small fitness center, or you can pay a small fee to use the Equitable Health and Swim Club across the street. The hotel's restaurant is the very good Limoncello, featuring Italian cuisine and an attached tavern, the Grotto. It feels secluded, but with the Theater District, Central Park, Times Square, and other attractions within a stone's throw, the Michelangelo is in the heart of the action. Check for special Internet and weekend rates.

152 W. 51st St., at the corner of Seventh Avenue (in the Theater District). ☎ *800-237-0990, 212-765-1900. Fax: 212-541-6604. Internet:* www.michel angelohotel.com. *Subway: 1/2 train to 50th Street stop, and then walk ½ block east on 51st Street; or N/R/W to 49th Street stop, and then walk 1 block north on Seventh Avenue; or B/D/E to Seventh Avenue stop, and then walk 2 blocks south on Seventh Avenue. Parking: Valet, $18 per day. Rack rates: $395–$495 double. AE, CB, DC, DISC, JCB, MC, V.*

Morgans
$$$ **Midtown East**

Located in a quiet Midtown oasis, Morgans has a sleek, minimalist atmosphere, with maple furniture and subdued colors characterizing the decor. The smallish bathrooms are classic black and white. Features include a fax machine in each room, 24-hour room service, a breakfast room, and complimentary access to the nearby New York Sports Club. The hotel is also endowed with one of the best gourmet restaurants in New York City, Asia de Cuba, with a bar that attracts a hip clientele.

237 Madison Ave. at 37th Street (near the Morgan Library, between the Empire State Building and the New York Public Library). ☎ *800-334-3408, 212-686-0300. Fax: 212-779-8352. Internet:* www.ianschragerhotels.com. *Subway: 4/5/6/7/S train to Grand Central stop, exit at 42nd Street, turn right, walk west to Madison Avenue, turn left, and walk 5 blocks south. Parking: $32 per day. Rack rates: $290–$330 double. AE, DC, DISC, MC, V.*

New York Marriott Marquis
$$$ **Midtown West**

For theatergoers, the gigantic Marriott Marquis (with more than 1,900 rooms) is a great place to stay — right in the heart of the Theater District. The revolving restaurant and lounge on top of the hotel offers a fantastic view of the surrounding neighborhood. In addition, the hotel has access to a health club (with whirlpool and sauna), and every room has a workstation. The Marriott Marquis is also well suited to the needs of travelers with disabilities. Keep in mind, though, that the rooms tend to be small, and traffic noise from Broadway can be a problem.

1535 Broadway between 45th and 46th streets (just north of Times Square). ☎ *800-843-4898, 212-398-1900. Fax: 212-704-8930. Internet:* www.nycmarriott.

com. *Subway: 1/2/3/7/N/Q/R/S/W train to Times Square stop, and then walk 2 blocks north on Broadway. Parking: $30 per day. Rack rates: $199–$375 double. AE, CB, DISC, JCB, MC, V.*

New York Times Square Hotel
$$ Midtown West

This reasonably priced, centrally located hotel is owned by the Super 8 motel chain. Rates include complimentary continental breakfast, use of the fitness and business centers, and free local phone calls (phones have voice mail and dataports, too). Rooms come with coffeemakers and irons. Children under 19 stay for free in their parents' room.

59 W. 46th St. between Fifth and Sixth avenues (2 blocks south of Rockefeller Center). ☎ *800-567-7720, 212-719-2300. Fax: 212-921-8929. Internet:* www. super8.com. *Subway: B/D/F/V train to 47th–50th streets/Rockefeller Center stop, walk 3 blocks south on Sixth Avenue, and turn left on 46th Street. Parking: $25 per day. Rack rates: $139–$209. AE, CB, DC, MC, V.*

Novotel New York
$$$ Midtown West

Near the Broadway theaters, Rockefeller Center, Times Square, and Central Park, Novotel New York places you in close proximity to many of the city's most famous attractions. The rooms, each of which comes with a king-size bed or two double beds and a sofa bed, are large, with fabulous views available from rooms on the upper floors. Other amenities include complimentary continental breakfast, a business center, a fitness room, and a children's activity center. Two children under 17 stay for free in their parents' room. More than 20 rooms at the hotel are equipped for travelers with disabilities.

226 W. 52nd St. at Broadway. ☎ *800-NOVOTEL, 212-315-0100. Fax: 212-765-5369. Internet:* www.novotel.com. *Subway: B/D/E train to Seventh Avenue stop, walk west on 53rd Street to Broadway, and turn left; or 1/2 train to 50th Street stop, and then walk 2 blocks north on Broadway; or N/R/W train to 49th Street stop, walk 1 block west to Broadway, turn right, and walk 2 blocks north. Parking: $16 per day. Rack rates: $209–$329 double. AE, CB, DC, JCB, MC, V.*

Pickwick Arms Hotel
$ Midtown East

At the Pickwick, you can stay in a pricey part of town for not a lot of money. Its roof garden and cocktail lounge help make up for the small rooms and lack of other amenities. Not all rooms have private baths; if you want one, reserve well in advance. This cheap, clean, stripped-down option will please budget-concious travelers, and it books up fast.

230 E. 51st St. between Second and Third avenues (between the United Nations and Rockefeller Center). ☎ *800-PICKWIK, 212-355-0300. Fax: 212-755-5029.*

Internet: www.pickwickarms.com. *Subway: 6 train to 51st Street stop, and then walk 1 block east on 51st to Third Avenue; or E/V train to Lexington Avenue/53rd Street stop, walk south 2 blocks on Third Avenue, and turn left. Parking: $35 per day. Rack rates: $140–$160 double. AE, CB, DC, MC, V.*

The Plaza Hotel
$$$$$ Midtown West

This landmark hotel is almost as famous as the Statue of Liberty. Some of its rooms are on the small side, but the amenities are first-rate throughout. Stay in this 1907 castlelike structure for the location (at the juncture of Central Park and Fifth Avenue's best shopping) and the feeling of Old New York. The most impressive rooms are obviously the more expensive, with gorgeous views of Central Park. Guests have free access to the nearby Atrium Health Club and pool and to a sumptuous full-service spa. The hotel also offers a choice of bars and restaurants, such as the bar at the classic Edwardian Room, the famed steakhouse the Oak Room, the more casual Oyster Bar and One C.P.S. brasserie, and the Palm Court, renowned for its royal-style high tea and its Sunday brunch. The prices may be high, but it's worth calling about weekend packages.

768 Fifth Ave. between 58th and 59th streets (on Central Park South). ☎ 800-759-3000, 212-759-3000. Fax: 212-759-3167. Internet: www.fairmont.com. *Subway: N/R/W train to Fifth Avenue/59th Street stop; or F train to 57th Street stop and then walk 1 block east on 58th Street; or 4/5/6 train to 59th Street stop, walk 3 blocks west to Fifth Avenue, and turn left; or E/V train to Fifth Avenue/53rd Street stop and then walk 5 blocks north on Fifth Avenue. Parking: Valet, $35 per day. Rack rates: $390–$700 double. AE, DC, DISC, JCB, MC, V.*

Portland Square Hotel
$ Midtown West

The same folks who run the Herald Square Hotel (see the listing earlier in this chapter) operate the Portland Square. However, the Portland Square has a few more amenities than its sibling and is close to the Theater District and Restaurant Row. The rooms are small, spare, and clean, and the hotel offers a business center with fax machines and computers, as well as a small exercise room.

132 W. 47th St. between Sixth and Seventh avenues (1 block south of Rockefeller Center). ☎ 800-388-8988, 212-382-0600. Fax: 212-382-0684. Internet: www.portlandsquarehotel.com. *Subway: B/D/F/V train to 47th–50th streets/ Rockefeller Center stop and then walk west on 47th Street; or N/R/W train to 49th Street stop, walk 2 blocks south on Seventh Avenue, and turn left. Parking: $24 per day. Rack rates: $94–$104 double. AE, JCB, MC, V.*

Radisson Empire Hotel
$$$ Upper West Side

The rooms at the Radisson Empire Hotel are fairly small, but they're nicely appointed with traditional furnishings, such as two-poster beds.

Guests have free access to the New York Sports Club. Central Park is a block away, and you're right across the street from all the cultural events offered at Lincoln Center. Children under 14 stay free in their parents' room, and the charge for an extra person is $20.

44 W. 63rd St. at Broadway (just off Lincoln Center and Central Park). ☎ *800-333-3333, 212-265-7400. Fax: 212-315-0349. Internet:* www.empirehotel. com. *Subway: A/B/C/D/1/2 train to Columbus Circle stop, walk 4 blocks north on Broadway, and turn left on 63rd Street. Parking: $25 per day. Rack rates: $260–$290 double. AE, CB, DC, DISC, JCB, MC, V.*

The Regent Wall Street
$$$$ Financial District

The historic landmark building that houses this elegant hotel started out as the New York Merchants Exchange back in 1842, and then became the New York Custom House, and then was transformed into the National City Bank in 1907. Today, the vault serves as the hotel's conference room. Large spaces and elegant luxury characterize every aspect of the hotel — the splendid ballroom, the restaurant, the terrace, the spa and health club, and the guest rooms (the smallest of them is 500 square feet). The marble bathrooms feature 6-foot bathtubs, showers, plush robes, and Aveda products. The rooms are decorated in relaxing colors and beautiful fabrics and feature such conveniences as private fax/printer/copy machines, Internet access to cable television, and CD and DVD players. The hotel was renovated in 1999.

55 Wall St. between William and Water streets (steps from the New York Stock Exchange and South Street Seaport). ☎ *212-845-8600. Fax: 212-845-8601. E-mail:* rwsreservations@regenthotels.com. *Internet:* www.regenthotels. com. *Subway: 1/2/4/5 train to Wall Street stop. Parking: Valet, $35 per day. Rack rates: $299–$450 double. AE, CB, DC, DISC, JCB, MC, V.*

The Royalton
$$$$ Midtown West

The fashionable atmosphere at the Royalton comes courtesy of the same folks who created Morgans (see the listing earlier in this chapter). Its emphasis on design and its close proximity to the Theater District attract a flashy clientele. Each room has a separate living and working space and comes with either a queen- or king-size bed; some rooms have additional features, such as working fireplaces.

44 W. 44th St. between Fifth and Sixth avenues (between the New York Public Library and Rockefeller Center). ☎ *800-635-9013, 212-869-4400. Fax: 212-869-8965. Internet:* www.ianschragerhotels.com. *Subway: B/D/F/V train to 42nd Street stop and then walk 2 blocks north on Sixth Avenue; or 7 train to Fifth Avenue stop and then walk 2 blocks north on Fifth Avenue. Parking: Valet, $28 per day. Rack rates: $315–$395 double. AE, DC, MC, V.*

Salisbury Hotel
$$$ Midtown West

Reasonably priced, spacious, and centrally located near the Broadway theaters, Rockefeller Center, and Central Park, the Salisbury is well suited for families. The hotel's apartment-sized rooms have kitchenettes, sinks, and small refrigerators. The regular rooms have walk-in closets, living space, and cable TV; the suites (one- or two-bedroom) include business centers. Children under 16 stay free in their parents' room; the extra-person charge is $20. Continental breakfast is complimentary, and a small fee gets you access to the health club at the Parker Meridien.

123 W. 57th St. between Sixth and Seventh avenues (between Central Park South and the Theater District). ☎ *800-NYC-5757, 212-246-1300. Fax: 212-977-7752. E-mail:* nycsalisbury@worldnet.att.net. *Internet:* www.nycsalisbury.com. *Subway: F train to 57th Street stop and then walk ½ block west on 57th Street; or N/R/Q/W train to 57th Street stop and then walk ½ block east on 57th Street. Parking: $18 per day. Rack rates: $289–$309 double. AE, DC, DISC, MC, V.*

Sheraton New York Hotel and Towers
$$$ Midtown West

The location of this hotel is great — you're only steps from the Broadway theaters, Times Square, Rockefeller Center, and Central Park. Recently renovated, the Sheraton New York offers large desks with voice mail and dataports in every room, a business center, a health club, free use of the pool at the Sheraton Manhattan across the street, and 24-hour room service. Additional amenities are available (at a higher price) on the Club Level, and above it, in the Towers. Two children under 19 stay free in their parents' room; an extra person costs $30.

811 Seventh Ave. at 53rd Street (off the Theater District, 1 block west of MOMA). ☎ *800-325-3535, 212-581-1000. Fax: 212-262-4410. Internet:* www.sheraton.com. *Subway: B/D/E train to Seventh Avenue stop. Parking: $30 per day. Rack rates: $195–$295 double. AE, CB, DC, DISC, JCB, MC, V.*

SoHo Grand Hotel
$$$ SoHo

Style is the operative word at this snazzy hotel that opened in 1996 and immediately became a cult hit for fashionable travelers. Everything in the small rooms is custom designed, the baths have pedestal sinks and traditional tiles, and the amenities include interactive TV and in-room movies as well as a fitness room. The hotel is at the southern edge of SoHo, giving you good access to trendy dining spots and evening activities, while the hotel's restaurant — the very good Canal House — and its bar are a popular evening rendezvous for the trendy.

310 W. Broadway between Grand and Canal streets (steps from Little Italy, TriBeCa, and Chinatown). ☎ *800-965-3000, 212-965-3000. Fax: 212-965-3141. Internet:*

www.sohogrand.com. *Subway: A/C/E train to Canal Street stop, walk 1 block east on Canal to West Broadway, and turn left. Parking: Valet, $35 per day. Rack rates: $239–$389 double. AE, CB, DC, DISC, JCB, MC, V.*

Trump International Hotel and Tower
$$$$$ **Upper West Side**

The word *luxury* doesn't begin to describe the amenities at this hotel. When you arrive, you're assigned a personal Trump Attaché to help you get organized and comfortable. (Your Attaché even remembers your personal preferences for future visits.) Take a peek at the surrounding neighborhood through the telescope in your room, or ask a chef from the hotel's restaurant to come up and fix you something to eat in your suite's kitchen. (The restaurant, Jean Georges, is a French-Asian delight considered to be among the best — if not *the* best — in the city.) Or kick back and enjoy the entertainment center in your room, work out in the huge fitness center, or take a dip in the 55-foot pool. For executives, each room comes with a fax machine, a computer, a two-line phone with dataport, personalized stationery and business cards, and complimentary cell phone service (you have to pay for the calls). Mr. Trump also wants families to feel welcome: The hotel offers children's programs, and children stay free in their parents' room. One luxury you won't want is your car — parking is $42 per day.

1 Central Park West at 60th Street (on Central Park, near Columbus Circle and south of Lincoln Center). ☎ **800-44-TRUMP,** *212-299-1000. Fax: 212-299-1150. Internet:* www.trumpintl.com. *Subway: A/B/C/D/1/2 train to Columbus Circle stop. Parking: Valet, $42 per day. Rack rates: $475–$565 double. AE, CB, DC, MC, V.*

W New York Union Square
$$$$ **Gramercy Park**

The new W New York Union Square is probably the most striking of the five W hotels that have opened in town. It's right in the heart of the action, near the art galleries in Chelsea and the fashion scene of the Flatiron District, and within easy reach of both uptown and downtown attractions. The decor successfully marries modernist style and luxury without forgetting comfort. The guest rooms come with all kinds of amenities, including comfy beds (with pillow-top mattresses and luxurious Egyptian cotton sheets), Aveda products and bathrobes in the bathrooms, irons, minibars, safes, large TVs with Internet access and VCRs, and cordless phones with dataports. Style is everywhere, including the lobby, where grass grows atop the reception counter.

201 Park Ave. South, at the northeast corner of Union Square. ☎ **212-253-9119.** *Fax: 212-253-9229. Internet:* www.whotels.com. *Subway: L/N/Q/R/W/4/5/6 train to 14th Street/Union Square stop, and then walk northeast to the corner of the square. Rack rates: $289–$419 double. AE, CB, DC, DISC, JCB, MC, V.*

The Waldorf-Astoria and Waldorf Towers
$$$$ Midtown East

Owned by the Hilton chain, the Waldorf is legendary. The rooms are quite large and have a traditional elegance about them. The bathrooms and closets are marble. The hotel offers a choice of connecting doubles for families. The Waldorf Towers is more expensive and lavish and has a complimentary continental breakfast and hors d'oeuvres, as well as butler service. A variety of restaurants and bars can be found inside the hotel. Access to a health club is available for a $30 surcharge. Children stay for free in their parents' room.

301 Park Ave. between 49th and 50th streets (1 block east of Rockefeller Center). ☎ *800-WALDORF, 212-355-3000. Fax: 212-872-7272. Internet:* www.hilton.com. *Subway: 6 train to 51st Street stop, and then walk 1 block west to Park Avenue. Parking: Valet, $37 per day. Rack rates: $395–$480 double. AE, CB, DC, DISC, JCB, MC, V.*

Washington Square Hotel
$ Greenwich Village

You need to know this up front: The rooms here are microscopic, but they're cheap, clean, and nicely decorated. No room service is available, but breakfast is included in the room rate, and the hotel organizes jazz packages and tours of Greenwich Village. The hotel is wonderfully located for taking advantage of the many downtown attractions, and you're only steps from all the important subway lines in Manhattan, which enables you to reach any other destination in town easily. An extra bed in the room costs $12.

103 Waverly Place between Fifth and Sixth avenues (off Washington Square, the center of the Village). ☎ *800-222-0418, 212-777-9515. Fax: 212-979-8373. Internet:* www.wshotel.com. *Subway: A/C/E/F/V/S train to West 4th Street stop, walk 1 block east on West 4th Street to Washington Square, turn left, and walk along the park to the hotel at the northwest corner. Parking: $22 per day. Rack rates: $120–$150 double. AE, JCB, MC, V.*

The Wyndham
$$ Midtown West

The Wyndham, with its elegant old front, promises old-fashioned good taste. You won't be disappointed with this favorite of European travelers. The rooms are large, and some of them have fireplaces. A family-run hotel, the Wyndham is conveniently located in the center of Midtown, close to Carnegie Hall, Central Park, and Lincoln Center. And at these affordable prices, you may just feel like a robber baron.

42 W. 58th St. between Fifth and Sixth avenues (1 block from Central Park South, north of MOMA). ☎ *212-753-3500. Fax: 212-754-5638. Subway: F train to 57th Street stop, walk 1 block north on Sixth Avenue, and turn right on 58th Street; or N/R/W to 5th Avenue/59th Street stop, walk 1 block south on Fifth Avenue, and turn right. Rack rates: $150–$170 double. AE, DC, MC, V.*

Where to Stay When There's No Room at the Inn

If none of the hotels that appeal to you has an available room, don't panic! With more than 230 hotels in town, you shouldn't have a problem finding accommodations. You can try some of the Web sites mentioned in Chapter 7 that specialize in discounted rooms or last-minute reservations. In addition, this section lists a few more good options.

The Algonquin

$$$ Midtown West   This turn-of-the-20th-century hotel has a grand literary tradition as headquarters for the acerbic Dorothy Parker and her famed Round Table. The rooms are smallish but have a pampered, old-world feel.

59 W. 44th St. between Fifth and Sixth avenues (steps from Times Square, the Theater District, Grand Central Terminal, and Rockefeller Center). ☎ *800-555-8000, 212-840-6800. Fax: 212-944-1419. Internet:* www.algonquinhotel.com.

Belvedere Hotel

$$ Midtown West   The rooms have kitchenettes, and some come with Nintendo, making this Theater District hotel an excellent and affordable choice for families.

319 W. 48th St. between Eighth and Ninth avenues. ☎ *888-468-3558, 212-245-7000. Fax: 212-245-4455. Internet:* www.newyorkhotel.com.

Crowne Plaza Manhattan

$$$ Midtown West   Owned by the Holiday Inn chain, the sleek Crowne Plaza is a midpriced choice in the heart of the Theater District known for great deals (check the Web site). Onsite is a health club with a pool and sauna.

1605 Broadway between 48th and 49th streets. ☎ *800-243-NYNY, 212-977-4000. Fax: 212-333-7393. Internet:* www.crowneplaza.com.

Gramercy Park Hotel

$$ Gramercy Park   The location can't be beat — a quiet, old-world block overlooking charming little Gramercy Park, to which guests and local residents have access. The rooms are slightly dated, but some have kitchenettes.

2 Lexington Ave., at the corner of 21st Street. ☎ *800-221-4083, 212-475-4320. Fax: 212-505-0535. Internet:* www.gramercyparkhotel.com.

The Mansfield

$$$ Midtown West   This inviting hotel has a warm, romantic atmosphere and a great location. Check the Web site or call for special promotions, which can make this an amazing deal.

12 W. 44th St. between Fifth and Sixth avenues (between Rockefeller Center and the New York Public Library). ☎ *877-847-4444, 212-944-6050. Fax: 212-764-4477. Internet:* www.mansfieldhotel.com.

Millennium Broadway

$$$$ Midtown West   This sleek Times Square hotel has posh Art Deco rooms and caters to business travelers with a business center and meeting rooms.

145 W. 44th St. between Sixth Avenue and Broadway. ☎ *800-622-5569, 212-768-4400. Fax: 212-768-0847. Internet:* www.millennium-hotels.com.

The Ritz-Carlton

$$$$ Financial District   The Ritz-Carlton's new downtown outpost is the city's only waterfront hotel, convenient to South Street Seaport and virtually across the street from the ferry to the Statue of Liberty and Ellis Island. But you pay handsomely for that convenience and the hotel's luxury.

2 West St. (at Battery Park). ☎ *800-241-3333, 212-344-0800. Fax: 212-344-3801. Internet:* www.ritz-carlton.com.

The Roger Williams

$$$ Midtown East   This sleek blond-wood hotel is owned by the same people who own the Mansfield (mentioned earlier in this section), so you get the same great deals, thoughtful in-room amenities (VCRs and CD players), and complimentary extras (free espresso, cappuccino, and cookies all day long, plus a VCR and CD library in the lobby).

131 Madison Ave. at 31st Street (4 blocks south of the Empire State Building). ☎ *888-448-7788, 212-448-7000. Fax: 212-448-7007. Internet:* www.rogerwilliams hotel.com.

TriBeCa Grand

$$$$ TriBeCa   Our pick for The Hotel Where You're Most Likely Run into a Rock Star, the TriBeCa Grand is a stylish luxury hotel with platform beds, warm colors, dataports, and wireless Internet access in every room.

2 Avenue of the Americas, between White and Walker streets (1 block north of Franklin Street). ☎ *877-519-6600, 212-519-6600. Fax: 212-519-6700. Internet:* www. tribecagrand.com.

Index of Accommodations by Price

$$$$$

The Carlyle (Upper East Side)
The Mark (Upper East Side)
The Plaza (Midtown East)
Trump International Hotel and Tower
  (Upper West Side)

$$$$

Hotel Elysée (Midtown East)
The Lowell (Upper East Side)
The Michelangelo (Midtown West)
Millennium Broadway (Midtown West)
The Regent Wall Street (Financial
  District)
The Ritz-Carlton (Financial District)
The Royalton (Midtown West)
Tribeca Grand (TriBeCa)
W New York Union Square (Gramercy
  Park)
The Waldorf-Astoria and Waldorf
  Towers (Midtown East)

$$$

The Algonquin (Midtown West)
Casablanca (Midtown West)
Crowne Plaza Manhattan (Midtown
  West)
Doubletree Guest Suites (Midtown
  West)
Drake Swissôtel (Midtown East)
The Franklin (Upper East Side)
Grand Hyatt New York (Midtown East)
Jolly Madison Towers Hotel (Midtown
  East)
The Kimberly (Midtown East)
The Mansfield (Midtown West)
Mayflower Hotel on the Park (Upper
  West Side)

Melrose Hotel
Morgans (Midtown East)
New York Marriott Marquis (Midtown
  West)
Novotel New York (Midtown West)
Radisson Empire Hotel (Upper West
  Side)
Roger Williams Hotel (Midtown East)
The Salisbury (Midtown West)
Sheraton New York Hotel and Towers
  (Midtown West)
SoHo Grand Hotel (SoHo)

$$

Belvedere Hotel (Midtown West)
Best Western Seaport Inn (South Street
  Seaport)
Chelsea Savoy Hotel (Chelsea)
Clarion Hotel (Midtown East)
Gramercy Park Hotel (Gramercy Park)
Hotel Beacon (Upper West Side)
Hotel Metro (Midtown West)
Incentra Village House (Greenwich
  Village)
Quality Hotel and Suites Rockefeller
  Center (Midtown West)
The Wyndham (Midtown West)

$

Chelsea Pines Inn (Greenwich Village)
Cosmopolitan Hotel (TriBeCa)
Herald Square Hotel (Midtown West)
Larchmont Hotel (Greenwich Village)
The Pickwick Arms Hotel (Midtown
  East)
Portland Square Hotel (Midtown West)
Washington Square Hotel (Greenwich
  Village)

Index of Accommodations by Location

Upper West Side

Hotel Beacon — $$
Mayflower Hotel on the Park — $$

Radisson Empire Hotel — $$$
Trump International Hotel and
  Tower — $$$$$

Upper East Side

The Carlyle — $$$$$
The Franklin — $$$
The Lowell — $$$$
The Mark — $$$$
Melrose Hotel — $$$

Midtown East

Clarion Hotel — $$
Drake Swissôtel — $$$
Grand Hyatt New York — $$$
Hotel Elysée — $$$$
Jolly Madison Towers Hotel — $$$
The Kimberly — $$$
Morgans — $$$
The Pickwick Arms Hotel — $
Roger Williams Hotel — $$$
The Waldorf-Astoria and Waldorf
    Towers — $$$

Midtown West

The Algonquin — $$$
Belvedere Hotel — $$
Best Western Manhattan — $$
Casablanca Hotel — $$$
Crowne Plaza Manhattan — $$$
Doubletree Guest Suites — $$$
Herald Square Hotel — $
Hotel Metro — $$
The Mansfield — $$$
The Michelangelo — $$$$

New York Marriott Marquis — $$$
Novotel New York — $$
The Plaza Hotel — $$$$$
Portland Square Hotel — $
Quality Hotel and Suites Rockefeller
    Center — $$
The Royalton — $$$$
Salisbury Hotel — $$$
Sheraton New York Hotel — $$$
The Wyndham — $$$

Chelsea/Flatiron District/ Gramercy Park

Chelsea Savoy Hotel — $$
Gramercy Park Hotel — $$
W New York Union Square — $$$$

Greenwich Village/SoHo

Chelsea Pines Inn — $
Incentra Village House — $$
Larchmont Hotel — $
SoHo Grand Hotel — $$$
Washington Square Hotel — $$

TriBeCa/Financial District/ South Street Seaport

Best Western Seaport Inn — $$
Cosmopolitan Hotel — $
The Regent Wall Street — $$$$
The Ritz-Carlton — $$$$
Tribeca Grand — $$$$

Chapter 9

Taking Care of the Remaining Details

*F*orgetting a few last-minute details can mean endless hassles. In this chapter, we help you make sure that you've got everything squared away, from getting insurance to packing what you need for your trip to New York.

Playing It Safe: Travel and Medical Insurance

 If you've paid for a large portion of your trip up front, trip cancellation insurance is a must; it usually costs approximately 6% to 8% of the total value of your vacation.

Your existing health insurance should cover you if you get sick away from home; if you belong to an HMO, check to see whether you're fully covered while away from home. Your homeowner's insurance should cover stolen luggage. Check your existing policies before you buy any additional coverage.

If an airline loses your luggage, it has to reimburse you up to $2,500 on flights within the U.S. Also, some credit cards (American Express and certain gold and platinum Visas and MasterCards, for example) offer automatic insurance against death or dismemberment in case of a plane crash.

If you still feel that you need more insurance, try one of the following companies, but don't pay for more insurance than you need. For example, if you only need trip cancellation insurance, don't purchase coverage for lost or stolen property. The following are reputable issuers of travel insurance:

- ✔ **Access America,** 6600 W. Broad St., Richmond, VA 23230 (☎ **800-284-8300;** Internet: www.accessamerica.com)

- ✔ **CSA,** P.O. Box 939057, San Diego, CA 92193-9057 (☎ **800-873-9855;** Internet: www.csatravelprotection.com)

- ✔ **Travel Guard International,** 1145 Clark St., Stevens Point, WI 54481 (☎ **800-826-1300;** Internet: www.travelguard.com)

- ✔ **Travel Insured International, Inc.,** P.O. Box 280568, East Hartford, CT 06128 (☎ **800-243-3174;** Internet: www.travelinsured.com)

Renting a Car: Don't Do It

One of the first questions that comes to mind when organizing a trip is: "Do I need to rent a car?" In New York, the answer is clear: "No! A thousand times no!" You just don't need one; New York is a great walking city, and you can take fast and cheap public transportation anywhere you need to go. Need we mention that gas is seriously expensive; parking can be a nightmare; and driving the city streets is — more often than not — a high-speed, high-stakes game of dodge 'em that's *not* for the weak of heart?

Making Reservations and Getting Tickets in Advance

The only way to ensure that you'll be able to see a specific show or eat at a particular restaurant is to arrange your visit ahead of time. Read on for tips.

Restaurants

Some famous restaurants are booked months in advance, particularly on weekend nights. Common sense tells you that when you read about a great new restaurant in *Gourmet, Bon Appétit, Food & Wine,* or a travel magazine, thousands of other people have, too. Line up a reservation before your trip.

If you're planning to dine at one of the city's top venues on a Saturday, make a reservation about a month ahead. For other popular restaurants, a few days in advance should suffice. (See Chapter 14 for specific recommendations on reservations.)

Events, sights, and shows

Several nationally distributed newspapers and magazines list cultural and other events in New York City, including the Friday and Sunday *New York Times* and the magazines *The New Yorker* and *New York*. You may find *Time Out New York* and the *Village Voice* at your local bookstore or library. Most of these publications offer their listings on Web sites, including the following:

- ✔ **Citysearch** (Internet: www.newyork.citysearch.com): You can find listings for entertainment, dining, and more at this site.

- ✔ **Gallery Guide** (Internet: www.gallery-guide.com): This site offers a monthly listing of what's going on at galleries and museums.

- ✔ **New York City Reference** (Internet: www.panix.com/clay/nyc/): In this list of thousands of New York–related links, you can find the Web sites of all the museums in New York and find out about current exhibits and other special features.

- ✔ **New York City Tourist** (Internet: www.nyctourist.com): This site offers a selection of useful information; however, it's a little more commercial than the other Web sites.

- ✔ **New York Today** (Internet: www.nytoday.com): This site is affiliated with the *New York Times*.

In addition, many attractions and organizations have Web sites that offer schedules and ticket information. You can get information about current theater happenings from NYC/On Stage (☎ **212-768-1818**) and Broadway Line (☎ **888-BROADWAY** or 212-302-4111), either of which will transfer you to a ticket vendor or booking agency after you've listened to schedules.

After you decide what you want to do, you can contact the following companies to make reservations and get tickets before you leave:

- ✔ **Manhattan Concierge,** 1350 Broadway, Suite 1203, New York, NY 10018 (☎ **800-NY-SHOWS** or 212-239-2570; you can buy online at www.manhattanconcierge.com).

- ✔ **Showtix,** 1501 Broadway, Suite 1915, New York, NY 10036 (☎ **800-677-1164** or 212-302-7000; Fax: 212-302-7069).

- ✔ **Telecharge,** P.O. Box 998, Times Square Station, New York, NY 10108-0998 (☎ **212-239-6200;** you can purchase tickets online at www.telecharge.com).

- ✔ **TicketMaster** (☎ **212-307-4100;** you can buy online at www.ticketmaster.com).

- ✔ **Tickets and Travel/Tickets Up Front USA,** 1099 N. Meridian St., Suite 150, Indianapolis, IN 46204 (☎ **800-876-8497** or 317-633-6406; Fax: 317-633-6409).

Sightseeing

If you want to take advantage of the free tours offered by Big Apple Greeter (see Chapter 18), remember that it gets a lot of requests, so you have to reserve at least a week in advance (☎ **212-669-2896**; Fax: 212-669-3685).

Let's Get Packing

If you want to blend in with the natives, somber, neutral colors are always appropriate. Note that there's no particular need to wear formal evening clothes to a Broadway show. For men, a jacket and tie will serve in any situation, and even those are unnecessary in all but the fanciest restaurants. Women may want to bring one nice dress; black is always a safe choice.

New Yorkers walk a lot and walk fast, and for the short time you're there you'll probably do the same. Be prepared to walk more than you ever have in your life and pack at least one pair of comfortable walking shoes; two is better. As a stylish alternative, bring a pair of comfortable flat shoes in addition to sneakers.

Pack clothes that you can layer so that you can take off or put on as much clothing as you need to suit the situation. New York weather is full of surprises. (For the daily temperature and the following day's weather forecast, call ☎ **212-976-1212** or try www.weatherchannel. com.) Pack a travel umbrella: As you can see from the chart in Chapter 2, you need to be prepared for rain.

In addition, keep in mind the following tips when packing for your trip:

✔ You'll be hard pressed to keep one of those full-size suitcases-on-casters upright on a rough New York sidewalk. A wheeled carry-on type of bag with a retractable handle is a better idea.

✔ Most hotels provide hairdryers and irons, ironing facilities, or service; call your hotel in advance to avoid carrying that extra weight.

✔ Pack important items (toiletries, medications, and return tickets) in your carry-on bag so that you'll have them if the airline loses your luggage. However, see the next item for more about the new carry-on rules.

✔ In the aftermath of September 11, airlines have cracked down on carry-on luggage. You're allowed to bring only one piece of carry-on luggage on the plane, plus one personal item such as a laptop, purse, briefcase, or diaper bag. As before, each item must fit in the overhead compartment or under the seat in front of you. Stricter security measures have increased the number of items banned from the passenger cabin as well. If you're unsure whether an item will be allowed on the plane, put it in your checked baggage. You can check the Transportation Security Administration's Web site (www.tsa.gov) for an up-to-date list of banned items.

✔ Pack your biggest, hardest items (usually shoes) first, and then fit smaller items in and around them. Put things that could leak in zippered bags. Make sure that the identification tag on the outside of your bag is up-to-date.

Part III
Settling into New York

The 5th Wave   By Rich Tennant

"Ooo-look at this—we've got a perfect view of the Chrysler Building, the Buick Building, and the Chevy Building."

In this part . . .

*B*eing in a new city is exciting but can be disconcerting: You lose your points of reference because things are not necessarily where and how you expect them to be. New York's sheer size can make it seem even less user-friendly at first, but once you get a sense of the city, you'll probably find it much more orderly and much less overwhelming than you imagined. Reading through this part will help you navigate New York like a local, whether that means finding your way in from the airport, train station, or highway; figuring out the transportation and the neighborhoods; or getting cash.

Chapter 10

Arriving and Getting Oriented

* *

In This Chapter

▶ Making your way into the city from the airport, train station, or highway

▶ Figuring out New York's neighborhoods

▶ Getting local information

* *

*T*ravelers used to have three main ways to arrive in New York: by sea, by land, or by air. Although many cruise ships come in and out of New York during the summer, arriving by sea is now a rare and magical event. (The *Queen Elizabeth 2* is the only ship that still has regular transatlantic crossings between the U.K. and New York. If you're coming from England and you have the five extra days required for the trip, it's probably the most glorious way to arrive in New York.) However, most people have the choice of plane, train, or car. (For details on getting to New York, see Chapter 5.)

Getting from the Airport to Your Hotel

Manhattan is so crowded and space is at such a premium that there's no room for an airport on the island. Instead, the airports are located away from the center of things — LaGuardia and Kennedy airports are in the borough of Queens, and Newark Airport is across the Hudson River in New Jersey. Two smaller local airports, a bit farther away, also serve New York: MacArthur Airport in Islip, Long Island (east of the city), and Westchester Airport in White Plains (north of the city).

From any of these airports, taking a taxi is the easiest and most hassle-free option, but also the most expensive. Another possibility is to use a car service or van service (see the following sections for information). At the cheaper end, you can take a bus or a train.

 Make sure that a uniformed, official taxi dispatcher hails your cab. Always stand in the official taxi line and take a licensed New Jersey Taxi or New York City yellow cab. If someone approaches you offering a cab ride, just keep walking toward the cab line; illegal drivers, who may take you on an unwelcome ride, abound at all three main airports. Remember that taxis are required by law to take no more than four people, and you should always tip 15% of the fare, regardless of whether the driver helped you with your bags. (See Chapter 11 for more tips on taking cabs in New York.)

From JFK

John F. Kennedy International (JFK) is New York's largest airport. Its several terminals are located along a great loop. At each terminal, you find a taxi stand, bus stops, and car service pickup points. After collecting your luggage, follow the "Ground Transportation" signs or the signs for the closest exit to the transportation of your choice.

A cab from JFK to Manhattan takes about 45 minutes, depending on the traffic (which can be fierce), and costs a flat rate of $35 plus tolls and tip. The toll is $3.50 for the Queens Midtown Tunnel and the Triboro Bridge; the Queensboro Bridge is free, as are the Williamsburg and Manhattan bridges, but they can get very crowded. Still, if your destination is downtown and the Williamsburg and Manhattan bridges are free of construction, they should be your best bets. Your cab driver should know the best and fastest way into town considering the traffic situation. If you arrive at night (between 8 p.m. and 6 a.m.), you have to pay a 50¢ night surcharge.

A private car service (a "limo" in New York–ese) is another option. Unbelievably, a ride in a private car can cost a little less than a cab ride. Also, the driver will meet you just outside the baggage claim area, so you don't have to wait in line for a cab. Following are some of the car companies that service JFK; call ahead for a reservation:

- ✔ **Allstate:** ☎ **800-453-4099** or 212-741-7440

- ✔ **American Ground Transportation:** ☎ **800-NYC-LIMO**

- ✔ **Sabra:** ☎ **212-777-7171**

Another possibility is to take a shared transportation service (a "mini-van" in New York lingo). Follow the "Ground Transportation" signs upon your arrival and sign up at one of the desks:

- ✔ **Gray Line Air Shuttle** (☎ **800-451-0455** or 212-315-3006; Internet: www.graylinenewyork.com) has vans that depart every 20 minutes and serve major hotels between 23rd and 63rd streets in Manhattan. The fare is $19 to the airport and $14 from the airport; children under 6 ride free. If you buy a round-trip Gray Line ticket at the airport when you arrive, you get the $14 fare both ways (for a total of $28) and save $5. Call 24 hours in advance for pickup; hourly pickup is available from hotels.

New York Metropolitan Area

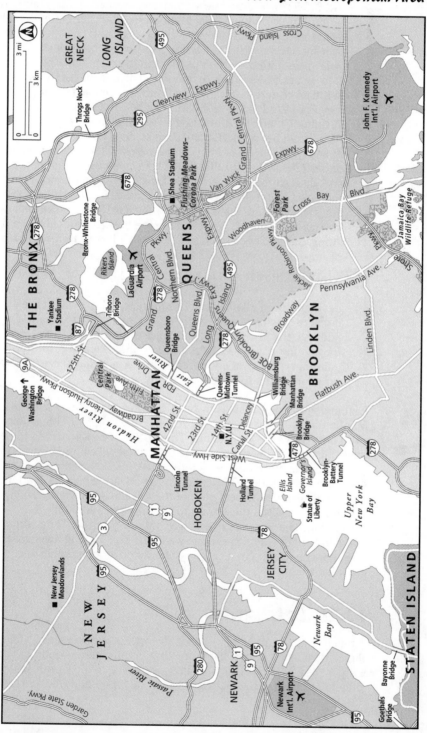

✔ **New York Airport Service** (☎ **800-872-4577,** 718-875-8200, or 212-875-8200; Internet: www.nyairportservice.com) offers regular bus service to and from Manhattan. The buses stop outside each terminal; follow the directions to ground transportation and wait by the sign. When boarding the bus at the airport, purchase your ticket either on the bus or from the dispatcher posted at the sign. Buses leave every 20 minutes. The bus makes three stops in Manhattan: across from Grand Central Terminal (the southeast corner of 42nd Street and Park Avenue), the Port Authority Bus Terminal (42nd Street and Eighth Avenue), and Penn Station (1 Penn Plaza between 31st and 33rd streets, just off Seventh Avenue). The price is $13 per person or $23 round-trip; children under 12 ride free ($1 discount for tickets purchased on the Web site; discounted rates available for students and seniors only from the ticket counters in Manhattan). Add $2 for the Midtown Hotel Shuttle, which serves hotels between 33rd and 57th streets. When you leave New York, you can take the bus from any of these three stops, but you need to call 24 hours in advance to reserve a hotel pickup.

✔ **Super-Shuttle** (☎ **800-BLUE-VAN** or 212-BLUE-VAN; Internet: www.supershuttle.com) has vans on call 24 hours a day to all destinations in Manhattan. The price is $13 to or from the airport if you're staying at a hotel; if you're staying at a residential address, the price is $15 from the airport and $22 to the airport for the first passenger in your party and $9 for each additional passenger; children under 3 ride free. You can reserve in advance for your pickup to head back to the airport.

Last and very much least is public transportation. Going from JFK to Manhattan by public transportation is *really* cheap (a $1.50 subway ride) but *really* time-consuming. This option is best reserved for those traveling light and with more time than money. The free blue-and-yellow shuttle bus stops at each terminal; just follow the signs for ground transportation. This bus leaves you at the subway station (the Howard Beach/JFK Airport stop of the A train, Rockaway branch). There you can catch the A train to the stop of your choice in Manhattan. The trip is easy enough, but not painless: Think about the stairs up and down to the subway and the bus, trailing luggage, and a ride that can take up to a couple of hours on a potentially very crowded train.

From LaGuardia

A much smaller and more pleasant airport, LaGuardia receives fewer flights than its other two New York–area counterparts — but, paradoxically, experiences more flight delays, according to the FAA. Just step outside the terminal at the baggage-claim level for ground transportation.

The fare for a taxi ride from LaGuardia to Midtown runs about $16 to $26 plus tolls and tip. The toll is $3.50 for the Queens Midtown Tunnel and Triboro Bridge; the Queensboro bridge is free, as are the Williamsburg and Manhattan bridges. Allow 30 minutes or more, depending on traffic.

A private car service (a "limo" in New York–ese) is also an option (see "From JFK," earlier in this chapter). Call ahead to one of these reliable car companies for a reservation:

- ✔ **Allstate:** ☎ **800-453-4099** or 212-741-7440
- ✔ **American Ground Transportation:** ☎ **800-NYC-LIMO**
- ✔ **Sabra:** ☎ **212-777-7171**

New York Airport Service (☎ **800-872-4577,** 718-706-9658, or 212-875-8200; Internet: www.nyairportservice.com) also serves LaGuardia. It offers the same service to and from LaGuardia as for JFK (see the preceding section). Buses leave every 20 minutes, and the cost is $10 or $17 round-trip (children under 12 free, $1 Internet discount, discounted rates for students and seniors available only from the service's ticket counters in Manhattan). Add $2 for the Midtown Hotel Shuttle service.

Shared transportation services are a good option from LaGuardia as well. Follow the "Ground Transportation" signs upon your arrival and sign up at one of the desks:

- ✔ **Gray Line Air Shuttle** (☎ **800-451-0455** or 212-315-3006; Internet: www.graylinenewyork.com) has vans that depart every 20 minutes and serve hotels between 23rd and 63rd streets. The fare is $13 from and $16 to LaGuardia airport; children under 6 ride free; round-trip is $26. Call 24 hours in advance for pickup; hourly pickup is available from hotels.

- ✔ **Super-Shuttle** (☎ **800-BLUE-VAN** or 212-BLUE-VAN; Internet: www.supershuttle.com) has vans on call 24 hours a day to all destinations in Manhattan. The price is $13 to and from the airport if you're going to a hotel; if you're staying at a private residence, the price is $15 from the airport and $22 to the airport for the first passenger in your party and $9 for each additional passenger. Children under 3 ride free. You can reserve in advance for pickup to go back to the airport.

As for public transportation, the **M60 bus** will get you from the airport to a choice of subway stops: first the Astoria Boulevard stop in Queens on the N/W line, then into Manhattan at one of the subway stops on 125th Street (4/5/6, 2/3, or A/B/C/D subway lines), and finally to the Cathedral Parkway/110th Street stop and the 116th Street/Columbia University stop on the 1 subway line. Another possibility: The **Q48** and

Q33 buses will bring you to a stop of the 7 train in Queens, which will eventually take you to Times Square. Curbside bus signs and stops are clearly marked. If you're using the bus-and-subway system's MetroCard, you're allowed free transfers to approved connecting buses and subways within two hours of initial use. In both cases, you face a complicated, two-hour odyssey that you shouldn't attempt unless you're really looking to save money.

From Newark

Although it's in New Jersey, Newark is closer to Manhattan than JFK, especially if your final destination is downtown or the west side of Manhattan. Newark is the newest of the three airports in the New York area and probably the best organized; after years of work, the **AirTrain,** a monorail train, finally has been completed. It connects Newark's three terminals with the long-term parking lots and with the Rail Link (the railroad station of Newark Airport). From there, you can catch a train directly into New York Penn Station. See the end of this section for details.

The airport taxi dispatcher sets the price of a cab — about $34 to $45 — from Newark to Manhattan based on your final destination in the city, to which you add toll and tip. You pay a $6 inbound-only toll (toward Manhattan) for either the Holland Tunnel or the Lincoln Tunnel, and you should tip 15%. You'll probably take a New Jersey cab on the way in and a New York cab on the way back. The trip takes about 40 minutes each way.

You can take a private bus as well. **Olympia Trails (☎ 877-894-9155,** 908-354-3330, or 212-964-6233; Internet: www.olympiabus.com) offers regular service between Newark and destinations in Manhattan for $11 each way or $21 round-trip (children under 30 inches free, seniors and the disabled $5 — but only if you buy your ticket at the ticket counters). Buses run every 20 minutes, and the ride takes 30 minutes or longer, depending on traffic. From the Grand Central Station stop (at 120 E. 41st St. between Park and Lexington avenues), you can transfer to Olympia Trails' Midtown Shuttle, which will take you to any destination between 30th and 65th streets for an additional $5 (you can purchase the ticket at the airport). Other stops in Manhattan are Penn Station (at the northwest corner of 34th Street and Eighth Avenue) and the Port Authority Bus Terminal (gates 316 and 317 at the Airport Bus Center, on 42nd Street between Eighth and Ninth avenues).

In the airport, follow the "Ground Transportation" signs and stop at the Olympia Trails counter, or go directly to the bus stop outside that corresponds to your destination; you can buy your ticket either at the counter or from the driver. If you're traveling from Manhattan, you'll find a dispatcher on duty at the bus stop at 34th Street and 8th Avenue and a counter in the Airport Bus Center; at the 41st Street stop, you can buy your ticket from the Western Union office or directly from the driver.

Another possibility is to take a mini-van. Follow the signs for ground transportation upon your arrival and sign up at one of the desks:

> **Super-Shuttle** (☎ 800-BLUE-VAN or 212-BLUE-VAN; Internet: www.supershuttle.com) has vans on call 24 hours a day to all destinations in Manhattan. The price is $13 to or from the airport if you're going to a hotel; if you're staying at a private residence, the price is $15 from the airport and $22 to the airport for the first passenger in your party and $9 for any additional passengers; children under 3 ride free. You can reserve in advance for pickup to go back to the airport.
>
> **Gray Line Air Shuttle** (☎ 800-451-0455 or 212-315-3006; Internet: www.graylinenewyork.com) has vans every 20 minutes serving hotels between 23rd and 63rd streets. The fare is $14 to and $19 from Newark Airport; children under 6 ride free; round-trip is $28.

You also can take public transportation: the **AirTrain** (☎ 800-772-2222 or 973-762-5100; Internet: www.airtrainnewark.com), the spanking new monorail, gets you from the airport (monorail stations are located in each terminal) to the Rail Link station served by Amtrak and New Jersey Transit, where you can catch a direct train to New York Penn Station (a 20-minute ride). Trains run every 20 minutes on weekdays and every half-hour on weekends; service is less frequent in the evening after 9 p.m. A one-way trip on New Jersey Transit is $11.55 for adults and $9.05 for children and seniors. Purchase tickets from the automated vending machines in the station; if you purchase a ticket from the conductor on the train, add $5 to the price.

An even cheaper option is to catch a New Jersey Transit train to Newark Penn Station (a five-minute ride; $6.80 adults and $5.80 children and seniors), where you can hop a PATH train to Manhattan. The PATH train works quite well and costs only $1.50. From Newark, the train makes four stops in New Jersey and five stops in Manhattan: Christopher Street (in Greenwich Village on Hudson Street), and then at 9th Street, 14th Street, 23rd Street, and 33rd Street, all along Sixth Avenue. Allow about 40 minutes for the trip between Newark Penn Station and 33rd Street.

Note that the PATH train is *very* crowded with commuters during rush hour; if you're toting luggage, paying the extra $3 to take the train from the airport directly to New York Penn Station is far easier.

From MacArthur Airport

The budget airline Southwest flies into MacArthur Airport, located in Islip, Long Island, 50 miles east of Manhattan. Taxi service into the city is not available from there, but you can reserve a private car (a limo, as we say in New York), which costs about $100 for a 1½-hour trip. Call **Colonial Transportation** (☎ 800-464-6900 or 631-589-3500; Internet: www.colonialtransportation.com) for reservations.

Another option is to take the shuttle, also run by Colonial
Transportation (a white van marked Express Service between Islip/
MacArthur and LIRR/Ronkonkoma) from outside the terminal to the
Ronkonkoma train station. There you can take the Long Island Rail
Road (☎ 718-217-5477) into New York Penn Station. A shuttle comes
every 20 minutes and costs $5; the train ride costs about $10, depend-
ing on the time of day. The trip takes about 1 hour and 45 minutes.

Finally, you can use the **Hampton Jitney** (☎ **800-963-0440** or
631-283-4600; Internet: www.hamptonjitney.com). Take a local cab to
the Jitney's bus stop in Ronkonkoma for about $15, and then catch the
bus (a 1½-hour ride) into Manhattan. The price of a ticket is $25.

From Westchester Airport

Many of the major U.S. airlines fly to this smaller airport located in
White Plains, New York. A taxi ride into the city costs about $85 plus
tolls and tip and takes about 1 hour and 15 minutes. You also can use
the **Bee-line Systems Bus** (☎ **914-813-7777**; Internet: www.west
chestergov.com/airport/groundtransportation.htm). For $8, it
can take you to Manhattan, where it makes several stops along Fifth
Avenue between 98th and 23rd streets, in about 1½ hours. Alternatively,
you can take the bus service to the White Plains train station and catch
a Metro North train to Grand Central Terminal. The bus connection is
$1.75, whereas the train ride is about $8 depending on the time of day.
For information about Metro North trains, call ☎ **800-638-7646** or
212-532-4900, or try www.mta.info.

Arriving by Train

As we mention in Chapter 5, Amtrak has regular service to New York
from several other cities in the United States. All Amtrak trains arrive
at Penn Station (between Seventh and Eighth avenues and 31st and
33rd streets), a large, noisy space with a fast-food outlets galore and
cramped waiting areas.

From the station, you can take a cab: Signs guide you to the taxi
stand — on Penn Plaza Drive, a passageway situated between Penn
Station (close to Eighth Avenue) and the Long Island Rail Road
Terminal (LIRR, close to Seventh Avenue).

Another option is public transportation; the station is well connected
with the 1/2/3/A/C/E trains and several buses. However, this isn't the
best alternative, especially if you're unfamiliar with the city and you
have a lot of luggage. Elevators are virtually unheard of in New York's
subway stations, so count on lugging your bags up and down multiple
flights of stairs.

Arriving by Car

We don't recommend having a car in New York for the reasons we outline in Chapter 9. If you decide to arrive by car, you'll immediately understand why we tried to dissuade you.

You know you're approaching New York when the traffic and signs multiply beyond all expectations. Open your eyes and sharpen your senses; getting into Manhattan if you're unfamiliar with the chaotic tangle of highways, thoroughfares, and parkways can be a nerveracking experience. Remember that there are no signs for Manhattan; signs give the names of specific tunnels, bridges, and streets instead.

 Before beginning your trip, it's a good idea to check with the Port Authority of New York and New Jersey, which is responsible for managing all the bridges and tunnels into the city. Since September 11, 2001, certain traffic regulations have restricted the times that singleoccupant vehicles can use some crossings. These restrictions probably will have been lifted by the time you arrive, but check www.panynj. com just to be sure. Or you can tune your car radio to WINS (1010 AM) or WCBS (880 AM), both of which have traffic updates every ten minutes all day long. Have we mentioned yet how much we recommend against driving?

If you arrive from the west or south, the New Jersey Turnpike is your jumping-off point to Manhattan. Take exit 14C for the Holland Tunnel (which lets you out around Canal Street in Manhattan), exit 16E for the Lincoln Tunnel (which deposits you in far-west Midtown at 42nd Street), or exit 18, the turnpike's end, for the George Washington Bridge (which lets you out at 181st Street, far uptown). The inbound-only toll (toward Manhattan) is $6; you pay no outbound toll (you're free to leave, so to speak).

From the north, take the Deegan Expressway (I-87); from the northeast, take the New England Thruway (I-95) to the Bruckner Expressway. To get to the east side of Manhattan, follow the signs to the Triboro Bridge ($3.50 toll in both directions), but then be careful to follow the signs to FDR Drive and avoid going on to Queens — unless that's your destination. FDR Drive runs along the East River all the way to the southern tip of Manhattan and has exits at different points. If you want to get to the west side of Manhattan, exit I-87 at the Sawmill River Parkway and follow it to the Henry Hudson Parkway, pass the Henry Hudson Bridge (a $1.75 toll), and you'll find yourself on the West Side Highway, which runs along the Hudson on the west side of the island to its southern tip and has exits at different streets.

When approaching a toll plaza, stay in the lanes marked "Cash" and *not* "EZ-Pass only." EZ-Pass is a toll payment system where you prepay your toll money; as you proceed through the toll, a scanner identifies your car by an electronic tag mounted on your rearview mirror and deducts the toll money from your account. No attendants man the EZ-Pass booths, so you can't pay cash in those lanes.

The Cross Bronx Expressway runs east-west and connects to the George Washington Bridge; you can use it to get to whichever side of the island you want, but its traffic jams are infamous (especially on days when the Yankees play at home).

Once you're on the West Side Highway or FDR Drive, take the exit closest to your destination — all exits have street names — and calm down: You've made it to New York!

Think your ordeal is over? Think again. Now you have to face the city traffic. Here are a few recommendations:

- ✔ **Arrive before or after rush hour** to avoid traffic jams. Rush hours are from about 8:00 to 10:00 a.m. and 4:30 to 7:00 p.m. on weekdays and from 2:00 to 9:00 p.m. on Fridays and Sundays; Saturday nights are pretty busy as well.

- ✔ **Park your car at your hotel** (some have good deals) or at one of the outdoor long-term parking lots on the west side (along the West Side Highway in the 50s and at Houston Street). In the latter case, you may want to pass by your hotel first to deposit your luggage, as finding a cab from those areas is not easy. The other option is to park in one of the many private garages scattered in the city, but expect to pay about $45 every 24 hours.

- ✔ **Remember that streets in New York are mostly one-way.** As a rule, even-numbered streets go east (think E for even and east) and odd-numbered ones go west, but exceptions exist. About every ten blocks is a two-way street: Canal, Houston, 14th, 23rd, 34th, 42nd, 57th, 72nd, 79th, and 86th. Alternate avenues go north and south: First goes up, Second goes down, Third up, Lexington down, Madison up, Fifth down, Sixth up, Seventh down, and so on. Park, Eleventh, and Broadway north of Columbus Circle travel in both directions. Below Houston Street, the grid pretty much ends and things get more complicated.

- ✔ **Be patient and aware.** Drivers in New York don't necessarily know how to drive and are often aggressive and rude. This is not surprising, however, because they have to fight their way against thousands of people on foot, bikes, and inline skates, all breaking all possible rules. Beware of taxis: They're renowned for changing lanes and picking up and dropping off passengers without even glancing around.

New York by Neighborhood

Getting to know New York and all its neighborhoods is easy (see the map "Manhattan Neighborhoods"). Most of the famous sights are on the island of Manhattan, bounded by the Hudson River to the west and the East River — guess where? — to the east. With a few exceptions (mostly downtown), the main avenues run north-south and the streets run east-west.

Downtown

The downtown area is a collection of neighborhoods bounded by water to the south, east, and west and Houston Street to the north. Wall Street and the Financial District are the oldest part of the city. Here you find some of the city's most important historical landmarks, including Trinity Church, South Street Seaport, and the Brooklyn Bridge. The Financial District area bustles during the day, but at night, it's just you and the streetlights. The South Street Seaport is lively at any time, especially in summer.

The area restricted to pedestrian and vehicular traffic because of the collapse of the Twin Towers is now quite small — a square limited to the streets adjacent to Ground Zero, the site of the World Trade Center. Pedestrians can walk all the way along the east side of Church Street, across on Warren Street (at the north of the site), along the Esplanade of the World Financial Center (by the Hudson River), and across on Carlisle Street and Rector Place (to the south of the area). You can find the latest information online at the official Web site of the City of New York, Office of Emergency Management (www.nyc.gov/html/oem/). For information about visiting Ground Zero, see Chapter 16.

After the disaster, some people have been concerned about air quality in the affected area. Officials say that the situation is back to normal; however, if you have a special concern, you can contact the city's Air Quality Hotline at ☎ 212-221-8635. The hotline is staffed Monday through Friday from 11 a.m. to 7 p.m.

TriBeCa, Chinatown, Little Italy, and the Lower East Side

TriBeCa is one of the trendiest parts of town. The name stands for "Triangle Below Canal" (that is, Canal Street). It's an area of residential lofts inhabited by artists and celebrities, as well as of some of the most fashionable and chic restaurants in town. Hip doesn't translate into big crowds, though; the neighborhood is very quiet. Some blocks remain deserted at night.

TriBeCa did sustain some damage in the September 11 attacks. In the immediate aftermath, many residents relocated, and businesses in the neighborhood suffered. However, TriBeCa's restaurants and nightspots have hung tough, and people are returning in droves.

Canal Street runs straight across the island, going through the heart of **Chinatown,** which lies to the east of TriBeCa. Chinatown is a sprawling neighborhood that bursts with shops selling Asian wares, cheap souvenirs, and counterfeit watches, bags, and sunglasses (more about this in Chapter 19). The streets are lined with Chinese, Thai, and Vietnamese restaurants, including dim sum places.

North of Chinatown and centered around Mott and Mulberry streets is **Little Italy,** where you find Italian shops and restaurants. The neighborhood has been squeezed by Chinatown, which has spread northward; as a result, younger, trendier Italians have created an Italian Renaissance over in the eastern part of SoHo and the southern part of the East Village.

To the east and north of Little Italy is the **Lower East Side,** a historic area that was a Jewish ghetto in the 19th century. The neighborhood is now a bubbling mix of hipster-trendy (alternative music clubs, trendy new restaurants) and somewhat dangerous; the farther east you go, the sketchier it gets.

Greenwich Village, the East Village, SoHo, and NoHo

SoHo (which stands for south of Houston Street — pronounced "HOW-ston," not "HUE-ston") is a beautiful neighborhood famous for its cast-iron architecture. Twenty-five years ago, artists moved here for the cheap real estate and large, airy studio spaces. It was once the center of the city's arts scene, which has migrated to West Chelsea. A few galleries remain in the area, but the neighborhood is known primarily for its swanky shops and restaurants. The eastern part of SoHo, rebaptized **NoLiTa** (north of Little Italy), is where young fashion and accessory designers have opened small shops and share the neighborhood with interesting eateries and new Italian restaurants. The neighborhood has merged north into **NoHo** (north of Houston), a small, fashionable area just east of Broadway and north of Houston Street. You can find some of the city's most trend-setting restaurants here.

Greenwich Village, also called simply "the Village," is a center of art, dining, shopping, jazz music, and gay life. The neighborhood is roughly bordered by Houston Street to the south and 14th Street to the north. Known for its architecture, the Village has the shortest street in the city (Weehawken, just one block long) and the narrowest house (on Bedford Street, where poet Edna St. Vincent Millay lived). It's an area that never sleeps yet still manages to give off a sense of quiet and beauty. Within the Village itself is the **West Village,** west of Seventh Avenue, which is the historic and de facto center of New York's gay community. It has a residential feel, with beautiful tree-lined streets and comfortable neighborhood cafes. East of Broadway, the Village becomes the **East Village,** a center for alternative music and dance clubs, which draws a younger, edgier crowd. More raw and less polished, it's seedy in places (St. Marks Place, in particular, is lined with

Manhattan Neighborhoods

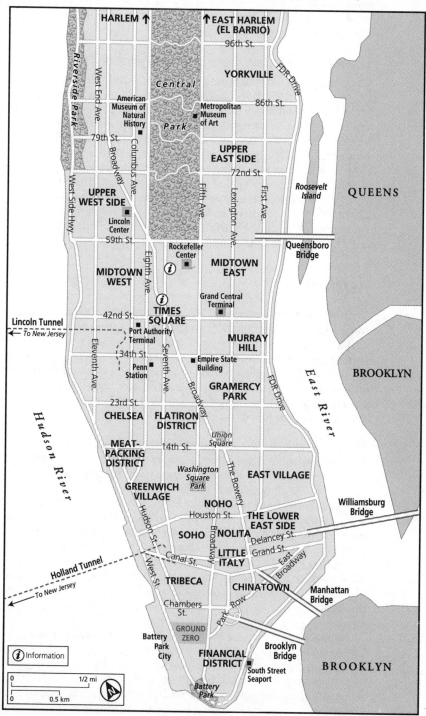

HARLEM ↑

↑EAST HARLEM
(EL BARRIO)

96th St.

Riverside Park

West End Ave.

Central

American
Museum of
Natural
History

Metropolitan
Museum
of Art

Park

YORKVILLE

86th St.

FDR Drive

Broadway

79th St.

Columbus Ave.

UPPER
EAST SIDE

72nd St.

West Side Hwy.

UPPER
WEST SIDE

Lincoln
Center

59th St.

Fifth Ave.

Lexington Ave.

First Ave.

Roosevelt
Island

QUEENS

Rockefeller
Center

ⓘ

Eighth Ave.

MIDTOWN
WEST

MIDTOWN
EAST

Queensboro
Bridge

ⓘ

Grand Central
Terminal

Lincoln Tunnel

← To New Jersey

TIMES
SQUARE

42nd St.

Port Authority
Terminal

MURRAY
HILL

Eleventh Ave.

34th St.

Seventh Ave.

Empire State
Building

East River

BROOKLYN

Penn
Station

23rd St.

GRAMERCY
PARK

CHELSEA

FLATIRON
DISTRICT

Broadway

FDR Drive

MEAT-
PACKING
DISTRICT

14th St.

Union
Square

Hudson River

GREENWICH
VILLAGE

*Washington
Square
Park*

The Bowery

EAST VILLAGE

NOHO

Williamsburg
Bridge

Houston St.

Hudson St.

SOHO

NOLITA

Broadway

THE LOWER
EAST SIDE

Delancey St.

Holland Tunnel

Canal St.

LITTLE
ITALY

Grand St.

East Broadway

To New Jersey

West St.

TRIBECA

CHINATOWN

Manhattan
Bridge

Chambers
St.

Park Row

GROUND
ZERO

Battery
Park
City

FINANCIAL
DISTRICT

Brooklyn
Bridge

ⓘ Information

South Street
Seaport

BROOKLYN

0   1/2 mi

0   0.5 km

*Battery
Park*

piercing and tattoo parlors) but has some excellent restaurants and a growing number of boutiques. The area between the East Village and West Village (that is, between Broadway and Seventh Avenues) is simply referred to as the Village.

Chelsea, the Flatiron District, and Gramercy Park

Chelsea, which extends from 14th Street to 26th Street and from the Hudson River to Fifth Avenue, is home to a large gay community, lots of art galleries, and many cutting-edge cafes and restaurants. East of Chelsea is the **Gramercy Park** area — a quiet, elegant, moneyed neighborhood known for its jewel of a park and handsome architecture. In between are **Union Square** and the **Flatiron District,** a lively hub of New York life that was home to New York's dot-com companies in the late 1990s, before the virtual economy went bust. This is where members of the fashion industry — models, advertising people, photographers, and so on — meet and eat. The area is bordered by the historic Flatiron Building to the north (at Broadway and Fifth at 23rd Street) and Union Square to the south.

Midtown

Midtown, roughly defined by 26th Street to the south and 59th Street to the north, is where most of the city's skyscrapers are located. The architecture is definitely big and modern — you can hardly see the sky. During the day, Midtown is a hectic place of commerce, seething with serious-looking people on their way to or from work. After dark, much of Midtown is deserted (except Times Square and the Theater District), and much of it is positively dull. But Midtown is huge, and such generalizations can be inaccurate.

Within Midtown to the southeast lies **Murray Hill,** just east of Fifth Avenue and below 42nd Street. It's a mixture of business and residential property, where a 40-story slab may rub up against a five-story apartment building. The area is safe and quiet — *very* quiet at night, so you'll probably have to find your entertainment elsewhere. Few sightseeing stops are located here, but you see many blocks of beautiful brownstones and a number of hotels. Above 42nd Street is **Midtown East,** which is more commercial and includes a number of famous shops that line 57th Street between Fifth and Lexington. The main attractions in this area are the United Nations, the renovated (and once-again breathtaking) Grand Central Terminal, and the Chrysler Building.

To the southwest lies the **Fashion** or **Garment District** (roughly between 26th and 42nd streets west of Fifth Avenue), with its array of fabric shops and wholesale fashion stores. At the heart of it, at the intersection of 34th Street, Broadway, and Sixth Avenue (also called the Avenue of the Americas), is **Herald Square,** a bustling (some would say choked with crowds) shopping area. Herald Square is the home of

Macy's, and with ongoing development, more national chain stores are appearing all the time. The Empire State Building is nearby and so is Penn Station (between Seventh and Eighth avenues at 32nd Street).

Farther north, on the west side, is **Times Square,** a once nasty — some would say colorful — place full of peep shows and sex shops until a business partnership completed an ambitious (and completely transforming) improvement campaign. Times Square is now a family-oriented area (remain alert, however; pickpockets abound) with renovated theaters and the famous neon, which is bigger, brighter, and louder than ever (including the largest TV screen in the world, the Sony Jumbotron). Just up Broadway is the legendary **Theater District.** The area churns with activity, and the scale is grand, so it's not the kind of place to step out for a casual stroll under the trees (there aren't any, anyway). Famed Restaurant Row is close by on 46th Street.

Just west of the Theater District is **Hell's Kitchen,** probably the most picturesquely named neighborhood in New York City. Once a rough-and-tumble immigrant community and the home turf of notorious Irish gangs, Hell's Kitchen has seen some gentrification of late. In an amusing example of New York's constant effort to reinvent itself, real-estate developers have pushed to rename the area "Clinton Hill" or "Theater District West" in an attempt to avoid associations with its seedier history. The name sticks, though. The area has some interesting ethnic nouvelle cuisine along Ninth Avenue, and excellent restaurants have been opening over the past couple of years, making it a gourmet destination.

East of the Theater District is **Central Park South** (namely 59th Street between Fifth and Eighth avenues), home to one of the most glamorous views in the city. The park is just across the street, Fifth Avenue's toniest stretch of shops is at the corner, and Rockefeller Center and MOMA (closed for renovation until 2005) are just beyond.

The Upper West Side

To the west of Central Park, the **Upper West Side** is bordered by Lincoln Center to the south and Columbia University and the Cathedral of St. John the Divine to the north. The area is home to some beautiful, historic residential buildings, such as the famous Dakota. Other streets are lined with brownstones, townhouses, and apartment buildings. Scattered throughout the area are a wealth of shops and restaurants. Also in this neighborhood, you find the American Museum of Natural History.

The Upper East Side

To the east of Central Park and stretching to the East River, the **Upper East Side**'s main draw is Museum Mile, a stretch of Fifth Avenue that includes the Metropolitan Museum of Art, the Guggenheim, the Museum of the City of New York, the International

Center of Photography, the Frick Museum, and the Jewish Museum, all within a walkable stretch. The Upper East Side also has its share of galleries, fancy shops, and restaurants. The neighborhood has an upper-crust, old-money feel and, west of Lexington Avenue, is generally pretty quiet after sundown. East of Lexington along Third, Second, and First avenues, you encounter a number of lively restaurants and clubs.

Harlem

Harlem stretches from about 98th Street to 155th Street, a historic neighborhood that has suffered greatly from lack of funds and a bad reputation. But much has changed during the past few years, and many destinations are completely safe to explore on foot, which is wonderful because this area has some stunning examples of early Dutch architecture and some exciting entertainment, including an African market (at 116th Street), restaurants (see Chapter 14), and landmark music venues like the Apollo Theater (☎ 212-802-5706). You can take a guided tour: You'll no doubt see much more that way. (See Chapter 18 for a choice of guided tours.)

Getting Information after You Arrive

The following places can help you get your bearings after you arrive in New York:

- ✔ **NYC & Company** (the former Convention & Visitors Bureau) has a **Visitor Information Center** (810 Seventh Ave. between 52nd and 53rd streets; ☎ 212-484-1222; Internet: www.nycvisit.com; open Monday through Friday 8:30 a.m. to 6:00 p.m., Saturday and Sunday 9:00 a.m. to 5:00 p.m.) where you can find useful printed material, pick up coupons for theaters and attractions, and buy tickets for New York's top sights, as well as the CityPass (see Chapter 16). Together with American Express and CitySearch.com, NYC & Co. has developed electronic kiosks at various locations in the city, called Ticket axis (see the second-to-last item in this list). Using the touch-screen, you can get directions and get information about attractions and events.

- ✔ The **Grand Central Partnership** (Grand Central Terminal, East 42nd Street and Vanderbilt Avenue; open Monday through Friday 8:30 a.m. to 6:30 p.m., Saturday and Sunday 9:00 a.m. to 6:00 p.m.) offers an information window inside Grand Central Terminal and a cart outside.

- ✔ The **Manhattan Mall** (Sixth Avenue and 32nd Street; open Monday through Saturday 10 a.m. to 8 p.m., Sunday 11 a.m. to 6 p.m.; ☎ 212-465-0500) offers traveler information on the first floor.

✔ The **34th Street Partnership** (Penn Station, Seventh Avenue between 31st and 33rd streets; open Monday through Friday 8:30 a.m. to 5:30 p.m., Saturday and Sunday 9:00 a.m. to 6:00 p.m.; ☎ 212-868-0521) has a window inside Penn Station and an information cart at the Empire State Building at Fifth Avenue and 32nd Street. You find carts at Greeley Square (32nd Street at Broadway and Sixth Avenue) in the summer and at Madison Square Garden (above Penn Station at Seventh Avenue and 32nd Street) in above-freezing weather. The carts open a little later and close a little earlier than the indoor window.

✔ **Ticket axis kiosks** are electronic touch-screen kiosks offering information and tickets at the touch of a finger. The number of locations is increasing, but at press time kiosks can be found at the Visitor Information Center (see the following item), New York Skyride (on the second floor of the Empire State Building), Intrepid Sea-Air-Space Museum, Circle Line, Museum of the City of New York, New York Hall of Science (in Queens), New York Botanical Gardens (in the Bronx), Museum of American Financial History (26 Broadway at Wall Street), and Brooklyn Museum of Art (Brooklyn).

✔ The **Times Square Visitor & Transit Information Center** (229 W. 42nd St. between Seventh and Eighth avenues; open daily 9 a.m. to 6 p.m.) can tell you everything you need to know about the Theater District, including information about discount tickets, hotels, and restaurants. (It even offers a walking tour of the area on Fridays at noon.)

Chapter 11

Getting Around New York

. . . .

. . . .

*Y*ou may not be used to riding a subway, taking a bus, or hailing a taxi to get where you want to go, but that's what New Yorkers do (few own cars, and those who do use them only on weekends to get out of the city), and you'll find yourself doing the same. The guidelines and tips in this chapter will have you navigating the island of Manhattan like a native in no time. Remember that taxis, subways, and most buses run 24 hours a day.

Traveling by Subway

The city has made a serious — and successful — effort to make the subways safe and as pleasant as possible. And you can't beat that it costs only $1.50 per ride, no matter how long the ride. (With proper identification, seniors and travelers with disabilities pay half price; up to three children under 3 feet, 8 inches tall ride for free when accompanied by a fare-paying adult.)

The nature of a subway, however, is that much of it is totally underground, which means that it can get hot down in the station, especially during the summer; it's noisy; and you may spot the occasional rat (they mostly stay down on the tracks where they belong).

Finding the entrance and getting on board

You can easily locate a subway entrance along the sidewalk by looking for a set of stairs that heads underground. Most stops also have signs above them that list the lines that run through those stations.

Some subway entrances close at night. Each stairway has a globe on top of it that's supposed to tell you whether the entrance is open (green for open, red for closed), but the globes aren't always accurate; look or head down the stairs to find out whether the entrance is open.

To ride, you must buy a token (which costs $1.50) and drop it into a turnstile as you enter the platform. Or you can use the increasingly popular MetroCard, which also allows you to transfer to a bus for free; see the section "Understanding the MetroCard," later in this chapter, for details.

The Cheat Sheet at the front of this book shows you the pertinent subway stops, and the other maps in this book also show subway stops. You can usually find a subway map inside each subway car, on the platform, and on the wall in the subway station. You also can get a detailed subway map from the ticket booth inside each station.

Five subway stops have been closed temporarily as a result of the collapse of the Twin Towers; the affected lines are the 1, N and R trains. But the subway system has been reorganized and actually works better that before, with a few new lines and stops having been added. By the time you read this, some of the closed stations may have reopened. For the latest information about service changes and upgrades, contact the **MTA New York City Transit** (☎ **718-330-1234;** Internet: www.mta.info).

There is no posted schedule for the subway. You just go down to the platform and wait; a train should come every few minutes (the trains are less frequent late at night). If you have to wait a while before the train comes along, just grumble about it like everybody else — it's part of the subway ritual.

Getting where you want to go

If you need directions in the subway, trying to get information from the token-booth attendant can be frustrating. The acoustics are horrible, the people behind you are impatient, and it's difficult to make yourself heard (and even harder to understand the resulting directions). Ask a friendly-looking person or a police officer instead.

Theoretically, once you're on the train, you'll be able to see a sign with the name of each stop on it as the train pulls into the station. However, sometimes the car is so crowded that you can't see out the car windows. Be familiar with your route: Know how many stops you're riding through and count them as you go.

The orientation of the subway system is mainly north-south (or uptown-downtown); there are only a few points at which the lines go straight east-west (at 53rd and 59th streets for varying distances via the E, F, N, R, V, and W trains; at 42nd Street via the S shuttle or the 7 train; at 14th Street via the L train; and at Houston Street via F train and the new S Grand Street Shuttle). This makes buses very useful (see the following section, "Taking the Bus").

Be aware that uptown and downtown tracks on the same line are not connected at all stations, but usually only at those stations where transfer is available to other subway lines. If you board going the wrong way and get out at a station without transfer, you may have to go outside, cross the street, and pay again.

Learn which are the **express trains** (which make only limited stops): the **A, 3, 4, and 5.** That way, you won't see your stop go by at 40 mph. It's also useful to know where the express trains stop. Take Columbus Circle, at 59th Street, the station where Uptown meets Midtown, close to glamorous Central Park South, Lincoln Center, and heavily touristed 57th Street. Seems like it should be an express stop, right? It is, but only for the A train. If you're riding the 3 train, the closest stops to Columbus Circle are 72nd Street to the north and Times Square (42nd Street) to the south.

One potentially confusing aspect of the new subway configuration: The system now has two S trains, both shuttle services that make only a few stops in Manhattan. One S shuttle runs along 42nd Street and takes passengers back and forth between two stations: Times Square and Grand Central. A completely separate S train (called the Grand Street shuttle) originates at West 4th Street in Greenwich Village and stops at Broadway–Lafayette Street in the East Village and Grand Street on the Lower East Side.

Staying safe

To keep yourself safe in the subway, heed this advice:

- ✔ Use the off-hours waiting areas late at night, which are usually close to the exits to the street. They're clearly marked with signs overhead.

- ✔ Don't tempt thieves by displaying money or valuables on the subway.

- ✔ Don't try to open a subway door that's closing. The conductor may close the door on your hand anyway, which can result in a bruised hand or arm — or something more serious. Just wait for the next train.

- ✔ Always stand a few feet back from the tracks on the subway platform.

Taking the Bus

The New York City bus system reaches far and wide, traveling to just about all points of the city on a north-south *and* an east-west grid. You even get a tour of the city as you ride! Remember, however, that because traffic can be horrific during the day, buses are much slower going than the subway.

To check out the bus routes, grab one of the free city bus maps available right by the front door of every bus and also in the booths at subway stations. If you want to scan the routes before you get to town, you can access full bus maps via the Internet at www.mta.info.

Bus stops are located every couple of blocks along each route. The stop is either a small, glass-walled shelter or a simple sign on a post (blue with a bus icon) stating the bus numbers. Each bus has a sign above the driver's windshield that flashes its route and end destination. Schedules for buses are posted at most bus stops and are relatively reliable. The buses run every 5 to 20 minutes or so, depending on the time of day.

Some buses are labeled "Limited" and make only a few major stops along the line; they're particularly useful when you want to go a long distance. Buses making express stops only have an orange "Limited" sign placed on the dashboard to the right of the driver. Limited bus stops also display the orange sign.

You may see express buses as well. These commuter buses go to the boroughs and have an X before their number; they are more expensive and not useful for transportation within Manhattan.

A bus ride costs $1.50, and you can pay with exact change (nickels, dimes, and quarters only — no pennies or dollar bills), a token, or a MetroCard (see the following section). Buses never take paper money; always have exact change in coins if you plan to pay with cash.

By far, the easiest way to pay is to use a MetroCard, which has the added advantage of enabling you to transfer between the bus and the subway for free if you want. Note that if you use tokens or change, you can ask for a transfer, and you'll be given a little paper card valid for a ride — but only on another bus, not for the subway.

All buses in Manhattan, and 95% of New York City buses, are equipped with wheelchair lifts and special areas where the seats in the back fold up to make room for securing wheelchairs on board. The buses also "kneel," scrunching down when they stop so that the first step is not quite so high up.

Understanding the MetroCard

The MetroCard farecard is a high-tech system that encodes a certain number of rides on a magnetic strip on the back of a thin plastic card. MetroCards are accepted on both buses and subways and have a lot of advantages over tokens: They don't weight a ton, you can slip the card in your wallet or pocket, you can buy and recharge it in an automatic vending machine, you get a free ride for every ten prepaid rides, and, last but not least, you get one free transfer between bus and subway (or vice versa) for each ride as long as you make the transfer within two hours of your initial boarding.

Two types of MetroCards are available for purchase:

✔ **Pay-Per-Ride** is the regular card we just described. These cards are sold at values from $3 to $80 (at vending machines and at the ticket booths inside subway stations) and can be "refilled" by a booth attendant or at an automatic vending machine for any value, again between $3 and $80. You may find it hard to believe, but there *is* such a thing as a free ride: Every time you put $15 or more on your card, you get an additional 10% free — meaning 11 rides for the price of 10.

Up to four riders can use the Pay-Per-Ride MetroCard if you want to buy just one instead of a fistful (a particularly useful feature if you're traveling with kids). For the first ride, you swipe the card as many times as you have people (up to four), and for the transfer you swipe it only once: It "remembers" and deducts the transfer for all the riders. Remember that the transfer is good for only two hours.

✔ **Unlimited-Ride** is also a prepaid card, but you get an unlimited number of rides for a fixed price. Unlike the Pay-Per-Ride card, it can't be recharged or used by multiple riders (after you use the card, you can't swipe it again for 18 minutes). The **One-day Fun Pass,** available from automatic vending machines in the subway and at many newsstands (but *not* from the token booth clerks), costs $4 and is valid from first use to 3 a.m. the next day. The **7-day MetroCard** costs $17 and is valid from first use to 12 a.m. seven days later. In case you decide not to go home, the **30-day MetroCard** costs $63.

In addition to being sold in the subway, MetroCards are sold at many hotels and in thousands of shops all over town (if a shop offers the card, it will have a sign in its window saying so). Note, though, that newsstands and shops sell precoded cards, usually in only $3, $6, and $15 denominations; also note that the Unlimited Ride 7-Day and 30-Day MetroCards are sold only at the ticket booths inside subway stations. Vending machines accept credit cards and ATM cards, but they can return only up to $6 in change if you pay with cash.

Seniors and disabled persons get a 50% discount with the MTA New York City Transit. You can apply for the discount by writing to Customer Assistance Division, MTA, 370 Jay St., 7th Floor, Brooklyn, NY 11201. Or you can download the application from the MTA Web site (www.mta.info), or call ☎ 718-243-4999. You can recharge your discounted MetroCard at the vending machines and ticket booths in subway stations.

The MetroCard has one corner snipped off and a small hole on one side. To use your MetroCard in the subway, swipe the card horizontally through the reader in the same direction you're traveling, with the cutoff corner on top and at the back (and between your fingers) and the little hole leading the way. To use your MetroCard on the bus, insert the card downward into the machine with the snipped-off corner up and to the left, the little hole on the bottom and the side with the magnetic strip facing you. The machine eats the card momentarily and then spits it back out and beeps — also displaying, for your information, how much money is left on your card.

Traveling by Taxi

Sometimes, taking a cab really is the most convenient form of transportation — when you're late getting somewhere and it isn't rush hour, when public transportation is not well located and you would have to transfer more than once, when you're in a group of three or four, or when it's late at night and you're tired.

Taking a cab costs you $2 for the initial charge, plus 30¢ per ⅕ mile or 20¢ per minute when stuck in traffic, plus a 50¢ night surcharge (from 8 p.m. to 6 a.m.). The average fare in Manhattan is $5.25.

At rush hours, getting a cab is a real battle; you see people sneakily position themselves just above you on the curb or quickly cross the street to snatch a cab away from you. In short, be prepared to fight, or stand back and enjoy the game. Also keep in mind that traffic can get so snarled at this time of day that it's usually faster to take the subway or, if your destination is within ten blocks or so, to walk.

To hail a cab, just stand at the curb and wave your hand at an oncoming cab. It's not necessary to whistle like they do in the movies. You'll know that a cab is available because the number on the cab's roof will be lit up. (This number is the "medallion number," which identifies each driver to New York's Taxi & Limousine Commission, the office that oversees taxi business.) If the words "off duty" are also lit on the sign, the driver is ending his shift and cannot stop to pick you up.

Celebrity greetings, taxi-style

What's it like to share a cab with the rich and famous? In New York, you can find out. When you settle into your seat for the ride, a disembodied voice floats through the vehicle, beseeching you to fasten your seat belt. And not just any voice: New York Yankees manager Joe Torre's, for example, or concert cellist Yo-Yo Ma's, or stand-up comic and *Saturday Night Live* alum Chris Rock's. All have taped public service messages for New York's Taxi and Limousine Commission, urging riders to wear their seat belts. The messages are activated when the driver turns on the meter for your ride, so sit back, buckle up, and enjoy the message.

Here are a few suggestions to make your ride as smooth as possible:

- ✔ When announcing your destination to the driver, speak clearly. Remember that English may not be your driver's first language.

- ✔ Try to know the cross-street of your destination ("Third Avenue and 41st Street"). Many drivers don't know the city as well as you might expect, and if you give a specific street address (like "1500 Broadway"), the driver may not immediately know the exact location.

- ✔ If your driver is driving too fast for you, ask him nicely to slow down. You have the right to a safe (as well as smoke-free and noise-free) trip.

- ✔ Have your money ready (you can track the charge on the meter; remember to add the 50¢ night surcharge). You want to disembark rapidly to avoid traffic jams.

- ✔ Have small bills with you when boarding a cab; drivers generally don't accept bills larger than $20.

- ✔ Tip 15%.

- ✔ Ask for a receipt: It will have the taxi registration number on it, which is a useful detail if you forget something in the car.

- ✔ Check that you have all your belongings before leaving. Taxi drivers are usually very honest, but the same is not necessarily true of the customers who use the cab immediately after you.

- ✔ Disembark from the curbside door to avoid the stream of traffic that will be dodging around your stopped vehicle on the other side.

- ✔ Wear a seat belt — accidents can happen.

- ✔ Remember your taxi's medallion number. If you leave anything behind in the cab or if you want to register a complaint, call the Taxi and Limousine Commission Consumer Hotline (☎ **212-NYC-TAXI**) and reference the medallion number to help identify your driver.

Seeing New York on Foot

Walking gives you time to take in New York's breathtaking skyscrapers, street life, and shops. Even better: It's free, and you can go wherever you want at your own pace.

When walking in New York, however, you need to exercise some caution. Always be careful when crossing the street; drivers sometimes get distracted. You also need to watch out for aggressive walkers on the sidewalk — some folks race along at Olympic speeds, which can lead to world-class collisions. If you're walking slowly or stopping to take in the scenery, be aware that the flow of traffic on the sidewalk (which could include bicyclists and inline skaters) won't stop with you. Finally, don't clog the sidewalk by walking three abreast unless you all walk very quickly.

As we mentioned, walking is sometimes faster than taking the bus, and sometimes even taking a taxi. Traffic can move through Midtown at a snail's pace — especially during rush hours — and pedestrians typically outdistance cars and buses by blocks.

If you plan to do a lot of walking, be sure to bring comfortable shoes! You'll not only be on your feet seeing the city all day, but you'll probably be on your feet indoors, too — you can rack up a lot of mileage inside the Metropolitan Museum of Art, for example.

See Chapter 20 for suggested walking itineraries.

Chapter 12

Money Matters

*I*n Chapter 3, we talk about how to plan a budget, including planning for that most taxing of problems: taxes. In this chapter, we discuss the merits of various forms of money, getting cash in New York, and what to do if the unthinkable happens and your wallet gets stolen.

Greenbacks and Other Ways to Pay

You have several options when it comes to paying for things during your trip. In this section, we tell you what you need to know about cash and other methods of payment.

ATMs and getting cash

An ATM card is by far the most convenient way to keep your wallet stocked with money. ATM machines are everywhere in New York, including banks, supermarkets, and delis, and you can get cash at any hour of the day or night. Most ATMs are linked to a national network that almost always includes your bank at home.

The two major networks in the U.S. are **Cirrus** (☎ **800-424-7787**; Internet: www.mastercard.com) and **PLUS** (☎ **800-843-7587**; Internet: www.visa.com); check the back of your ATM card to see which network your bank belongs to. From the 800 numbers and Web site addresses for these networks, you can get specific locations of ATMs to use during your vacation. If your own bank doesn't have branches in New York, call to find out if it's affiliated with a bank in the city. Doing so may save you the extra $1.50 or more charge for using a nonaffiliated ATM. Many banks limit the amount of money per day that you can withdraw from an ATM; before you depart, be sure you know your bank's daily withdrawal limit.

ATM machines are scarce at airports and in some neighborhoods, including the far West Village, SoHo, the East Village, and far northern Manhattan. Wherever you are, try to use an indoor machine, where security is better. Also, remember that everybody in New York takes cash — including pickpockets and thieves. To minimize the chance of an unexpected cash outlay, carry only what you need and put the rest in your hotel room safe.

Some credit cards let you get cash advances at ATMs. However, interest rates for cash advances are often significantly higher than rates for credit card purchases. More important, you start paying interest on the advance the moment you receive the cash.

Traveler's checks

Traveler's checks have only one major advantage: Many banks now charge a fee ranging from $1.50 to $3 whenever a non–account holder uses their ATMs. Your own bank may assess an additional fee for using an ATM that's not at one of its branches. This means that in some cases, you'll be charged twice just for using your bankcard while you're on vacation. In such cases, it may be cheaper (but certainly less convenient) to revert to traveler's checks.

Not every merchant accepts traveler's checks because the merchant incurs a small fee when cashing them. Also, don't forget your ID — you'll need to show it each time you cash a check.

You can get traveler's checks at almost any bank. Three main companies offer them:

- ✔ **American Express:** You pay a service charge ranging from 1% to 4%, although AAA members can obtain checks without paying a fee at most AAA offices. You also can get American Express traveler's checks over the phone by calling ☎ **800-221-7282.**

- ✔ **MasterCard:** Call ☎ **800-223-9920** for a location that sells these checks near you.

- ✔ **Visa:** These checks are available at banks across the country. The service charge ranges from 1.5% to 2%. Call ☎ **800-732-1322** for more information.

Credit cards

Credit cards offer a safe way to carry money and provide a convenient record of all your travel expenses when you arrive home. Using your credit card to pay for most expenses may have additional advantages, too. Many credit cards give you some form of insurance against dishonest commercial behavior, and you can earn frequent-flyer miles or get money back for every dollar you spend. Beware, though, of nasty surprises at the end of the month.

Most restaurants and shops accept a variety of credit cards. Just check the stickers on the door or ask the waiter or clerk to make sure that the restaurant or shop takes the card you want to use.

You can pay many merchants directly from your bank account by using a debit card, which can help you cut down on cash purchases without running up your credit card balances.

What to Do if Your Wallet Gets Stolen

Losing your wallet is extremely unpleasant, but it's really nothing to get in a panic about. Take the following simple steps:

- ✔ Call your credit card company right away to report the theft. **Citicorp Visa**'s U.S. emergency number is ☎ **800-645-6556**. **American Express** cardholders and traveler's check holders should call ☎ **800-221-7282** for all money emergencies. **MasterCard** holders should call ☎ **800-307-7309**. Or you can call 800 information at ☎ 800-555-1212 to find out your card's 800 number. The credit card company may be able to wire you a cash advance off your credit card immediately, and in many places the company can get you an emergency credit card in a day or two.

- ✔ If you purchased traveler's checks, call the emergency number provided with your checks and report the serial numbers of the stolen checks.

- ✔ Call the police. Your wallet may be a lost cause, but you may need a police report number for credit card or insurance purposes.

Part IV
Dining in New York

The 5th Wave   By Rich Tennant

"...and for our entree special, we're offering New York's famous foot-long Veal Oscar."

In this part . . .

*I*n New York, people take eating seriously. There's even a name — foodies — for serious stomach stokers. (Next they'll be calling avid readers bookies.) The proof, as they say, is in the pudding: You can find more than 17,000 eating establishments in the city, and that figure continues to grow by about 150 per year. So tuck into the following chapters, where you'll find descriptions of New York's best dining areas, specialties, and deals, as well as complete, detailed reviews of our favorite spots for lunch, dinner, and "noshing" (snacking).

Chapter 13

Getting the Lowdown on New York's Dining Scene

*T*he quality of the average meal in a New York restaurant is so high that you really have to go out of your way for a bad experience. On the other hand, it's easy to pay too much for your food here. High prices don't ensure high quality, although the reverse tends to be true — it's tough to find world-class food for a mere couple of bucks. In this chapter, we give you all the tips you need to wade through the New York dining jungle and sort through its thousands of restaurants.

What's Hot Now

It seems like every other restaurant that opens in New York is a **bistro** or **brasserie** of some description — French, Belgian, or hybrid. The trend began a few years ago and continues unabated. (We give you a selection in Chapter 14, from upscale celeb hangouts to casual lunch joints.) Bistros usually serve such traditional favorites as mussels, steak au poivre, the Belgian fish stew known as *waterzooi,* and, of course, frites — the light, crispy French fries that Belgians are so fond of. Atmosphere is a big deal in bistros; the most successful are those with a Hemingway-in-Paris-in-the-1920s feel.

An ongoing experiment with fusion cooking has brought about a **"new" American cuisine.** Fusion marries different flavors and cuisines in exotic new ways (fusing Mediterranean or Asian foods or cooking styles with traditional French or American ones, for example). You can find some of the best entries in this category of dining in the restaurant listing in Chapter 14.

Smoke 'em if you can

Only restaurants with fewer than 35 seats can have a smoking section, which must be well ventilated. If a restaurant has a bar, you may be able to smoke there. However, make sure to ask about the smoking policy at the bar if you're uncertain.

Another trend in fusion cuisine is to add **Indian spices and preparations** to a variety of dishes. The result is the opening of new gourmet (and expensive) modern Indian restaurants, as well as the addition of dishes with an Indian flavor to the menus of many classic gourmet restaurants.

On the cheaper end, **fish-and-chips restaurants** seem to be multiplying. Is it the British heritage or the New England influence?

New York has plenty of pizza joints; sadly, most offer pies with the consistency of a wet towel and weighted down with cheese that resembles the stuff that comes out of a caulking gun. **Brick-oven pizza,** on the other hand, is as close to the real deal back in Italy as you get: crispy, with crustlike bread and an emphasis on savory, high-quality toppings. Brick-oven pizzas have become so popular over the last few years that city officials had to limit the number of wood-fired ovens to reduce air pollution. The gourmet pizza craze goes hand in hand with a surge of interest in specialty breads; several **gourmet bakeries** have opened around town (see Chapter 15 for a quick overview).

Once-hot innovations have stuck around long enough to become permanent favorites: **gourmet coffee, Italian cuisine, Japanese sushi and sashimi** (raw fish served with or without rice), **wraps, bagels,** and **Sunday brunch.**

Sunday brunch is so popular, in fact, that getting a table can be a long, drawn-out affair. Go early to avoid the crowds — before 11 a.m. for spots downtown and before 10 a.m. for family spots in upper Manhattan.

Discovering New York's Dining Areas

Some neighborhoods offer more restaurants and variety than others. The following neighborhoods are the biggies for dining in New York.

Greenwich Village

The Village is probably the number-one dining destination in New York. The sheer number of restaurants, the variety of cuisine, and the quality of the food make it a sure bet for any taste and any purse. The neighborhood being on the trendy side, some restaurants are very expensive, but most are mid-range (for New York, that is), and many are really cheap.

Within the village, the area between Sixth Avenue and Hudson Street is lined with places to eat; your best bets are on the parallel streets of Greenwich Avenue (to the north), West 4th Street, Bleecker Street, and Bedford. Some of the side streets in between also offer hidden jewels. The short block of Cornelia Street is a perfect example: **Pó,** the Italian restaurant first opened by the well-known chef Mario Batali, is at number 31 (☎ **212-645-2189**); **Home,** at number 20 (☎ **212-243-9579**), opens its garden in fair weather and serves food that tastes just like Mother used to make — assuming that your mother was a gourmet chef who made everything from scratch and knew her nouvelle cuisine. **Pearl Oyster Bar,** 18 Cornelia St. (☎ **212-691-8211**), is small, but its superb seafood has made it a hit. At 30 Cornelia, **Little Havana** (☎ **212-255-2212**) adds a Cuban mix to what's being called the Village's version of Midtown's Restaurant Row (see "Eating Where the Locals Eat," later in this chapter). The only thing missing from this one-block summary of New York cuisine is a French restaurant — no, wait, at number 18 is **Le Gigot** (☎ **212-627-3737**), a small but highly regarded French bistro.

Another smaller but equally good spot is the area just south of Washington Square bounded by Sixth Avenue to the west, LaGuardia Place to the east, and Houston Street to the south.

The East Village

Less elegant and less expensive, the East Village is a prime dining destination, especially popular with the young and arty crowd. Restaurants line Second Avenue and Avenue A south of 14th Street — First Avenue has a smaller concentration for some reason. Also within the area are some interesting ethnic pockets (see "New York's Ethnic Eats," later in this chapter).

Gramercy Park and the Union Square/Flatiron District

Gramercy Park and the Union Square/Flatiron District are a fiefdom of fashion and photography workers, and those folks know how to eat. Of the many excellent places, none rates so highly as the renowned (and pricey) **Union Square Café,** 21 E. 16th St. (☎ **212-243-4020**), where you're unlikely to get a reservation unless you're willing to dine as late as 11 p.m. At **Gramercy Tavern** (see Chapter 14), reservations are necessary weeks in advance to sample its hearty New American fare. You'll find mouthwatering South American creations at **Patría,** 250 Park Ave. South at 20th Street (☎ **212-777-6211**), and Indian-influenced new American cuisine at **Tabla,** 11 Madison Ave. at 25th Street (☎ **212-889-0667**).

TriBeCa

This neighborhood, with its curious mix of towering industrial buildings and pricey loft spaces, is increasingly active in the restaurant scene. TriBeCa is home to many of New York's most expensive and famous restaurants, such as **Chanterelle,** 2 Harrison St. between Hudson and Greenwich streets (☎ **212-966-6960**), and **Montrachet,** 239 W. Broadway between White and Walker streets (☎ **212-219-2777**). Both offer prix fixe (fixed-price) menus — the lunch version at Montrachet is available only on Fridays, but the dinner version available Monday through Saturday is an excellent deal.

TriBeCa is also where Robert De Niro opened his stylish (but we think overrated) restaurants **TriBeCa Grill,** 375 Greenwich St. at Franklin Street (☎ **212-941-3900**), and **Nobu,** 105 Hudson St. at Franklin Street (☎ **212-219-0500**). Nobu is an expensive (and, yes, exquisite) Japanese restaurant; if you'd like to try it, you need to make reservations now, before you turn this page. As an alternative, try **Nobu Next Door;** its no-reservation policy makes it easier to get in, but you'll still have a wait for a table.

In the aftermath of the September 11 terrorist attacks, many of TriBeCa's restaurants suspended normal operations to cook for rescue workers and law-enforcement officials in round-the-clock shifts. In the weeks and months following, access to downtown was restricted and many patrons stayed away, some out of a lingering sense of apprehension. Loyal residents kept area restaurants afloat during these hard times; the crowds have since returned, and the dining scene is as vibrant as ever.

The meatpacking district

This rough-and-tumble area still contains meatpacking businesses (although fewer and fewer), but it's also home to some of the city's most fashionable new restaurants. The popular **Pastis,** 9 Ninth Ave. at Little West 12th Street (☎ **212-929-4844**), is a dead ringer for a real French bistro, plunked down in the meatpacking district as if it had been there for years. The food is as authentic as the atmosphere. An old standby that's still going strong is **Florent** (see the review in Chapter 14).

Grand Central Terminal

Recently, a fashionable dining scene has developed in an unlikely setting: Grand Central Terminal. The station has always been famous because of its historic **Oyster Bar** (see Chapter 14), but now, after a glamorous renovation, Grand Central has become a food hub as well as a train hub. Overlooking the main concourse, you find **Michael**

Jordan's The Steakhouse NYC on one side (☎ 212-655-2300), where you can enjoy a buffalo steak followed by a cigar; and the attractive **Metrazur** on the other (☎ 212-687-4600), which has refined food at moderate prices.

Attached to Grand Central, in the Met Life building, are two other classy restaurants: **Tropica** (☎ 212-867-6767), specializing in Caribbean seafood; and **Naples 45** (☎ 212-972-7001), which serves pizza the way the Neapolitans invented it — a classically simple combination of tomato, basil, and mozzarella atop a wood-fired crust.

Eating Where the Locals Eat

Because ethnic food is cheap, good, and widely available, it plays an important role in the everyday life of most New Yorkers. Even the most celebrated, so-called New York specialties are in reality imported ethnic foods: pizza (Italy), pastrami and bagels (northern Europe), and dim sum (China). In Chapter 15, we name our selections for the best bagels and pizza slices in Manhattan — although ubiquitous, the quality of both varies *a lot.* In Chapter 14, we point you toward the best brick-oven pizza and delicatessen fare. See the following section for dim sum selections.

Another celebrated tradition is the famous New York Sirloin steak. The best steakhouse in New York is **Peter Luger Steak House,** 178 Broadway at Driggs Avenue in Williamsburg, Brooklyn (reservations necessary; ☎ 718-387-7400). We name our best Manhattan alternatives in Chapter 14.

One of New York's most popular attractions is, of course, the Theater District. Its nearby dining annex is the famous Restaurant Row, on 46th Street between Eight and Ninth avenues. It's a great spot for pre- and post-theater dining and offers affordable choices. Some of the best bets are **Orso,** 322 W. 46th St. (☎ 212-489-7212), and **Becco,** 355 W. 46th Street (☎ 212-397-7957), for great Italian food (reserve in advance if you can get in); **Lotfi's,** 358 W. 46th St. (☎ 212-582-5850), for Moroccan food; and **Joe Allen,** 326 W. 46th St. (☎ 212-581-6464), for good pub fare.

See also our review of **Les Sans Culottes** in Chapter 14 — a great place for "all-you-can-eats."

Enjoying New York's Ethnic Eats

Ethnic food rules in New York. Nationalities from all over the world are represented — 1,001 nationalities were present in the city at the last count. This makes deciding where to go a challenge; here are your best options.

Chinese cuisine

The streets in Chinatown are lined with Chinese groceries, Chinese restaurants, and eateries from other East Asian countries. It's safe at night and always busy, but beware of pickpockets on crowded Canal Street.

Dim sum, a traditional and festive Chinese breakfast/lunch, is a great way to try many authentic Chinese foods. After you take your seat, usually at a table with other groups, waiters wheel carts filled with tiny dishes by you. If you like what you see, you pick one or two items from the cart. The waiter puts a little stamp on your bill (dim sum prices run from about $1 to $4 per item). Try a tapioca for dessert — on second thought, take two! Besides the **Golden Unicorn** (reviewed in Chapter 14), other good places for dim sum are **Triple Eight Palace,** 88 E. Broadway between Division and Market streets (☎ 212-941-8886), and **Nice Restaurant,** 35 E. Broadway between Catherine and Market streets (☎ 212-406-9510).

A hot — literally — attraction is soup dumplings. This Shanghai breakfast specialty, served here for lunch and dinner, consists of a dumpling filled with a spoonful of hot broth and a combination of minced crab, pork, or shrimp. To avoid burning your mouth on the hot broth, put the dumpling on a soup spoon, nibble a little piece so that the broth flows into the spoon, and then eat it. The best places to try soup dumplings are Evergreen Shanghai and Joe's Shanghai. **Evergreen Shanghai** has branches at 63 Mott St. between Canal and Bayard streets (☎ 212-571-3339), 10 E. 38th St. between Fifth and Madison avenues (☎ 212-448-1199), 785 Broadway at 10th Street (☎ 212-473-2777), and a newer uptown location at 1378 Third Ave. between 78th and 79th streets (☎ 212-585-3388). **Joe's Shanghai** is at 9 Pell St. between Bowery and Mott streets (☎ 212-233-8888) and at 24 W. 56th St. between Fifth and Sixth avenues (☎ 212-333-3868).

In addition to the restaurants we recommend in this section, you can find excellent Shanghai cuisine at **Goody's** (see the review in Chapter 14). If you want to splurge, the best and most elegant Chinese restaurant in New York — authentic Chinese, that is — is **Canton,** 45 Division St. between Bowery and Market streets (☎ 212-226-4441). For other Chinese restaurants, both in Chinatown and elsewhere, see Chapter 14.

Indian cuisine

Two neighborhoods in the city have become synonymous with Indian food, but Little India, in the East Village (around 6th Street between First and Second avenues), may hold the largest concentration of Indian restaurants.

Probably the best on the row is the new, modern **Banjara,** 97 First Ave. at 6th Street (☎ 212-477-5956), but it's also more expensive than the competition. Old favorites are **Mitali East,** 334 E. 6th St. (☎ 212-533-2508), and, just around the corner, **Haveli,** 100 Second Ave. between 5th and 6th streets (☎ 212-982-0533) — not technically on the strip, but one of the best Indian restaurants in the area. Also excellent and slightly off the row is **Raga,** 433 E. 6th St. between Avenues A and First (☎ 212-388-0957). Many of the restaurants on the strip feature live Indian music on certain days of the week.

Many of the restaurants in Little India don't have liquor licenses, but you can bring beer and wine with you. The convenience store at the northwest corner of First Avenue and 6th Street has an unbelievable variety of beer, including several Indian brands (Taj Mahal and Kingfisher are very popular).

Another concentration of Indian restaurants is at "Curry Hill," the area surrounding Lexington Avenue in the mid-20s, where the Indian restaurants range from cafeteria-style takeout joints to elegant restaurants. Try **Pongal,** at 110 Lexington Ave. between 27th and 28th streets (☎ 212-696-9458) and 81 Lexington Avenue at 26th Street (☎ 212-696-5130); or **Mavalli Palace,** 46 E. 29th St. between Madison and Park avenues (☎ 212-679-5535), for excellent vegetarian Southern Indian fare at friendly prices.

Japanese cuisine

New Yorkers love Japanese food, and you can find good, reliable Japanese restaurants in every neighborhood in Manhattan. The East Village has an especially large collection; a "Little Tokyo" zone has recently grown up on East 9th Street between Second and Third avenues. In this one block are six restaurants — perhaps more by the time you read this — including the popular **Hasaki,** 210 E. 9th St. (☎ 212-473-3327). Perhaps the most interesting of them all is **Otafuku,** 236 E. 9th St. (☎ 212-353-8503), a take-out window and restaurant that serves *takoyaki* (octopus balls) and *okonomiyaki* (Japanese savory pancakes). We recommend several other Japanese restaurants in Chapter 14.

Other great ethnic eats

As you wander the city, you come across both common and unusual culinary destinations. A few of the more unique spots we favor are **Paõ,** 322 Spring St. at Greenwich Street (☎ 212-334-5464), a small, charming Portuguese spot in SoHo; **Flor's Kitchen,** 149 First Ave. between 9th and 10th streets (☎ 212-387-8949), an authentic Venezuelan café; **Persepolis,** 1423 Second Ave. between 74th and 75th streets (☎ 212-535-1100), which serves fine Persian food; the delicious Afghan restaurant **Pamir,** nearby at 1437 Second Ave. between 74th and 75th streets (☎ 212-734-3791), with a second location at 1065 First Ave. at 58th Street (☎ 212-734-3791); and **Tibet on Houston,** 136 W. Houston St. between MacDougal and Sullivan streets (☎ 212-995-5884), for interesting and tasty Tibetan food.

Dressing to Dine

During the week, people wear just about everything to go out to eat. On the weekends, dress tends to be a little more upscale, but still fairly casual. In a few restaurants, men are required to wear a jacket (and, more rarely, a tie).

To avoid the risk of feeling underdressed if you're going to an elegant restaurant, call ahead and ask about appropriate attire.

Saving Money

Yes, prices in New York are high, but you can eat well without spending a lot of money if you follow a few simple rules — and you never need to sacrifice quality. The best and most famous restaurants are expensive, but you don't need to pay through the nose if you keep these tips in mind:

- ✔ **Go for the prix-fixe menu** at top restaurants (see the sidebar in Chapter 14). Usually the best deals are at lunch, when many of the best restaurants in New York offer a special deal — a three-course meal for $20.

- ✔ **Eat ethnic food,** which generally costs less than food at American restaurants.

- ✔ **Discover "all-you-can-eat" places.** Most Indian restaurants offer such stuff-yourself buffets for lunch.

- ✔ **Skip the national fast-food chains and go for local food.** A bagel with cream cheese is good, cheap, and filling; so is a good slice of pizza (check Chapter 15 for more light choices).

- ✔ **Order takeout.** Thousands of takeout places all over Manhattan deliver to hotel rooms for free. (Don't forget to tip.)

Making Reservations

Reservations are always recommended for dinner. At lunch, for a party of two, you usually don't need a reservation. On Fridays and Saturdays, you often need to reserve a few days in advance, especially if you're with a larger party. At the most popular venues, reserve a table a week or more in advance. If you really want to dine in a particular popular restaurant, make a reservation before you depart for New York.

If you don't have a reservation, or if the restaurant doesn't take reservations, arrive early to avoid a long wait (before 12:30 p.m. for lunch and before 7:00 p.m. for dinner). For dinner at restaurants in the Theater District, go at about 8:00 p.m.; after the Broadway shows begin, restaurants in the area empty fast.

Chapter 14

New York's Best Restaurants

In This Chapter

▶ Searching out the best restaurant neighborhoods

▶ Finding out about the best restaurants in town

▶ Reading quick restaurant indexes by location and price

The listings in this chapter include our favorites among the best restaurants in the city. We give you a sampling of pricey gourmet choices, but we also understand that weary travelers sometimes just want to be fed economically but tastily and then hit the sack after a long day.

All the listings in this chapter are for good (often excellent) restaurants where you can get a satisfying meal. We don't list any crummy places just because they're cheap; nor do we list any outrageously expensive places at which you pay an arm and a leg for a couple of leaves of well-arranged lettuce. What we do list are restaurants that offer good-quality food for a fair price.

Naturally, the price of a meal depends on what you order. If you order expensive wine and the most expensive dish on the menu, you'll spend more, of course. The listings in this chapter offer two price indicators for each restaurant: a number of dollar signs, which gives you an idea of what a complete meal costs, and the price range of the entrees on the menu. Those two pieces of information can help you choose a place that's right for you and your budget.

One dollar sign ($) means inexpensive, and five dollar signs ($$$$$ — the maximum) means extravagant. The symbols reflect what one person can expect to pay for an appetizer, entree, dessert, one drink, tax, and tip. The difference between one category and the next often has much to do with extras such as location, type of cuisine, service, decor, atmosphere, view, and, of course, trendiness. Here's a more complete key to the dollar-sign ratings that we use in this chapter:

- ✔ **$ (Dirt Cheap):** These popular places have been around for a while and are located in not-too-fancy neighborhoods. They offer plain, good food in a simple setting. Expect to spend between $15 and $25 per person for a really full meal. Many ethnic restaurants fall in this category.

- ✔ **$$ (Inexpensive):** These restaurants are great bargains. They're cheaper than they might otherwise be either because they're located a little outside the prime dining areas or because they offer relatively simple fare. Don't expect designer decor; do expect to pay $25 to $35 for your meal.

- ✔ **$$$ (Medium):** These restaurants are probably your best bets for a fine, relatively fancy dinner that doesn't cost a fortune (say, $35 to $45 per person). In most of these restaurants, the food is classy, the decor is nice, the service is good, and the location is central. In a few cases, the food is plentiful and the place is famous.

- ✔ **$$$$ (Expensive):** These restaurants are among the best in New York: top food, top chefs, top service, top location, and top decor. A meal at one of these places will cost you about $45 to $60 per person.

- ✔ **$$$$$ (Where the Stars Dine):** These glamorous, top-of-the-top restaurants have achieved world renown, usually for all of the following: the chef's celebrated skills, the atmosphere, the service, the location, and the view. You get a unique experience that you may remember for the rest of your life (and you'll probably run up a good bill on your credit card, too).

As a quick-reference guide, here's a summary:

$	=	Under $25
$$	=	$25–$35
$$$	=	$35–$45
$$$$	=	$45–$60
$$$$$	=	Over $60

Our dollar signs give you a rough idea of how much a meal will cost, but don't use them as the only factor in your decision; restaurants may offer prix fixe meals or other deals that aren't reflected in their price rankings.

As you peruse the listings, check the maps in this chapter to pinpoint a restaurant's location. The maps also note the locations of the restaurants listed in Chapters 13 and 15. The indexes at the end of this chapter can help you select a restaurant by location or price.

 For more dining choices, consult the list of restaurants in our rundown of dining advice in Chapter 13. For quickie meal or snack, see our recommendations in Chapter 15.

New York Restaurants from A to Z

In this listing of our favorite restaurants, you're sure to find something to please your palate.

Angelica Kitchen
$ **East Village ORGANIC VEGETARIAN**

You don't have to be a vegetarian or vegan to enjoy the delicious fare served here. Angelica Kitchen offers a cheese-free onion soup that will match any French restaurant's, and many excellent fruit-based desserts as well. Try the "daily seasonal creation" or the lunch or dinner special, with soup, salad, homemade bread, and spread — the cornbread is outstanding. One specialty is the Dragon Bowl: a healthy helping of rice or noodles, vegetables, a little of everything. It's quite filling but won't drag you down; we guarantee that you'll wake up the next day filled with energy.

300 E. 12th St. between First and Second avenues. ☎ 212-228-2909. Reservations accepted for parties of 6 or more Mon–Thurs. Subway: L/N/Q/R/W/4/5/6 train to 14th Street/Union Square stop, walk east on 14th Street to Second Avenue, turn right, and turn left on 12th Street. Main courses: $7–$15. No credit cards. Open: Daily 11:30 a.m.–10:30 p.m.

Aquagrill
$$$ **SoHo SEAFOOD**

Among the top seafood restaurants in town, this elegant and trendy spot in SoHo has attracted crowds of New Yorkers since its opening. The reason? Fantastic food at moderate prices and friendly service where you would expect a snooty atmosphere. Go for one of the chef's creations and/or the raw bar, which offers an ample choice of very fresh seafood. A word of warning: Forget about going on a Saturday night without making a reservation well in advance.

210 Spring St. at Sixth Avenue. ☎ 212-274-0505. Reservations necessary. Jackets suggested. Subway: C/E train to Spring Street stop. Main courses: $16–$30. AE, MC, V. Open: Tues–Sun noon–3 p.m., Sat–Sun until 4 p.m., Tues–Sun 6:00–10:45 p.m., Fri–Sat until 11:45 p.m.

Downtown Dining

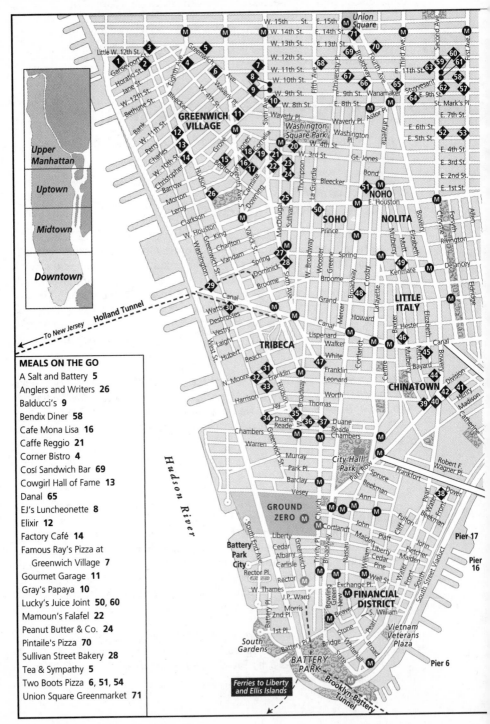

MEALS ON THE GO

A Salt and Battery **5**
Anglers and Writers **26**
Balducci's **9**
Bendix Diner **58**
Cafe Mona Lisa **16**
Caffe Reggio **21**
Corner Bistro **4**
Cosí Sandwich Bar **69**
Cowgirl Hall of Fame **13**
Danal **65**
EJ's Luncheonette **8**
Elixir **12**
Factory Café **14**
Famous Ray's Pizza at
   Greenwich Village **7**
Gourmet Garage **11**
Gray's Papaya **10**
Lucky's Juice Joint **50, 60**
Mamoun's Falafel **22**
Peanut Butter & Co. **24**
Pintaile's Pizza **70**
Sullivan Street Bakery **28**
Tea & Sympathy **5**
Two Boots Pizza **6, 51, 54**
Union Square Greenmarket **71**

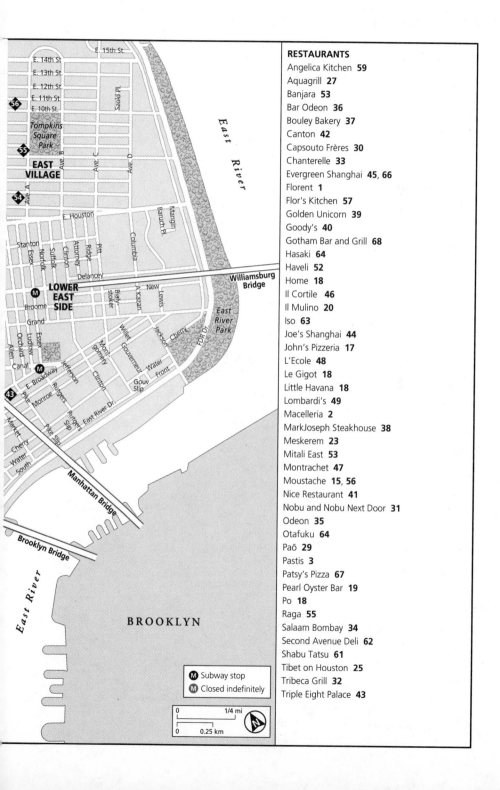

RESTAURANTS
Angelica Kitchen **59**
Aquagrill **27**
Banjara **53**
Bar Odeon **36**
Bouley Bakery **37**
Canton **42**
Capsouto Frères **30**
Chanterelle **33**
Evergreen Shanghai **45, 66**
Florent **1**
Flor's Kitchen **57**
Golden Unicorn **39**
Goody's **40**
Gotham Bar and Grill **68**
Hasaki **64**
Haveli **52**
Home **18**
Il Cortile **46**
Il Mulino **20**
Iso **63**
Joe's Shanghai **44**
John's Pizzeria **17**
L'Ecole **48**
Le Gigot **18**
Little Havana **18**
Lombardi's **49**
Macelleria **2**
MarkJoseph Steakhouse **38**
Meskerem **23**
Mitali East **53**
Montrachet **47**
Moustache **15, 56**
Nice Restaurant **41**
Nobu and Nobu Next Door **31**
Odeon **35**
Otafuku **64**
Paō **29**
Pastis **3**
Patsy's Pizza **67**
Pearl Oyster Bar **19**
Po **18**
Raga **55**
Salaam Bombay **34**
Second Avenue Deli **62**
Shabu Tatsu **61**
Tibet on Houston **25**
Tribeca Grill **32**
Triple Eight Palace **43**

Ⓜ Subway stop
Ⓜ Closed indefinitely

0 — 1/4 mi
0 — 0.25 km

Midtown Dining

RESTAURANTS

Becco **16**
Carmine's **18**
Carnegie Deli **2**
Churrascaria Plataforma **8**
Delegate's Dining Room **46**
Diwan Grill **48**
Evergreen Shanghai **40**
Gramercy Tavern **32**
Hell's Kitchen **9**
Joe Allen **14**
Joe's Shanghai **64**
John's Pizzeria **19**
Kum Gang San **37**
Les Sans Culottes **5, 61**
Lotfi's **13**
Marichu **47**
Mavalli Palace **36**
Meskerem **10**
Metrazur **42**
Michael Jordan's
   The Steakhouse NYC **42**
Naples 45 **50**
Orso **15**
Oyster Bar **42**
Palm **45**
Palm Too **45**
Palm West **7**
Pamir **60**
Patria **31**
Patsy's Pizza **21, 38**
Pongal **35**
Remi **55**
Republic **26**
Sushisay **57**
Tabla **34**
Tamarind **33**
Tropica **50**
"21" Club **56**
Union Square Cafe **25**
Verbena **29**
Zarela **59**

Ⓜ Subway stop

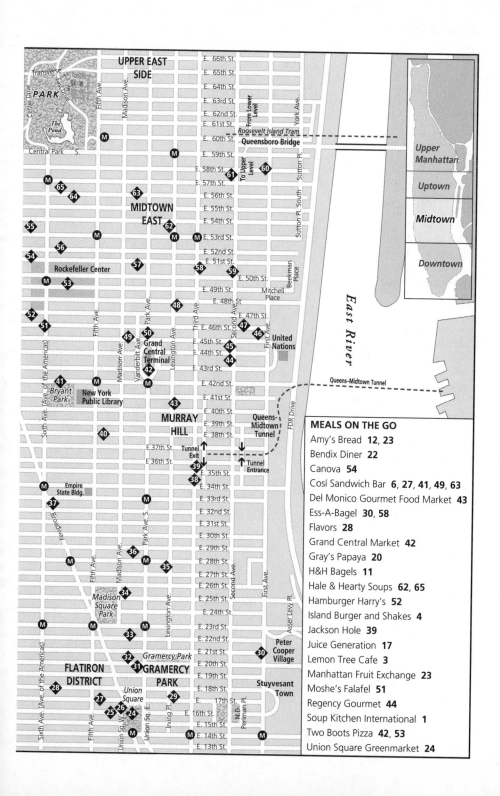

UPPER EAST SIDE

E. 66th St.
E. 65th St.
E. 64th St.
E. 63rd St.
E. 62nd St.
E. 61st St.
E. 60th St.
E. 59th St.
E. 58th St.
E. 57th St.
E. 56th St.
E. 55th St.
E. 54th St.
E. 53rd St.
E. 52nd St.
E. 51st St.
E. 50th St.
E. 49th St.
E. 48th St.
E. 47th St.
E. 46th St.
E. 45th St.
E. 44th St.
E. 43rd St.
E. 42nd St.
E. 41st St.
E. 40th St.
E. 39th St.
E. 38th St.
E. 37th St.
E. 36th St.
E. 35th St.
E. 34th St.
E. 33rd St.
E. 32nd St.
E. 31st St.
E. 30th St.
E. 29th St.
E. 28th St.
E. 27th St.
E. 26th St.
E. 25th St.
E. 24th St.
E. 23rd St.
E. 22nd St.
E. 21st St.
E. 20th St.
E. 19th St.
E. 18th St.
E. 17th St.
E. 16th St.
E. 15th St.
E. 14th St.
E. 13th St.

Transverse
PARK
Center Drive
The Pond
Central Park S.

Fifth Ave.
Madison Ave.

From Lower Level
York Ave.
Roosevelt Island Tram
Queensboro Bridge
To Upper Level
Sutton Pl.
Sutton Pl. South

MIDTOWN EAST

Rockefeller Center
Grand Central Terminal
New York Public Library
Bryant Park

MURRAY HILL

Queens-Midtown Tunnel
Tunnel Exit
Tunnel Entrance

Empire State Bldg.

Madison Square Park

FLATIRON DISTRICT
GRAMERCY PARK
Gramercy Park
Union Square

Fifth Ave.
Sixth Ave. (Ave. of the Americas)
Broadway
Madison Ave.
Park Ave.
Park Ave. S.
Lexington Ave.
Third Ave.
Second Ave.
First Ave.
Union Sq. W.
Union Sq. E.
Irving Pl.
N.D. Perlman Pl.

Beekman Place
Mitchell Place
United Nations
Asser Levy Pl.
FDR Drive

Peter Cooper Village
Stuyvesant Town

East River

Upper Manhattan
Uptown
Midtown
Downtown

MEALS ON THE GO

Amy's Bread **12**, **23**
Bendix Diner **22**
Canova **54**
Cosí Sandwich Bar **6**, **27**, **41**, **49**, **63**
Del Monico Gourmet Food Market **43**
Ess-A-Bagel **30**, **58**
Flavors **28**
Grand Central Market **42**
Gray's Papaya **20**
H&H Bagels **11**
Hale & Hearty Soups **62**, **65**
Hamburger Harry's **52**
Island Burger and Shakes **4**
Jackson Hole **39**
Juice Generation **17**
Lemon Tree Cafe **3**
Manhattan Fruit Exchange **23**
Moshe's Falafel **51**
Regency Gourmet **44**
Soup Kitchen International **1**
Two Boots Pizza **42**, **53**
Union Square Greenmarket **24**

Uptown Dining

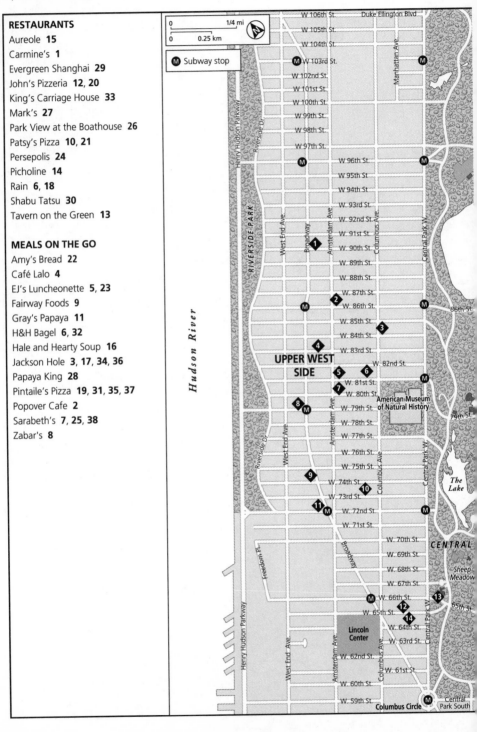

RESTAURANTS

Aureole **15**

Carmine's **1**

Evergreen Shanghai **29**

John's Pizzeria **12, 20**

King's Carriage House **33**

Mark's **27**

Park View at the Boathouse **26**

Patsy's Pizza **10, 21**

Persepolis **24**

Picholine **14**

Rain **6, 18**

Shabu Tatsu **30**

Tavern on the Green **13**

MEALS ON THE GO

Amy's Bread **22**

Café Lalo **4**

EJ's Luncheonette **5, 23**

Fairway Foods **9**

Gray's Papaya **11**

H&H Bagel **6, 32**

Hale and Hearty Soup **16**

Jackson Hole **3, 17, 34, 36**

Papaya King **28**

Pintaile's Pizza **19, 31, 35, 37**

Popover Cafe **2**

Sarabeth's **7, 25, 38**

Zabar's **8**

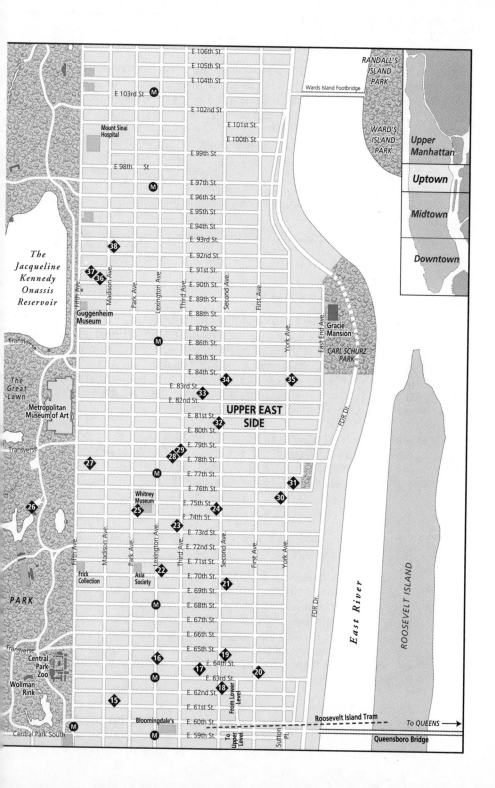

Dining in Little Italy

For a little taste of Italy, try Little Italy, which is just a short distance from SoHo. Most of the Italian restaurants and shops in this neighborhood are clustered on Mulberry Street, particularly at the crossing with Grand Street. There, you find "typical" Italian restaurants lined up one after the other. Unless you venture farther, where it gets a little deserted at night, the neighborhood is very safe. Good spots in addition to those listed in this chapter (Il Cortile and Lombardi's) are the very traditional **Da Nico,** 164 Mulberry St. between Broome and Grand streets (☎ 212-343-1212); **Il Fornaio,** 132A Mulberry St. between Grand and Hester streets (☎ 212-226-8306), a less expensive choice; **Il Palazzo,** 151 Mulberry St. between Grand and Hester streets (☎ 212-343-7000), which has a nice garden; and **Puglia,** 189 Hester St. at Mulberry Street, 1 block north of Canal Street (☎ 212-226-8912).

Capsouto Frères

$$$ Downtown   FRENCH

Housed in a landmark 1891 building not far from the Hudson River, this atmospheric jewel serves excellent French food in a refined atmosphere. The spacious dining room's large windows and high ceilings provide a lovely setting for classic French cuisine. The prix fixe lunch ($20.02) and dinner ($30.02) are excellent bargains. You can walk there from the subway along busy Canal Street, but because the restaurant is a little out of the way, we recommend treating yourself to a cab.

451 Washington St. at Watts Street. ☎ *212-966-4900. Reservations recommended. Subway: 1/2 train to Canal Street stop, walk 3 blocks west to Washington Street, and turn south for 1 block. Main courses: $15–$19.75. AE, DC, MC, V. Open: Mon 6–10 p.m., Tues–Sun noon–10 p.m., Fri–Sat until 11 p.m.*

Carmine's

**$$$ Theater District/Midtown West, Upper West Side
SOUTHERN ITALIAN**

You'll love this dining room's old-fashioned ambience, although it gets loud and mobbed at rush hour. Orders come on large oval platters in huge portions; families will love that each entree is big enough to feed three or four. The fried calamari — which comes in a foot-high pile — is as startling as it is tasty. The antipasto is also delicious, as are many of the main courses and salads. Unless you're very hungry, your party of two will find the helpings a little too large or will have to settle for sharing only one dish.

Midtown: 200 W. 44th St. between Broadway and Eighth Avenue. ☎ *212-221-3800. Reservations recommended before 6 p.m.; after 6 p.m. accepted only for parties of six or more. Subway: N/Q/R/S/W/1/2/3/7 train to Times Square stop, walk 2 blocks north on Seventh Avenue, and turn left on 44th Street. Main courses (family style;*

each serves three or four): $15–$47. AE, DC, MC, V. Open: Tues–Sat 11:30 a.m.–midnight, Sun–Mon closes at 11 p.m. Upper West Side: 2450 Broadway between 90th and 91st streets. ☎ *212-362-2200. Subway: 1/2/3 train to 96th Street stop, and then walk 5 blocks south on Broadway. Main courses: Lunch $9–$11, dinner (family style; each serves about three) $15–$47. AE, DC, MC, V. Open: Daily 11:30 a.m.–midnight, Sun–Mon until 11:00 p.m.*

Carnegie Delicatessen and Restaurant
$ Theater District/Midtown West   DELI

You may have to fight your way into this incredibly popular restaurant, but sampling its famous pastrami, corned beef, matzo balls, blintzes, and borscht will be worth it. Expect sandwiches a mile high and satisfaction to match. The cheesecake isn't bad either.

854 Seventh Ave. at 55th Street. ☎ *800-334-5606, 212-757-2245. Internet:* www.carnegiedeli.com. *Reservations not accepted. Subway: N/R/Q/W train to 57th Street stop, and then walk 2 blocks south on Seventh Avenue; or B/D/E train to Seventh Avenue stop, and then walk 2 blocks north on Seventh Avenue. Main courses: $12–$20. No credit cards. Open: Daily 6:30 a.m.–4:00 a.m.*

Churrascaria Plataforma
$$$ Theater District/Midtown West   BRAZILIAN

Who can turn down all-you-can-eat Brazilian BBQ? Huge portions of meat and innards of every kind — from steaks to hearts, from chicken and lamb to sausage and ham — are served right at your table. This meat feast is accompanied by a king-size salad bar that includes such nontraditional items as paella and octopus stew. Want another reason to come here? Kids under 5 eat free, and kids ages 5 to 10 pay half price. Henry VIII would have loved this place.

316 W. 49th St. between Eighth and Ninth avenues. ☎ *212-245-0505. Reservations recommended. Subway: C/E train to 50th Street stop, walk 1 block south on Eighth Avenue, turn right on 49th Street, and walk 1 block west. Main courses: Prix fixe lunch $27.95, prix fixe dinner $38.95. AE, DC, MC, V. Open: Daily noon–midnight.*

Delegates' Dining Room
$$ Midtown East   INTERNATIONAL

It's a little out of the way, but the Delegates' Dining Room is an excellent excuse to visit the United Nations. This restaurant, an upscale cafeteria with magnificent views, is one of the city's best-kept secrets. It's open only for lunch and offers a great all-you-can-eat buffet for $23. The buffet includes many appetizers, entrees, side dishes, delicious desserts, and an assortment of cheeses. The best time to go is when the restaurant hosts one of its international events (a regular occurrence; check in advance): A visiting foreign chef of world renown "on loan" from one of the best restaurants in the world prepares the menu. The only drawback is the often lengthy security check at the building's entrance: Allow at least an extra 15 minutes.

United Nations Plaza, Visitors' Entrance, First Avenue at 46th Street. ☎ 212-963-7626. Reservations required. Jackets suggested. Subway: 4/5/6/7/S train to 42nd Street/Grand Central stop, take the Lexington exit, walk 3 blocks east to First Avenue, turn left, and walk north to the Visitors' Entrance. Main courses: $15–$26. AE, MC, V. Open: Mon–Fri 11:30 a.m.–2:30 p.m.

Diwan Restaurant
$$$ Midtown East   INDIAN

You get a lot for your money here: quiet elegance, attentive and respectful service, a large and comfortable dining room, and, most important, delicious Indian food. The buffet lunch lets you eat as much as you want of a vast array of delicacies for $13.95. Don't forget to try the tandoori chicken, probably the best in town, or the delicious vegetarian stews.

148 E. 48th St. between Lexington and Third avenues. ☎ 212-593-5425. Reservations not necessary. Subway: 6 train to 51st Street, walk 3 blocks south on Lexington Avenue, and turn left on 48th Street. Main courses: $12.95–$16.95. AE, MC, V. Open: Daily 11:30 a.m.–2:30 p.m. and 5:30–10:30 p.m.

Florent
$$ Greenwich Village   FRENCH BISTRO

Expect lots of atmosphere in this restaurant, where cross-dressers, truckers, artists, and you all enjoy the feel of Paris together. You get imaginative, French-inspired food at all hours, plus the floor show provided by the other patrons. The quality of the food is inconsistent; at times it seems as if the restaurant is coasting on its reputation as the alternative-lifestyle after-hours hangout. Try the steak au poivre.

69 Gansevoort St. between Greenwich and Washington streets (Greenwich is the southern continuation of Ninth Avenue). ☎ 212-989-5779. Reservations recommended. Subway: A/C/E/L train to 14th Street stop, walk 1 block south on Eighth Avenue, turn right on West 13th Street for 1 short block, and turn left on Gansevoort Street. Main courses: $8.95–$21.95. No credit cards. Open: Mon–Fri 9 a.m.–5 a.m., Sat–Sun 24 hours.

Golden Unicorn
$$ Chinatown   CHINESE/DIM SUM

Dim sum is the order of the day at the Golden Unicorn. These delicacies are rolled around on little carts, and when something strikes your fancy, the waiters hand it over and mark it (in Chinese) on a little scorecard that serves as your bill. You can order regular dishes from the menu as well, and the quality is likewise good. The restaurant also offers banquets (the Chinese-style prix fixe dinner) in the evening. Expect long lines on Sunday as Chinese and other families make a day of it.

18 E. Broadway, 3 blocks south of Canal Street at Chatham Square. ☎ *212-941-0911. Reservations accepted for large parties. Subway: J/M/N/Q/R/W/Z/6 train to Canal stop, walk 4 blocks south on Confucius Plaza (the southern continuation of the Bowery) to Chatham Square, and turn left on East Broadway. Main courses: $7.95–$35. AE, DC, DISC, JCB, MC, V. Open: Daily 9 a.m.–10 p.m., dim sum until 4 p.m.*

Goody's

$$ Chinatown   CHINESE/SHANGHAI

At this Manhattan branch of a well-established, Queens-based restaurant, the specialty is hot soup dumplings — little steamed pastry pouches filled with pork and crab stuffing as well as an impossibly rich and aromatic broth. (The trick is to bite a hole in the dumpling and suck out the steaming broth without burning your mouth!) But Goody's serves many other goodies, particularly the authentic Shanghai specialties that you won't find in most other restaurants. As a bonus, the waiters are friendly and the prices reasonable. We love the pork buns and the yellowfish — two Shanghai cuisine staples — which are prepared in various tasty ways.

1 E. Broadway at Chatham Square. ☎ *212-577-2922. Reservations accepted for large parties. Subway: J/M/N/Q/R/W/Z/6 train to Canal stop, walk 4 blocks south on Confucius Plaza (the southern continuation of the Bowery) to Chatham Square, and turn left on East Broadway. Main courses: $4.95–$12.95. No credit cards. Open: Daily 9 a.m.–10 p.m.*

Gotham Bar & Grill

$$$$$ Greenwich Village/Union Square   CONTEMPORARY AMERICAN

Style, elegance, and originality are the key words that describe this glamorous restaurant and its exquisite food. Chef Alfred Portale is one of the founding fathers of "new American" cuisine and the originator of many a trend. The impeccable attention to flavors and presentation of the dishes show why this once-trendy restaurant has become a classic. If the dinners are delicious, the desserts are cosmic — not only delectable but also so beautiful that it's almost (only almost) a shame to cut into them. Certainly, the place is expensive, but the $20 prix fixe lunch is a wonderful way to experience Gotham without breaking the bank.

12 E. 12th St. between Fifth Avenue and University Place. ☎ *212-620-4020. Reservations recommended. Jackets suggested. Subway: L/N/Q/R/W/4/5/6 train to 14th Street/Union Square stop, walk 2 small blocks south on University Place, and turn right. Main courses: $29–$35. AE, DC, MC, V. Open: Mon–Fri noon–2:15 p.m. and 5:30–10:00 p.m. (Fri until 11:00 p.m.), Sat–Sun 5:00–10:00 p.m. (Sat until 11:00 p.m.).*

Gramercy Tavern

$$$$ **Gramercy/Flatiron District/Union Square CONTEMPORARY AMERICAN**

Impeccable service, top-quality food, and a rich, rustic ambience make this one of the best (and most popular) restaurants in New York. It's quite expensive, and you have to plan well in advance to get a reservation. But you're rewarded with a truly superior experience: The wonderful food is matched by an interior in warm woods, with tasteful and slightly whimsical decoration under high ceilings. It really is like a tavern, elegant and comfortable. The staff is impeccably professional yet warm. Game and seafood are prepared with imaginative combinations of flavors — for example, rabbit with rosemary and olives and foie gras with sour cherries. The cheese tray is excellent, as are the desserts (we love the pear and berry cobbler for two).

An affordable way to experience Gramercy Tavern is to eat in the bar at the front — an old-fashioned affair with tall stools and a long mirror behind it. The bar menu is cheaper and simpler but no less delicious. The tavern is even open later than the adjoining restaurant. It's a great deal for lunch or for light fare anytime.

Restaurant: 42 E. 20th St. between Broadway and Park Avenue South. ☎ *212-477-0777. Reservations required well in advance. Jackets required. Subway: N/R train to 23rd Street stop, walk 3 blocks south on Broadway, and turn left on 20th Street; or 6 train to 23rd Street stop, walk 3 blocks south on Park Avenue South, and turn right on 20th Street. Main courses: Lunch $19–$21, prix fixe $36 and $55; dinner prix fixe only $65–$90. AE, DC, MC, V. Open: Lunch Mon–Fri; dinner daily. Tavern: Reservations not necessary. Jackets suggested. Main courses: $13–$22. AE, DC, MC, V. Open: Tavern and restaurant Mon–Sat noon–11 p.m. (Fri–Sat until midnight), Sun 5–11 p.m.*

Hell's Kitchen

$$$ **Theater District/Midtown West MEXICAN**

Don't let the name fool you: This restaurant is a slice of heaven (and the neighborhood is perfectly friendly and safe). Billing itself as "progressive Mexican cuisine," Hell's Kitchen serves up delicious and inventive twists, such as an avocado leaf–crusted tuna tostada salad with mango vinaigrette. The desserts are wonderful — try the coconut flan over a macaroon with a raspberry coulis. The restaurant has a warm, cozy interior, a relaxed atmosphere, and easygoing but attentive service.

679 Ninth Ave. at 47th Street. ☎ *212-977-1588. Reservations recommended. Subway: C/E train to 50th Street stop; then walk south on Eighth Avenue, turn right on 47th Street, and walk 1 block west. Main courses: $14–$20. AE, MC, V. Open: Daily 5–11 p.m. (Thurs–Sat until midnight).*

Il Cortile

$$$ Little Italy   NORTHERN ITALIAN

You may be able to find flashier restaurants in Little Italy, but we can't think of one that serves better food than Il Cortile. Although you pay a little more at the end of the night, you'll be thankful for the superior quality and variety of the dishes — plus, the portions are generous. The menu goes beyond traditional dishes to make some interesting statements, as in the shrimp with pine nuts, spinach, and mozzarella wrapped with prosciutto. Ask to be seated in the airy indoor garden.

125 Mulberry St. between Canal and Hester streets. ☎ 212-226-6060. Reservations recommended for parties of 4 and more. Subway: 6/J/M/Z train to Canal Street stop, walk 3 blocks east on Canal, and turn left on Mulberry Street; or N/Q/R/W train to Canal, walk 3 blocks west on Canal, and turn right on Mulberry Street. Main courses: $14–$30. AE, DC, DISC, JCB, MC, V. Open: Daily noon–midnight, Fri–Sat until 1 a.m.

Il Mulino

$$$$ Greenwich Village   ITALIAN

Rated the top Italian restaurant in the city every year for almost two decades, Il Mulino is indeed one of the very best restaurants in New York. The space and decor are surprisingly uninspiring, but the food makes up for everything. The service is professional, congenial, and Old World. At lunch, the restaurant is a favorite for Italian executives on expense accounts. Be forewarned: It isn't difficult at all to part with a cool $100 for lunch if you have wine and one of the daily specials, like ravioli with porcini mushrooms in a truffle cream sauce. Reservations are absolutely necessary at dinner, and the wait can be long even with a reservation. Most impressive is the quality of the ingredients and the superb preparation. You'll never go near spaghetti sauce in a jar again! Jackets are required and ties are suggested for the evening. At lunchtime, the dress code is more relaxed.

86 W. 3rd St. between Thompson and Sullivan streets. ☎ 212-673-3783. Reservations required. Jackets required. Subway: A/C/E/F/V/S train to West 4th Street stop, walk 1 block south on Sixth Avenue, turn left on West 3rd Street, and walk 2 blocks east. Main courses: $25–$57. AE, MC, V. Open: Mon–Fri noon–2:30 p.m., Mon–Sat 5:00–11:00 p.m., closed in July.

Iso

$$$ East Village   JAPANESE

Here you get the best sushi, for the price, on the island. It's fresh and well presented; cooked-fish entrees are also available. If you and a companion are *very* hungry, the sushi-sashimi for two is a great deal. If you have room for dessert, the restaurant offers great Western-style desserts for a finish. Come early to avoid the crowd of regulars.

175 Second Ave. just north of 11th Street. ☎ *212-777-0361. Reservations not accepted. Subway: 6 train to Astor Place stop, walk east to Second Avenue, and turn left. Main courses: $13–$23.50. AE, MC, V. Open: Mon–Sat 5:30 p.m.–midnight.*

John's Pizzeria
$ Greenwich Village, Midtown West, Lincoln Center/ Upper West Side, Upper East Side PIZZA

One of the perennial contenders for best pizza in town. Expect a wait at the original downtown location, with its celebrity photos and testimonials; the other stops on this chain are a little more upscale and a little less crowded. (The Midtown branch is housed in a converted church, with lovely vaulted ceilings and some beautifully preserved stained glass.) What do the people come for? Our verdict: the best thin-crust pie in town, with super-fresh ingedients and great prices.

Downtown: 278 Bleecker St. between Sixth and Seventh avenues. ☎ *212-243-1680. Reservations accepted for parties of six or more. Subway: A/C/E/F/V/S train to West 4th Street/Washington Square stop, walk 1 block south on Seventh Avenue, and turn right on Bleecker. Upper West Side: 48 W. 65th St. between Columbus Avenue and Central Park West.* ☎ *212-721-7001. Subway: 1/2 train to 66th Street/Lincoln Center stop, walk 1 block south on Columbus Avenue or Broadway, and turn left on 65th Street. Upper East Side: 408 E. 64th St. between First and York avenues.* ☎ *212-935-2895. Subway: N/R/W train to Lexington Avenue stop, walk 1 block north on Lexington Avenue, turn right, and walk 3 blocks east on 64th Street. Midtown: 260 W. 44th St. at Eighth Avenue.* ☎ *212-391-7560. Subway: N/Q/R/S/W/1/2/3/7 train to Times Square stop, walk 2 blocks north on Seventh Avenue, turn left on 44th Street, and walk 1 block west. Main courses: $6–$15.75. No credit cards. Open: Daily 11:30 a.m.–12:30 a.m., Fri–Sat until 1:00 a.m.*

Kings Carriage House
$$$ Upper East Side CONTEMPORARY ENGLISH

Tucked away in a real stone carriage house, this small restaurant is a well-kept secret. With its quaint and charming interior, it's a perfect choice for a romantic dinner or a quiet, cozy occasion. Its real strength is the food: The menu changes daily, and each dish is delectably prepared. Moreover, the chef choses his dishes with the harmony of the whole meal in mind. The result is a perfect dinner experience.

251 East 82nd St. between Second and Third avenues. ☎ *212-734-5490. Reservations recommended. Subway: 4/5/6 train to 86th Street stop, walk 4 blocks south on Third Avenue, and turn left. Main courses: $14.95–$23.95. AE, MC, V. Open: Mon–Sat noon–3:00 p.m. and 6:00–10:30 p.m., Sun 2:00–10:00 p.m., closed Sun in July and Aug.*

Kum Gang San

$$ **Koreatown/Herald Square** **KOREAN**

Kum Gang San is one of the best Korean restaurants around. The special fare here is an authentic Korean barbecue that you cook yourself at a tableside grill. It's quite different from the woklike plate for Japanese *shabu* (see "Shabu Tatsu," later in this chapter) and, to our taste, more satisfactory. In addition to the meat, your barbecue order comes with side dishes — rice, vegetables, and pickles. Also available are many other tasty Korean specialties. Children love this place — the waterfall and white piano add to the charm, and really young ones are provided with high chairs.

49 W. 32nd St. at Broadway. ☎ *212-967-0909. Reservations recommended. Subway: B/D/F/N/Q/R/V/W train to 34th Street, and then walk 2 blocks south on Broadway. Main courses: $9.95–$21.95. AE, MC, V. Open: Daily 24 hours.*

L'Ecole

$$ **SoHo** **FRENCH**

Future master chefs finish their training here, the official restaurant of the French Culinary Institute. They may be students, but they're hardly amateurs: The food is exceptional and served in classic style. Before 8 p.m., the prix fixe (fixed price) dinner is a four-course menu with several choices of appetizers, entrees, and desserts; after 8 p.m., there's a five-course tasting menu with no choices but a different combination every evening. Keep in mind that the restaurant stops serving early: 9:30 p.m. Monday through Thursday (hey, those are school nights, after all!) and 10 p.m. Friday and Saturday. Lunch is a good deal, with a small à la carte menu, a prix fixe option, and a choice of sandwich and salad of the day. The lunchtime "Salute to healthy cooking" menu takes dishes from one of the school's cookbooks.

462 Broadway just north of Grand Street. ☎ *212-219-3300. Reservations recommended. Jackets suggested for dinner. Subway: 6 train to Spring Street stop, walk 2 blocks east on Spring Street to Broadway, turn left, and walk 1½ blocks south. Main courses: Lunch $9–$14, dinner prix fixe only $29.95. AE, DC, MC, V. Open: Mon–Fri 12:15–2:30 p.m., Mon–Thurs 6:00–9:30 p.m. (opens Thurs at 5:30 p.m.), Fri–Sat 5:30–10:00 p.m.*

Les Sans Culottes

$$ **Midtown East, Theater District/Midtown West** **FRENCH**

This French restaurant welcomes you with a free huge basket of raw veggies, salami, sausages of all sorts, country paté, and delicious French bread and dipping vinaigrette. The rest of the meal is optional and decent, but frankly not that exceptional. We love to go just for the free appetizers. Of course, if you have just the appetizers, you have to pay for it, and it's well priced at about $10. Add some good French wine and a dessert, and you still get out having spent less than $50 for two. Sounds like a bargain, don't you think? Two new locations near Times Square are perfect for pre- and post-theater dinner.

Midtown East: 1085 Second Ave. between 57th and 58th streets. ☎ 212-838-6660. Reservations not necessary. Subway: N/R/4/5/6 train to 59th Street stop, walk 2 blocks east, turn right on Second Avenue, and walk 2 blocks south. Midtown West/Theater District: 329 W. 51st St. between Eighth and Ninth avenues. ☎ 212-581-1283. Subway: C/E train to 50th Street stop, walk 1 block north on Eighth Avenue, and turn left on 51st Street. Midtown West/Theater District: 347 W. 46th St. between Eighth and Ninth avenues. ☎ 212-247-4284. Subway: C/E train to 50th Street stop, walk 4 blocks south on Eighth Avenue, and turn right on 46th Street. Main courses: $9.50–$18.95. AE, MC, V. Open: Tues–Sun 11:45 a.m.–3:30 p.m. (Sun until 2:30 p.m.), Mon–Sat 4:30–11:30 p.m. (Mon until 10:00 p.m.), Sun 2:30–10:30 p.m.

Lombardi's

$ Little Italy PIZZA

Lombardi's serves what many consider to be the best pizza in New York, and that's saying something. These pies are thin and crispy, made with real Italian toppings (no wonder: the family that originated this restaurant in 1905 came from Naples). The house specialty is the fresh clam pizza, a tomatoless "white pizza" overflowing with garlic and large whole clams, which draws people from all five boroughs as well as from around the world. Although our "best pizza" vote ultimately goes to John's (see our review earlier in this chapter), we still admit that the clam pizza is worth a trip to Lombardi's.

32 Spring St. between Mott and Mulberry streets. ☎ 212-941-7994. Reservations accepted for parties of six or more. Subway: 6 train to Spring Street stop, and then walk 1 block east on Spring Street. Main courses: $11.50–$21. No credit cards. Open: Mon–Thurs 11:30 a.m.–11:00 p.m., Fri–Sat closes at midnight, Sun closes at 10:00 p.m.

Macelleria

$$$ West Village/Meatpacking District ITALIAN/STEAKHOUSE

With a name that means "slaughterhouse" or "meatmonger" in Italian, Macelleria is right at home in the Meatpacking District, home to some of the city's hot new restaurants. This is a very authentic Italian steakhouse, with high-quality food, a chic (verging on spartan) atmosphere, and service so professional it might unsettle you. (Waiters keep an eye on you from a distance and don't come to remove your plate unless you signal — Italians find that civilized.) The steaks are impossibly tender, grilled with herbs and perfectly flavored.

48 Gansevoort St. between Greenwich and Washington. ☎ 212-741-2155. Reservations recommended on weekends. Subway: A/C/E/L train to 14th Street stop, walk 1 block south on Eighth Avenue, turn right on West 13th Street for 1 short block, and make a left on Gansevoort Street. Main courses: $16.95–$32.95. AE, MC, V. Open: Daily noon–2 a.m.

Marichu

$$$ Midtown East   SPANISH/BASQUE

Off the beaten path but near the United Nations, this charming restaurant serves up elegant yet earthy Basque cuisine. It's a secret well kept by the diplomats of the nearby embassies. Once here, you'll make some surprising culinary discoveries of your own: a salad of monkfish pieces with bechamel sauce wrapped in warm lettuce with vinaigrette, or spinach and shrimp cannelloni, or an interesting version of Mexico's traditional chile rellenos (stuffed peppers, which in this case are stuffed with cod). The service is excellent — at once old-fashioned and professional. In good weather, be sure to ask for a table in the garden.

342 E. 46th St. between First and Second avenues. ☎ *212-370-1866. Reservations recommended. Jackets recommended. Subway: 4/5/6/7/S train to 42nd Street/ Grand Central stop, take the Lexington Street exit, walk 3 blocks north, turn right on 46th Street, and walk 2½ blocks east. Main courses: $14.50–$23. AE, DC, DISC, MC, V. Open: Mon–Fri noon–2:30 p.m. and 5:30–10:00 p.m. (Fri until 11:00 p.m.), Sat 5:30– 11:00 p.m.*

MarkJoseph Steakhouse

$$$$ Downtown   STEAKHOUSE

South Street Seaport used to be an area where you wouldn't want to eat — except maybe to grab a quick hotdog or ice cream. No longer: This new steakhouse gets our rave review for its tasty cuts of meat. Why not try the — *gulp* — porterhouse steak for four? The menu contains solid fish dishes for the noncarnivores in your party as well. Prices, however, run as high as the compliments.

261 Water St. off Peck Slip. ☎ *212-277-0020. Reservations recommended. Subway: A/C/J/M/Z/1/2/4/5 train to Fulton Street/Broadway Nassau stop, walk down Fulton to Water Street, and turn left; then walk east 2 blocks to Peck Slip. Main courses: $20–$36. AE, DC, JBC, MC, V. Open: Mon–Wed 11:30 a.m.–10:00 p.m., Thurs–Fri 11:30 a.m.–11:00 p.m., Sat 5:00–11:00 p.m.*

Mark's

$$$$$ Upper East Side   CONTEMPORARY AMERICAN

Upscale experimental cuisine and elegant decor characterize Mark's. The creations of chef David Paulstich include many dishes in which fruit interacts with meat or fish to create pleasing new flavors. More traditional fare is also available on the menu. The three-course pre-theater prix fixe dinner for $34 is an exceptional value, as are the well priced prix fixe lunch and brunch. The later prix fixe dinner is more expensive at $58.

25 E. 77th St. between Fifth and Madison avenues, in the Mark Hotel. ☎ *212- 879-1864. Reservations recommended. Jackets recommended. Subway: 6 train to 77th Street stop, and then walk west 2½ blocks on 77th Street to Madison Avenue. Main courses: $22–$34. AE, CB, DC, JBC, MC, V. Open: Daily 7:00 a.m.–10:30 p.m.*

Meskerem

$ Greenwich Village, Midtown West/Theater District ETHIOPIAN

Conveniently located near many theaters and hotels, Meskerem dispenses traditional Ethiopian fare, ranging from tongue-tingling, spicy berber ribs to melt-in-your-mouth steak tartare. Here's the treat: You get neither dishes nor silverware; instead, your food is served on communal platters and sopped up with flat, spongy, crepelike *injera* bread. Tear off chunks to make mini-wraps from the hearty, well-spiced stews of your choice: lamb, beef, chicken, fish, or vegetables. The vegetable stew and the lamb are great, and the vegetable combo (a sampler of four to six dishes, more than enough for two people, for about $10) is an amazing value. We love being allowed to eat with our hands. If you wish, though, you can ask for a fork. Another smaller location is downtown, in the heart of Greenwich Village.

Greenwich Village: 124 Macdougal St. between West 3rd and Bleecker streets. ☎ 212-777-8111. Subway: A/C/E/F/V train to West 4th Street stop, walk 1 block east on West 3rd to Macdougal, and turn right. Midtown West: 468 W. 47th St. between Ninth and Tenth avenues. ☎ 212-664-0520. Reservations recommended. Subway: C/E train to 50th Street stop, walk 3 blocks south on Eighth Avenue, turn right on 47th Street, and walk 1½ blocks west. Main courses: $8.50–$12.95. DISC, MC, V. Open: Daily 11:30 a.m.–midnight.

Moustache

$ Greenwich Village/East Village MIDDLE EASTERN

You may have to wait in line — especially for dinner on weekends — at this popular neighborhood outpost. The exposed-brick walls, copper-topped tables, and world music ooze a low-key, pleasant atmosphere. Follow the lead of the regulars and order a few dips with pita bread that's baked fresh to order (and miles better than the store-bought cardboard you're used to). Also on the menu are several types of sandwiches, as well as Moustache's trademark "pitzas" topped with a variety of exotic ingredients.

Greenwich Village: 90 Bedford St. between Barrow and Grove streets. ☎ 212-229-2220. Subway: 1/2 train to Christopher Street/Sheridan Square stop, walk 2 blocks west on Christopher, turn left on Bedford, and walk 1½ blocks. East Village: 265 E. 10th St. between First Avenue and Avenue A. ☎ 212-228-2022. Subway: L train to First Avenue stop, walk 4 blocks south on First Avenue, and turn left; or 6 train to Astor Place stop, walk 2 blocks east on St. Mark's Place, turn left, walk 2 blocks north on First Avenue, and turn left. Reservations not accepted. Main courses: $8.95–$16.95. No credit cards. Open: Daily noon–midnight.

The Odeon and Bar Odeon

$$$ TriBeCa FRENCH/AMERICAN

If you get inside this Art Deco diner, you will enjoy reliably good food — free-range chicken, seared tuna, and steak frites, as well as spinach ravioli and pizza with baby artichokes. You may see a famous face or two mingling in the crowd. Brunch is very popular and less expensive than dinner; try the grilled apple and chicken sausage. Luckily, Bar Odeon, a sibling restaurant, opened across the street, where the waits are shorter and the atmosphere more casual (alas, fewer celebrity sightings, though).

The Odeon: 145 W. Broadway at Thomas Street. ☎ *212-233-0507. Reservations recommended. Bar Odeon: 136 W. Broadway between Duane and Thomas streets.* ☎ *212-233-6436. Subway: 1/2 train to Franklin Street stop, and then walk 3 blocks south on West Broadway. Main courses: $15–$27. AE, DC, DISC, MC, V. Open: Daily noon– 2:00 a.m., Fri–Sat until 3:00 a.m., Sun opens at 11:30 a.m. for brunch.*

Oyster Bar
$$$ Midtown East   SEAFOOD

Located on the lower level of Grand Central Terminal, this landmark restaurant features a white-tiled dining room with arched ceilings and a cozy side room with wood-paneled walls. Only the freshest fish is served here, but the best reason to go is, of course, the namesake oysters: delicious, plentiful (at least a dozen kinds on any given day), and presented to you by a knowledgeable waitstaff. Another good reason is lunch, particularly for the famous clam chowder (dirt cheap at $4.75), but be prepared for *serious* crowds.

Grand Central Terminal, lower level (enter Grand Central on 42nd Street between Lexington and Vanderbilt avenues or on Vanderbilt and Lexington avenues between 42nd and 44th streets). ☎ *212-490-6650. Reservations recommended. Subway: 4/5/6/7/S train to 42nd Street/Grand Central stop, take an exit toward the railroad trains, and follow the signs to the lower concourse. Main courses: $14–$30. AE, CB, DC, DISC, JCB, MC, V. Open: Mon–Fri 11:30 a.m.–9:30 p.m., Sat 5:00–10:00 p.m.*

Palm (Palm Too and Palm West)
$$$$ Midtown East and West   STEAKHOUSE

One of the best steakhouses in Manhattan, Palm is a real old-time haunt, with sawdust on the floor and caricatures of famous people lining the walls. The atmosphere is masculine (but, unlike some steakhouses, *not* dominated by pathetically macho executives); the service is brusque but competent. The food is excellent, the menu including perfectly aged meat, lobsters so big that you'll be glad they're dead, and mouth-watering side dishes. The Palm restaurants are slightly cheaper than other famous steakhouses, and they offer a great lunch deal. If you don't find room in the main dining room, go across the street to the second dining room (Palm Too); same people, same service, same quality food. There's also a branch in the Theater District (Palm West).

Palm: 837 Second Ave. between 44th and 45th streets. ☎ *212-687-2953. Palm Too: 840 Second Ave. between 44th and 45th streets.* ☎ *212-697-5198. Palm West: 250 W. 50th St. between Broadway and Eighth Avenue.* ☎ *212-333-7256. Reservations recommended. Subway: 4/5/6/7/S train to 42nd Street/Grand Central stop, walk 3* blocks east to Second Avenue, turn left, and walk 3 blocks north. Main courses: $19.95–$29.95. AE, DC, MC, V. Open: Mon–Fri noon–11:30 p.m., Sat 5:00–11:30 p.m.

Park View at the Boathouse
$$$$ Upper East Side AMERICAN

You've seen this place in the movies, anytime the characters are in New York and are having lunch on a lake. Perched on the water's edge at Central Park's rowing pond, the Boathouse can be quite romantic; new ownership and a new chef have brought better food and bigger crowds. But then again, people come here more for the ambience than for the food. Lunch, not crowded during the work week, is a much better bet than dinner, which is more crowded and more formal. By the way, walking to the Boathouse from 72nd Street after dark is safe and actually very pleasant. (Don't start wandering behind bushes or down secondary paths far from the main road, though.) If you don't want to walk, the shuttle bus operates from Fifth Avenue and 72nd Street at night.

On the lake in Central Park at East Park Drive and 73rd Street. ☎ 212-988-0575. Reservations recommended. Jackets suggested. Subway: 6 train to 68th Street/Hunter College stop, walk 3 blocks west to Central Park, turn right, enter the park at 72nd Street, and follow East Park Drive to the lake. Main courses: $17.50–$26. AE, DC, DISC, MC, V. Open: Mon–Fri noon–3:30 p.m. and 5:30–9:00 p.m., Sat–Sun 11:00 a.m.–4:00 p.m. and 6:00–10:00 p.m.

Patsy's Pizza
$ Greenwich Village, Harlem, Midtown East, Upper East Side, Upper West Side PIZZA

The original Patsy's restaurant in Harlem is great, and it's still slinging pizza out of its much-praised brick oven after more than 60 years. The young sibling branches around town aren't far behind; the pizza is crispy and topped by a variety of fresh ingredients, the salads are enticing, and the choice of pastas is varied enough to satisfy anyone. Patsy's is one of the big three names in New York pizza, although we still prefer John's (see the listing earlier in this chapter).

Harlem: 2287–91 1st Ave. between 117th and 118th streets. ☎ 212-534-9783. Subway: 6 train to 116th Street stop, walk 3 blocks east on 116th Street, turn left on First Avenue, and walk 2 blocks north. Greenwich Village: 67 University Place between 10th and 11th streets. ☎ 212-533-3500. Reservations accepted for parties of six or more. Subway: 4/5/6/N/R/L to 14th Street/Union Square stop, and then walk 3 blocks south on University Place. Upper West Side: 61 W. 74th St. between Columbus Avenue and Central Park West. ☎ 212-579-3000. Subway: 1/2/3/9 train to 72nd Street stop, walk 2 blocks north on Broadway, turn right on 74th Street, and walk 2 blocks east. Upper East Side: 1312 Second Ave. at 69th Street. ☎ 212-639-1000. Subway: 6 train to 68th Street/Hunter College stop, walk 2 blocks east on 68th Street, turn left on Second Avenue, and walk 1 block north. Midtown:

509 Third Ave. between 34th and 35th streets. ☎ *212-689-7500*. Subway: 6 train to 33rd Street stop, walk 1 block east, turn left on Third Avenue, and walk 2 blocks north. Chelsea: 318 W. 23rd St. between Eighth and Ninth avenues. ☎ *646-486-7400*. Subway: C/E train to 23rd Street stop, and then walk half a block west. Main courses: $9.50–$17. No credit cards. Open: Daily 11:30 a.m.–midnight, Fri until 1:00 a.m., Sun closes at 11:00 p.m.

Picholine

$$$$$ Lincoln Center/Upper West Side   FRENCH/MEDITERRANEAN

Chef Terrence Brennan offers exciting Mediterranean food in an elegant dining room. Try any of his inventive dishes (ones that you certainly wouldn't find at home), and then enjoy the gourmet cheeses matured in the restaurant's own cheese-aging cellar under the supervision of a cheese master.

35 W. 64th St. between Broadway and Central Park West. ☎ *212-724-8585*. Reservations required. Jackets suggested. Subway: 1/2 train to 66th Street/Lincoln Center stop, walk 2 blocks south on Broadway to 64th Street, and turn left. Main courses: $26–$36. AE, DC, MC, V. Open: Tues–Sat 11:45 a.m.–2:00 p.m. and daily 5:15–11:00 p.m. (Thurs–Sat until 11:45 p.m., Sun until 9:00 p.m.).

Great fixed-price deals at top restaurants

New York's popular Restaurant Week, held every June, pioneered the idea of offering prix fixe (fixed price) lunches at a price mirroring the digits of the current year ($20.02 in 2002, $20.03 in 2003, and so on). Happily, some of the best restaurants in New York have adopted the idea; even better, several have extended the offer throughout the year, making it possible to have a superior culinary experience for an affordable price.

Among the $20 prix fixe lunch deals, our favorite is the one at Contemporary American powerhouse restaurant **Aureole**, 34 E. 61st St. between Madison and Park avenues (☎ **212-319-1660**). Not surprisingly, this restaurant has been rated one of the best in New York for years; the only drawback is that you have to wait until after 2 p.m. to take advantage of the deal.

If you want to eat earlier but still eat for only $20, by all means choose one of the following: **Gotham Bar & Grill** (see the listing earlier in this chapter); **Mark's** (see the listing earlier in this chapter); **Montrachet,** 239 W. Broadway between Walker and White streets (☎ **212-219-2777**; French), on Fridays only; **Nobu,** 105 Hudson St. at Franklin Street (☎ **212-219-0500**; New Japanese), if you're patient enough to get a reservation; or **Patría,** 250 Park Ave. South at 20th Street (☎ **212-777-6211**; Contemporary South American). If the ambience matters more to you than the food itself, try **Tavern on the Green** (see the listing later in this chapter).

Rain

$$$ Upper East Side/Upper West Side   PAN-ASIAN

Thai, Malaysian, and Vietnamese cuisines mingle on the tables — and within some of the dishes — at this popular restaurant. Ceiling fans turn lazily in the dining room; the atmosphere seems lifted straight out of a Graham Greene novel. Dishes include Malaysian chicken satay (spiced chicken cooked on bamboo skewers) and whole fish cooked to a crispy turn and served with a three-flavored sauce (you never get just one taste sensation here). For dessert, we never pass up the fried coconut ice cream. Walk-ins are welcome and often crowd the bar and its comfortable rattan chairs, but reservations are recommended during peak times.

Upper East Side: 1059 Third Ave. between 62nd and 63rd streets. ☎ 212-223-3669. Subway: 4/5/6 train to 59th Street stop, walk 1 block east on 59th Street, turn left on Third Avenue, and walk 3½ blocks north. Upper West Side: 100 W. 82nd St. between Amsterdam and Columbus avenues. ☎ 212-501-0776. Subway: 1/2 train to 79th Street stop, walk 3 blocks north on Broadway, turn right on 82nd Street, and walk 2 blocks east. Reservations recommended. Main courses: $12–$24. AE, DC, DISC, MC, V. Open: Daily noon–3 p.m. (Sat–Sun until 4 p.m.) and 6–11 p.m. (Fri–Sat until midnight, Sun until 10 p.m.).

Remi

$$$$ Theater District/Midtown West   ITALIAN/VENETIAN

This elegant Venetian restaurant, in the heart of the Theater District, is one of the finest Italian restaurants in the city. The Venetian theme carries over to the menu, which is heavy on such heavenly seafood dishes as shellfish risotto and tuna-filled ravioli. Remi draws a fashionable crowd and fills up at peak times (lunch and pre-theater dinner), so for those who are on the run, Remi offers a menu to go, with a takeout selection of its marvelous cuisine.

145 W. 53rd St. between Sixth and Seventh avenues. ☎ 212-581-4242. Reservations required. Jackets suggested. Subway: B/D/E train to Seventh Avenue stop, and then walk east on 53rd Street. Main courses: $17.50–$29. AE, CB, DC, JBC, MC, V. Open: Mon–Fri noon–2:30 p.m. and 5:30–11:30 p.m. (Mon until 11 p.m.), Sat 5:00–11:30 p.m., Sun 5:00–10:00 p.m.

Republic

$ Union Square   PAN-ASIAN

This bustling Asian restaurant, right on Union Square, is easy to find and easy to like: noodles, rice dishes, pad thai — the Asian specialties borrow from Chinese, Thai, and Vietnamese cuisine. The restaurant is a cavernous space filled with sleek tables and benches where you sit picnic style (you may have company — a great way to meet New Yorkers). It gets really busy at peak times, but the turnaround is pretty quick. And if you can't hack the crowds, guess what? Republic does takeout.

37 Union Square West between 16th and 17th streets. ☎ *212-627-7172. Reservations accepted for groups of ten or more. Subway: L/N/Q/R/W/4/5/6 train to Union Square stop; the restaurant is on the northwest corner of the square. Main courses: $7.50–$13. AE, MC, V. Open: Sun–Wed 11:30 a.m–11:00 p.m., Thurs–Sat 11:30 a.m.–11:30 p.m.*

Salaam Bombay

$$ TriBeCa   INDIAN

One of the best Indian restaurants in Manhattan, this TriBeCa find offers excellent food in a lovely setting. The sky (or, more appropriately, your stomach) is the limit with the $12.95 self-serve buffet lunch — a great bargain. The Northern Indian specialties tend to be somewhat less spicy than the other dishes. Go on a weekend to enjoy live Indian sitar music.

317 Greenwich St. between Duane and Reade streets. ☎ *212-226-9400. Reservations not necessary. Subway: 1/2 train to Chambers Street stop, walk 1 block west on Chambers, turn right on Greenwich, and walk 1½ blocks north. Main courses: $12.95–$22.95. AE, MC, V. Open: Daily noon–3:00 p.m and 5:30–11:00 p.m.*

Second Avenue Deli

$ East Village   DELI

Come to Second Avenue Deli to enjoy the corned beef that made this restaurant famous, as well as its other kosher specialties (no butter, milk, or cheese is used here). The chopped liver and the matzoh ball soup are tops, and the gigantic sandwiches are great, too (tongue, anyone?). Service is New York brusque, but people put up with it because the place oozes history. Weekends here are quite crowded.

156 Second Ave. at 10th Street. ☎ *212-677-0606. Reservations recommended for large parties. Subway: 6 train to Astor Place stop, walk 2 blocks east to Second Avenue, and turn left. Main courses: $7.50–$21. AE, MC, V. Open: Daily 7 a.m.– midnight, Fri–Sat closes at 2 a.m.*

Shabu Tatsu

$$ East Village, Upper East Side   JAPANESE

These restaurants feature a renowned chef — you! Shabu cooking is done on a woklike grill built into the table in front of you. The food is tasty, with all the little pickles and sauces that come with the raw slices of meat, veggies, and seafood. Kids will enjoy the hands-on experience. A real chef oversees things, of course; if you don't feel like cooking, you can order ready-made entrees from the menu.

East Village: 216 E. 10th St. between First and Second avenues. ☎ *212-477-2972. Subway: 6 train to Astor Place stop, walk east to Second Avenue, turn left, and walk north to 10th Street. Upper East Side: 1414 York Ave. at 75th Street.* ☎ *212-472-3322. Subway: 6 train to 77th Street stop, walk 4 long blocks east on*

77th Street, and turn right on York Avenue. Reservations accepted for parties of 4 or more. Main courses: $9.50–$18. AE, DC, MC, V. Open: Sun–Thurs 5:00–11:45 p.m., Fri–Sat 3:00 p.m.–2:00 a.m.

Sushisay
$$$$ Midtown East   JAPANESE/SUSHI

What makes this place tick is a combination of perfect service, stark decor, and unbelievably fresh fish; you'll experience Japanese know-how at its best. You may feel like you've been transported to one of the best sushi bars of Tokyo — with prices to match. Top-quality sushi comes at a high cost in Midtown, but after all, eating it here means that you save on the plane ticket to Japan. Try to get a spot at the sushi bar — it's very authentic, and the show is spectacular. Dress up for this place.

38 E. 51st St. between Madison and Park avenues. ☎ 212-755-1780. Reservations recommended. Jackets recommended. Subway: 6 train to 51st Street stop, and then walk 2 blocks west on 51st Street; or E/F train to Lexington Avenue stop, walk 2 blocks south on Lexington, turn right on 51st Street, and walk 2 blocks west. Main courses: $25–$45. AE, DC, MC, V. Open: Mon–Fri noon–2:15 p.m. and 5:00–10 p.m., Sat 5:30– 9:00 p.m.

Sylvia's
$$ Harlem   SOUTHERN

Sylvia's is the place for stick-to-your-ribs home cooking. The gospel brunch on Sunday is so famous that you may have to wait in line for quite some time with travelers from all around the world. Try the pancakes and fried chicken for brunch, or the ribs if you want something more substantial. If you go for dinner on Sunday night, there's open-mike gospel after hours.

328 Lenox Ave. (1 block west of Fifth Avenue) between 126th and 127th streets. ☎ 212-996-0660. Reservations accepted for parties of ten or more. Subway: 2/3 train to 125th Street stop, and then walk 1 block north on Lenox Avenue. Main courses: $9–$16. AE, DISC, MC, V. Open: Mon–Sat 7:30 a.m.–10:30 p.m., Sun brunch 12:30–7:00 p.m.

Tamarind
$$$ Flatiron District   CONTEMPORARY INDIAN

Indian flavoring is hot these days, and not just spicy hot. Tamarind is one of the restaurants that have created the latest trend of contemporary — read ground-breaking — Indian cuisine, and one of the best. Delete from your mind your typical Indian neighborhood restaurant, and prepare your palate for a special experience; the food is delicious and the combinations of flavors stimulating and satisfying. The pleasant decor is a definite plus. The downside? Well, your local Indian restaurant is a lot cheaper, but this is a world apart.

41–43 E. 22nd St. between Broadway and Park Avenue South. ☎ *212-674-7400. Reservations recommended. Subway: 6 train to 23rd Street stop, walk 1 block south on Park Avenue, and turn right. Main courses: $16.95–$25.95. AE, MC, V. Open: Daily 11:30 a.m.–3:00 p.m., Sun–Thurs 5:30–11:30 p.m., Fri–Sat 5:00 p.m.–midnight.*

Tavern on the Green

$$$$ Upper West Side   CONTEMPORARY AMERICAN

Try this New York institution for a romantic supper or a special night on the town. You can look forward to a beautiful setting and a night to remember, although the food is reliable if not interesting. (If you don't believe us, check it out on the Web — this is another New York institution with a Web site.) The menu changes seasonally and has a few inventive dishes as well as old standbys like roast chicken and prime rib. A children's menu is available.

In Central Park at 67th Street. ☎ *212-873-3200. Internet:* www.tavernonthe green.com. *Reservations recommended. Jackets recommended. Subway: 1/2 train to 66th Street/Lincoln Center stop, walk west to the park entrance, and follow the path. Main courses: $22–$33. AE, CB, DC, DISC, MC, V. Open: Mon–Fri 11:30 a.m.–3:00 p.m., Sun–Thurs 5:00–10:00 p.m., Fri–Sat 5:00–11:30 p.m., brunch Sat–Sun 10:00 a.m.–3:30 p.m.*

"21" Club

$$$$ Midtown West   AMERICAN

You may pay more than you'd like for your meal here, but this restaurant, a landmark and former speakeasy, makes up for the price of its food with its historic ambience. Everybody, from presidents to poets, has eaten here. The cuisine is American and the wine cellar superb. Eat here and feel like a true power broker. In fact, to get a feel for the place, rent the quintessential New York power-broker movie *Sweet Smell of Success,* which features the restaurant prominently.

21 W. 52nd St. between Fifth and Sixth avenues. ☎ *212-582-7200. Reservations required. Jackets required. Subway: B/D/F/V train to 47th–50th streets/Rockefeller Center stop, walk 3 blocks north on Sixth Avenue, and turn right; however, you may want to take a cab to such an illustrious spot. Main courses: $25–$44. AE, CB, DC, DISC, JCB, MC, V. Open: Mon–Fri noon–2:30 p.m., Mon–Sat 5:30–10:00 p.m., closed in Aug.*

Verbena

$$$$ Gramercy/Flatiron District/Union Square   CONTEMPORARY AMERICAN

Gramercy Park, probably the most romantic neighborhood in Manhattan, provides the backdrop for this fabulous restaurant. A mild country touch enhances the innovative cooking; the menu is seasonal, but if you're there in the fall or early winter, be sure not to miss the butternut squash ravioli with cheese and cinnamon. In spring and summer, the garden terrace is a wonderful setting for a meal.

54 Irving Place between 17th and 18th streets. ☎ *212-260-5454. Reservations recommended. Jackets suggested. Subway: L/N/Q/R/W/4/5/6 train to 14th Street/Union Square stop, walk 1 block east to Irving Place, turn left, and walk 1 block north. Main courses: $18–$29. AE, DC, MC, V. Open: Tues–Sat 5:30–10:00 p.m., Sun 11:30 a.m.–3:00 p.m. and 5:30–8:00 p.m.*

Zarela

$$$ Midtown East   MEXICAN

At this restaurant, creative dishes accompany traditional ones revisited with innovative spirit and style. The duck with a sauce of apricots, prunes, pineapples, red chilies, and tomatoes is fantastic; so is the shrimp braised with poblano, onions, and queso blanco. How about deep-fried oysters with chipotle mayonnaise? Leave room for one of the extraordinary desserts — among the best in the city (try the Aztec treasure pie). The margaritas are stunning (literally; they pack a punch), and the service is friendly and attentive. The proprietor wrote two books on Oaxacan cuisine, so only about 10 million people know this place — reserve ahead! Lunch is a good bet: same food, smaller prices.

953 Second Ave. between 50th and 51st streets. ☎ *212-644-6740. Reservations required. Subway: 6 train to 51st Street stop, walk 2 blocks east on 51st Street, and turn right on Second Avenue. Main courses: $13.95–$18.95. AE, DC. Open: Mon–Fri noon–3:00 p.m. and 5:00–11:00 p.m., Sat 5:00–11:30 p.m., Sun 5:00–10:00 p.m.*

Exploring Restaurants on Your Own

If you prefer to follow your nose and live in the moment, we heartily recommend it. New York is perfect for this kind of activity, and there are many more good restaurants than we could ever fit in one book.

In Chapter 13, we give you guidelines on ethnic eats and tips for where to find restaurants just by walking around. The Village — East and West — is probably the best bet for scouting out a place to eat. Not only is this neighborhood great for a walk, but the concentration of restaurants is such that you won't need to go far to hit pay dirt. Another excellent area for elegant dining is the east 60s, particularly between Third and Madison avenues. For a wider range of choices, head for the west 50s between Fifth and Sixth avenues or around Broadway.

Other good hunting grounds are Second Avenue between 70th and 89th streets, Third Avenue between 74th and 93rd streets, Columbus and Amsterdam in the 70s and 80s, and in the 40s and 50s along Ninth Avenue. Happy hunting!

Index by Price

If price is your primary concern, use the following list to help you select a restaurant that's within your budget.

$$$$$

Gotham Bar & Grill (Greenwich Village/Union Square)
Mark's (Upper East Side)
Picholine (Lincoln Center/Upper West Side)

$$$$

Gramercy Tavern (Gramercy/Flatiron District/Union Square)
Il Mulino (Greenwich Village)
MarkJoseph Steakhouse (Downtown)
Palm (Midtown East)
Palm Too (Midtown East)
Palm West (Midtown West)
Park View at the Boathouse (Upper East Side)
Remi (Theater District/Midtown West)
Tavern on the Green (Upper West Side)
"21" Club (Midtown West)
Verbena (Gramercy/Flatiron District/Union Square)

$$$

Aquagrill (SoHo)
Capsouto Frères (Downtown)
Carmine's (Theater District/Midtown West, Upper West Side)
Churrascaria Plataforma (Theater District/Midtown West)
Diwan Restaurant (Midtown East)
Hell's Kitchen (Theater District/Midtown West)
Il Cortile (Little Italy)
Iso (East Village)
Kings Carriage House (Upper East Side)
Macelleria (West Village/Meatpacking District)
Marichu (Midtown East)
Odeon (TriBeCa)
Oyster Bar (Midtown East)

Rain (Upper East Side, Upper West Side)
Tamarind (Flatiron District)
Zarela (Midtown East)

$$

Delegates' Dining Room (Midtown East)
Florent (Greenwich Village)
Golden Unicorn (Chinatown)
Goody's (Chinatown)
Gramercy Tavern (Tavern Room) (Gramercy/Flatiron District/Union Square)
Kum Gang San (Koreatown/Herald Square)
L'Ecole (SoHo)
Les Sans Culottes (Midtown East, Theater District/Midtown West)
Salaam Bombay (TriBeCa)
Shabu Tatsu (East Village, Upper East Side)
Sylvia's (Harlem)

$

Angelica Kitchen (East Village)
Carnegie Delicatessen and Restaurant (Theater District/Midtown West)
John's Pizzeria (Greenwich Village, Midtown West, Lincoln Center/Upper West Side, Upper East Side)
Lombardi's (Little Italy)
Meskerem (Theater District/Midtown West)
Moustache (Greenwich Village/East Village)
Patsy's Pizza (Harlem, Greenwich Village, Midtown East, Upper East Side, Upper West Side)
Republic (Union Square)
Second Avenue Deli (East Village)

Index by Location

Use the following list to select a restaurant in a particular part of town that you want to visit.

Chinatown
Golden Unicorn — $$
Goody's — $$

Downtown
Capsouto Frères $$$
MarkJoseph Steakhouse $$$$

TriBeCa
Odeon — $$$
Salaam Bombay — $$

SoHo
Aquagrill — $$$
L'Ecole — $$

Little Italy
Il Cortile — $$$
Lombardi's — $

East Village
Angelica Kitchen — $
Iso — $$$
Moustache — $
Second Avenue Deli — $
Shabu Tatsu — $$

Greenwich Village
Angelica Kitchen — $
Florent — $$
Gotham Bar & Grill — $$$$$
Il Mulino — $$$$
Iso — $$$
John's Pizzeria — $
Meskerem — $
Moustache — $
Patsy's Pizza — $
Second Avenue Deli — $
Shabu Tatsu — $$

West Village/Meatpacking District
Florent — $$
Macelleria — $$$

Gramercy/Flatiron District/Union Square
Gotham Bar & Grill — $$$$$
Gramercy Tavern — $$$$
Gramercy Tavern (Tavern Room) — $$
Republic — $
Tamarind — $$$
Verbena — $$$$

Midtown East
Delegates' Dining Room — $$
Diwan Restaurant — $$$
Les Sans Culottes — $$
Marichu — $$$
Oyster Bar — $$$
Palm — $$$$
Palm Too — $$$$
Patsy's Pizza — $
Sushisay — $$$$
Zarela — $$$

Midtown West/Theater District
Carmine's — $$$
Carnegie Delicatessen and Restaurant — $
Churrascaria Plataforma — $$$
Hell's Kitchen — $$$
John's Pizzeria — $
Les Sans Culottes — $$
Meskerem — $
Palm West — $$$$
Remi — $$$$
"21" Club — $$$$

Koreatown/Herald Square
Kum Gang San — $$

Lincoln Center
John's Pizzeria — $
Picholine — $$$$$

Upper East Side
John's Pizzeria — $
Kings Carriage House — $$$
Mark's — $$$$$
Park View at the Boathouse — $$$$
Patsy's Pizza — $
Rain — $$$
Shabu Tatsu — $$

Upper West Side
Carmine's — $$$
John's Pizzeria — $
Patsy's Pizza — $
Picholine — $$$$$
Rain — $$$
Tavern on the Green — $$$$

Harlem
Patsy's Pizza — $
Sylvia's — $$

Chapter 15

On the Lighter Side: Snacks and Meals on the Go

● ●

In This Chapter

▶ Having breakfast

▶ Snacking New York style

▶ Sampling street food

▶ Discovering other quick-grab treats

● ●

We feel that it's best to stay away from the national fast-food chains — why eat generic when you can have a New York taste sensation? If you're in a rush or you want something light, many of the options we list in this chapter are much more interesting and satisfactory than fast food — and probably healthier.

The restaurants and dining spots that we mention in this chapter are shown on the maps in Chapter 14. Check there to verify locations.

Breakfast and Brunch

Breakfast opportunities in New York are plentiful, pleasurable, and usually affordable, especially if you take advantage of the ubiquitous breakfast special. At local diners, the special costs about $4; expect to pay $3.95 for your eggs and coffee and $5.95 for a larger combination with sausage, bacon, and/or corned beef hash.

One of our favorite breakfast spots is the **Bendix Diner,** 167 First Ave. between 10th and 11th streets (☎ 212-260-4220). Another surefire winner is **EJ's Luncheonette,** which serves diner food at great prices, with a particularly good breakfast. Their three locations are well spaced around town, at 1271 Third Ave. at 73rd Street (☎ 212-472-0600), 447 Amsterdam Ave. between 81st and 82nd streets (☎ 212-873-3444), and 432 Sixth Ave. between 9th and 10th streets (☎ 212-473-5555).

Brunch choices abound in the city; here are some of the best bets:

✔ For a laid-back Village experience, try **Anglers and Writers,** 420 Hudson St. at St. Luke's Place in the West Village (☎ **212-675-0810**), or **Danal,** 90 E. 10th St. between Third and Fourth avenues (☎ **212-982-6930**), which is also nice for regular meals.

✔ For an upscale brunch, try **Capsouto Frères** (see Chapter 14) — you won't be disappointed, neither in quality nor in quantity.

✔ For gourmet food at a moderate cost, try **Sarabeth's,** which has three locations: 423 Amsterdam Ave. between 80th and 81st streets (☎ **212-496-6280**); at the Hotel Wales, 1295 Madison Ave. between 92nd and 93rd streets (☎ **212-410-7355**); and inside the Whitney Museum, 945 Madison Ave. between 74th and 75th streets (☎ **212-570-3670**).

✔ The teddy bear decor at the **Popover Café,** 551 Amsterdam Ave. between 86th and 87th streets (☎ **212-595-8555**) will no doubt win over the kids; the namesake popovers (served with strawberry butter) make it worth the trip for adults. Older children and teens will get a kick out of the **Cowgirl Hall of Fame,** with its kooky Greenwich Village–meets–Texas atmosphere, at 519 Hudson St. at 10th Street (☎ **212-633-1133**). Cowgirl is strictly an eggs-and-burgers kind of joint.

The Best Bagels in New York

Bagels are a true New York institution. You can't leave town without trying one, but beware: Once you've tasted a real one, those frozen supermarket imposters will never seem adequate again. Bagels make a great breakfast — whether your topping of choice is a fried egg and bacon, lox and onions, or a simple "schmear" (light coating) of cream cheese — but they're a perfect snack anytime. Look for the "hot bagel" sign in the window: It means that the bagels are baked on the premises. Don't settle for anything less!

Hundreds of places around the city sell bagels, but why not go straight for the best? The two best bagels in the city are baked by **H&H Bagels** and **Ess-A-Bagel.** H&H has three locations: 2239 Broadway at 80th Street (☎ **212-595-8003**; open daily 24 hours), 1551 Second Ave. at 80th Street (☎ **212-734-7441**), and 639 W. 46th St. between Eleventh Avenue and the West Side Highway (☎ **212-595-8000**). Ess-A-Bagel has two locations: 831 Third Ave. at 51st Street (☎ **212-980-1010**) and 359 First Ave. at 21st Street (☎ **212-260-2252**).

A Slice of Heaven: New York Pizza

Countless restaurants in New York serve pizza by the slice — a quick, affordable meal or snack. (The three pizza restaurants we review in

Chapter 14 are strictly whole pies only.) The big name in New York pizza is Ray. Wherever you go, you see that name attached to pizza places. The name refers to the historical Famous Ray's Pizza of Greenwich Village, 465 Sixth Ave. at 11th Street, which became famous for serving slices loaded down with cheese and is still in business. Other establishments use Ray's name for the notoriety. A typical Ray's slice is very *Americano* — big, doughy, heavy on the toppings, and with really thick cheese. Unfortunately, the quality varies greatly from restaurant to restaurant.

You can get what's called a "gourmet" slice (with veggie, meat-lover, pineapple, or other weird toppings) at the following places:

- **Pintaile's Pizza,** 29 E. 91st St. between Madison and Fifth avenues (☎ 212-722-1967; Internet: www.pintailespizza.com), is ideally located for a little break from Museum Mile. Other locations are at 1577 York Ave. between 83rd and 84th streets (☎ 212-396-3479), 1443 York Ave. between 76th and 77th streets (☎ 212-717-4990), 1237 Second Ave. between 64th and 65th streets (☎ 212-752-6222), and 124 Fourth Ave. between 12th and 13th streets (☎ 212-475-4977).

- **Two Boots** has the best and most innovative toppings. Branches are at 74 Bleecker St. between Broadway and Lafayette (☎ 212-777-1033), 201 W. 11th St. at Seventh Avenue South (☎ 212-633-9096), two places on Avenue A between 2nd and 3rd streets at numbers 37 (☎ 212-505-2276) and 42 (☎ 212-254-1919), the lower level of Grand Central Terminal (☎ 212-557-7992), and 30 Rockefeller Plaza between 49th and 50th streets (☎ 212-332-8800).

Delis and Salad Bars

The New York deli descended from the meat-oriented delicatessens found in Eastern Europe. Today in New York, *deli* is often a loose term that describes the many corner stores that sell vegetables, basic grocery items, and junk food, with a sandwich counter and a self-service salad bar (such stores are also called *bodegas,* the Spanish word that translates literally as wine cellar or tavern). Delis are a great place to have a healthy, relatively inexpensive lunch that can include a wide variety of American and Asian foods.

Because delis and salad bars cater mainly to office workers, most of the best ones are clustered in central Midtown. On the west side, try **Flavors,** 8 W. 18th St. between Fifth and Sixth avenues (☎ 212-647-1234), or the 24-hours-a-day **Canova,** 140 W. 51st St. between Sixth and Seventh avenues (☎ 212-969-9200) — perfect for a midnight snack. On the east side, the best choices are **Del Monico Gourmet Food Market,** Lexington Avenue between 41st and 42nd streets (☎ 212-661-0510), and **Regency**

Gourmet, 801 Second Ave. between 42nd and 43rd streets (☎ 212-661-3322), which has a great selection of fresh baked and grilled fish and is open 24 hours.

If you're in the vicinity of Grand Central Station or the New York Public Library, it's worth seeking out **Grand Central Market,** on the main floor of the terminal (the easiest access is from 42nd Street and Lexington Avenue; no phone). This gourmet food hall is actually a collection of small, specialized vendors in adjoining stalls. The food is unbelievably fresh, and you can purchase both ready-made food (crab cakes, salads, and desserts) and fresh meat, fish, and produce. It's a bit pricey, but given that prices in Midtown are high across the board, it's really an excellent value.

Gyros and Falafel

Middle Eastern cuisine is plentiful in New York. Many delis, shops, and street carts sell *gyros* (pita bread filled with roasted lamb meat, sesame sauce, lettuce, and tomatoes) and *falafel* (chickpea fritters served in a pita pocket).

While MacDougal Street in Greenwich Village has several falafel shops (all of which are good), the most legendary — and the smallest — is **Mamoun's,** 119 MacDougal St., near the corner of West 3rd Street (☎ 212-674-8685). If you find yourself in Midtown at lunchtime during the week, try **Moshe's Falafel,** a sidewalk stand at the southeast corner of 46th Street and Sixth Avenue. A little farther west in Midtown is the bare-bones **Lemon Tree Café,** 769 Ninth Ave. between 51st and 52nd streets (☎ 212-245-0818), where you can get a big falafel sandwich overstuffed with lettuce and other veggies for about $5. Lemon Tree also serves kabobs, gyros, and a wide selection of vegetarian dishes.

Street Cart Food

Street carts are staked out on corners all over the city selling a variety of foods — you can get coffee, muffins, and bagels in the morning; hot dogs, sandwiches, pretzels, *knishes* (potato dumplings), ice cream, and even gourmet soups are sold at lunch and dinnertime. Should you be put off by the local nickname for frankfurters sold from street carts ("dirty water dogs")? That's for you to decide. Carts selling fresh fruits and vegetables are open for business all day long.

Hot dogs, pretzels, and knishes should never cost you much more than $1.50. If someone tries to charge you $2 or more, you're being ripped off.

How clean are the carts?

An increasing number of hepatitis cases have been reported in the last few years, largely brought on by poor hygienic conditions during food preparation. Although the city has reacted with stricter rules and the situation is improving, you still need to keep an eye on what and where you eat. Don't eat at restaurants that look dirty, and look around for customers; if the place is crowded, it's also likely to be safe. These basic rules are particularly important for street carts — one of the major sources of problems — and for sandwiches and salad bars in delis.

Gourmet Sandwiches

Many places in New York sell tasty sandwiches made with freshly baked bread and combinations of appetizing and exotic ingredients. One of the nuttier places is **Peanut Butter & Co.,** 240 Sullivan St. between Bleecker and West 3rd streets (☎ **212-677-3995**), where you can have huge peanut butter sandwiches in 14 varieties — with fruit, nuts, and all kind of extra toppings. Yes, even in the realm of the humble PB&J, New York just has to be different.

Have you ever had a job where you went to the same place for lunch for years and never got sick of it? That's how people feel about **Così Sandwich Bar.** The tasty flatbread comes out of a brick oven on the premises and gets stuffed with olive oil, prosciutto, and other Italian and non-Italian specialties. If the chain keeps expanding the way it has been in recent years, you won't *not* be able to stumble upon a franchise. Following is a partial list: 60 E. 56th St. between Madison and Park avenues (☎ **212-588-0888**); Paramount Plaza, 1633 Broadway at 51st Street (☎ **212-397-2674**); 38 E. 45th St. between Madison and Vanderbilt avenues (☎ **212-949-7400**); 11 W. 42nd St. between Fifth and Sixth avenues (☎ **212-265-2674**); 3 E. 17th St. between Broadway and Fifth Avenue (☎ **212-414-8468**); and 841 Broadway at 13th Street (☎ **212-614-8544**).

Soup

The most famous soup maker in New York is Al Yeganeh, proprietor and chef at **Soup Kitchen International,** 259A W. 55th St. between Broadway and Eighth Avenue (no phone; takeout service only), spoofed in the TV sitcom *Seinfeld.* Prices are high relative to soup sold in other restaurants, but the thing is, the soup really is as good as they say. In fact, it's *so* good that the owner can afford to close the place for the summer and go on vacation! Note that the taciturn Yeganeh was deeply offended by the thinly veiled *Seinfeld* parody (which stuck him with the nickname "Soup Nazi"), so it's not a good subject to bring up within his earshot. And finally, yes: Please have your money ready and step to the extreme left after ordering.

Another excellent choice is **Hale and Hearty Soups,** with locations all around town. Two conveniently central locations are 55 W. 56th St. between Fifth and Sixth avenues (☎ 212-245-9200) and 849 Lexington Ave. between 64th and 65th streets (☎ 212-517-7600). Eight soups are offered every day — including vegetarian and low-fat choices — along with tossed-to-order salads and freshly made sandwiches.

Hamburgers and Hot Dogs

Tired of sushi, nouvelle cuisine, and hefty tabs? Hamburgers are always a welcome, hearty alternative. One of the best deals in Manhattan is **Island Burgers and Shakes,** 766 Ninth Ave. between 51st and 52nd streets (☎ 212-307-7934), a tiny surfer-looking hangout where you can have a softball-sized burger and an extra-thick shake at an excellent price.

Another great hamburger haven is **Hamburger Harry's,** 145 W. 45th St. between Sixth and Seventh avenues (☎ 212-840-0566), a large, loud place famous for its tasty mesquite-grilled hamburgers, its kid-friendly approach, and its good prices (for New York, that is; charging $7 or $8 for a hamburger may be a punishable offense in your town). Don't skip the curly fries, which are delicious, and remember that the place is closed on Sundays.

A perennial winner in the "Best Burger in New York" contest is **Corner Bistro,** 331 W. 4th St. at Hudson Street (☎ 212-242-9502), an aged dark-wood tavern and neighborhood hangout that gets quite crowded later at night. And **Jackson Hole,** 517 Columbus Ave. between 84th and 85th streets (☎ 212-362-5177), has the kind of assembly-kit retro atmosphere (vintage soda-pop signs and movie posters, for example) that makes the hamburgers, shakes, and free pickles go down easy. (They do a great turkey burger there, too.) Other branches on the east side are at 521 Third Ave. at 35th Street (☎ 212-679-3264), 232 E. 64th St. between Second and Third avenues (☎ 212-371-7187), 1270 Madison Ave. between 90th and 91st streets (☎ 212-427-2820), and 1611 Second Ave. between 83rd and 84th streets (☎ 212-737-8788).

You can't really cross the street in Manhattan without encountering a hot dog vendor camped out with his cart. But for a real New York Hot Dog Experience, stop by **Gray's Papaya**, 2090 Broadway at 72nd Street (☎ 212-799-0243). The concept — that people would actually want to consume hot dogs and papaya juice *at the same time* — seems straight out of some culinary Twilight Zone, but at $1.95 for two dogs and a fruit drink, the eats don't get much cheaper — or more bizarre. Other locations are at 539 Eighth Ave. at 37th Street (☎ **212-904-1588**) and 402 Sixth Ave. at 8th Street (☎ **212-260-3532**). All locations are open 24 hours. Even more amazing, Gray's has a direct competitor: **Papaya King** (the favorite hot dog of Kramer on *Seinfeld*), with locations at 179 E. 78th St. at Third Avenue (☎ **212-369-0648**) and 121 W. 125th St. between Lenox and Seventh avenues (☎ **212-665-5732**).

Gourmet Breads

In today's New York, you can buy — and often eat on the premises — fantastic freshly baked gourmet breads and other oven specialties in places all over town. One, the **Bouley Bakery,** 120 W. Broadway at Duane Street (☎ **212-964-2525**), serves delicious breads, and the adjoining restaurant is known for first-rate contemporary French food prepared by one of the top chefs in New York. Other examples include **Sarabeth's** (see the "Breakfast and Brunch" section earlier in this chapter), where you can buy many different excellent sweet baked goods and have a gourmet meal; and the **Sullivan Street Bakery,** 73 Sullivan St. between Spring and Broome streets (☎ **212-334-9435**), which makes to-die-for thin-crust Italian breads with toppings like zucchini, mushrooms, and potatoes. **Amy's Bread,** Lexington Avenue between 70th and 71st streets (☎ **212-537-0270**), offers a magnificent choice of baked goods; try the authentic scones or the wonderful potato and dill bread. Other Amy's locations are at 672 Ninth Ave. between 46th and 47th streets (☎ **212-977-2670**) and inside Chelsea Market at 75 Ninth Ave. between 15th and 16th streets (☎ **212-462-4338**).

Coffee Break and Tea Time

If it's coffee you crave, you can get your fix just about anywhere at any time. There's a **Starbucks** on just about every corner — just walk out your hotel door and you're bound to run into one. Other franchise shops (**New World Coffee, Timothy's Coffees of the World,** and **Au Bon Pain**) are scattered around town as well.

For the non-drinker, the caffeine addict, and all those who've wanted to step inside that Edward Hopper painting *Nighthawks,* there are many cafes and coffee temples that stay open late. On Christopher Street is the plush **Factory Café,** 104 Christopher St. between Bleecker and Hudson streets (☎ **212-807-6900**), with pastries, coffee, and sofas and armchairs. The Village is full of such hangouts, many steeped in the neighborhood's rich counterculture history. **Caffe Reggio,** 119 MacDougal St. between Bleecker and West 3rd streets (☎ **212-475-9557**), dates back to the 1920s and hosted a number of folk artist performances in the 1960s. **Café Mona Lisa,** 282 Bleecker St. at Seventh Avenue South (☎ **212-929-1262**), has the kind of charmingly decrepit easy chairs and loveseats that will make you want to nurse your cappuccino for hours. Further uptown is **Café Lalo,** 201 W. 83rd St. between Broadway and Amsterdam Avenue (☎ 212-496-6031), where online pen pals Meg Ryan and Tom Hanks had their first in-person meeting in *You've Got Mail.* There are hundreds more cafes in the city, and one of the pleasures of spending time in New York is the great pleasure that comes from stumbling upon a charming little place you can call your own.

If it's a nice cuppa tea you're after, the place to go is the tiny **Tea & Sympathy,** 108 Greenwich Ave. between 12th and 13th streets (☎ 212-807-8329). The cups and teapots may be a little the worse for wear, and the tables so close together you may feel like sharing your scone with the guy sitting next to you, but all that contributes to the mellow, super-friendly atmosphere. (Note that the same folks have opened an authentic fish-and-chips shop next door called — I'm not making this up — **A Salt and Battery,** ☎ 212-691-2713. The fish is delicious, and way fresher than that joke.)

Smoothies and Fresh Juices

Health-conscious visitors will have plenty to celebrate in this city, where people order beet-and-wheatgrass juice with the kind of seriousness and panache normally exhibited at a cocktail lounge. Among the best places to find fresh juices and healthy smoothies are **Elixir,** 523 Hudson St. between West 10th and Charles streets (☎ 212-352-9952); **Juice Generation,** 644 Ninth Ave. between 45th and 46th streets (☎ 212-541-5600); and **Lucky's Juice Joint,** at 75 W. Houston St. between West Broadway and Wooster Street (☎ 212-388-0300) and at 170 Second Ave. between 10th and 11th streets (no phone).

Fruits and Grocery Items

As we mentioned in the section "Delis and Salad Bars" earlier in this chapter, local corner markets (also called *bodegas*) usually sell a decent selection of fresh fruits and vegetables. For seasonal, super-fresh items right off the farm, you can try the **Union Square Greenmarket,** a farmer's market that runs Mondays, Wednesdays, Fridays, and Saturdays at Union Square between 14th and 17th streets and Broadway and Park Avenue. Or you can head west to the **Manhattan Fruit Exchange** in the Chelsea Market, 75 Ninth Ave. between 15th and 16th streets (☎ 212-989-2444), where you find organic fruits and vegetables as well as healthy snacks at affordable prices.

And of course, Manhattan is a haven for gourmet supermarkets. At the following places, you can get not only high-quality ingredients (if you're staying at a place with a kitchen and feel like whipping up a meal or two), but also delicious premade main courses, salads, soups, and desserts. The most well-known is **Zabar's,** 2245 Broadway at 80th Street

(☎ **212-787-2000**), where you can get more than two dozen varieties of smoked salmon as well as a wide range of specialty kitchen equipment, if you're looking to turn over a culinary leaf when you get back home. Just down the road is **Fairway Foods,** 2127 Broadway at 74th Street (☎ **212-595-1888**), known for its encyclopedic selection of fresh cheeses (the bread is good, too, if you want to head over to Central Park and make a picnic out of it). **Balducci's,** 424 Sixth Ave. at 9th Street (☎ **212-673-2600**), once a mom-and-pop grocery store, is now a gourmet market of the highest quality (the whole roast chicken for $6 is an unbelievable deal). **Gourmet Garage,** 117 Seventh Ave. South at West 10th Street (☎ **212-699-5980**), has slightly more affordable prices and a good selection of store-brand items like chips and salsa.

Part V
Exploring New York

The 5th Wave   By Rich Tennant

"Hey! Stop that running and put that cigarette out! This is the Statue of Liberty. You can't run around here doing anything you want."

In this part . . .

Now that you've settled into your hotel room and confirmed tonight's dinner plans, you're ready to do what you went to all this trouble for in the first place: see the city.

In Chapter 16, we describe New York's major attractions. In Chapter 17, we point out additional attractions that may not interest everybody, but just might interest you. In Chapter 18, we recommend the best guided tours to see it all. Then, of course, there's shopping to consider; you'll find the best of it described in Chapter 19. Finally, in Chapter 20 we suggest five ready-made itineraries for the sightseers who need a little extra help organizing their time.

Chapter 16

New York's Top Sights

In This Chapter

▶ Attractions by neighborhood and type

▶ The top attractions in New York City

*T*urn to this chapter for help in planning your sightseeing. We tell you which sights are located in which neighborhoods (and show you with maps), what you're going to see at each attraction, and anything else you may need to know to get the most out of your visit. The maps in this chapter also show the locations of several attractions discussed in Chapter 17 and in other chapters of this book.

For information about visiting the viewing platform at Ground Zero, the former site of the World Trade Center, see the section "A Solemn Site," later in this chapter.

The Top Sights from A to Z

American Museum of Natural History
Upper West Side

You'll need at least two hours to take in even a small sampling of this vast museum, which spans four city blocks. In addition to special exhibitions, the museum features an astonishing permanent collection of taxidermied wildlife (including a famous herd of African elephants), an enormous exhibition dedicated to biodiversity, interactive exhibits for kids, and displays of gems, dinosaur fossils, and meteorites, among other treasures. It also has an IMAX theater. The new planetarium — a huge sphere housed in a glass box several stories tall — is part of the Rose Center for Earth and Space. In the top half of the sphere is the state-of-the-art Space Theater, which airs a breathtaking space show; in the bottom half is the Big Bang, a multisensory re-creation of the first moments of the universe.

Downtown Attractions

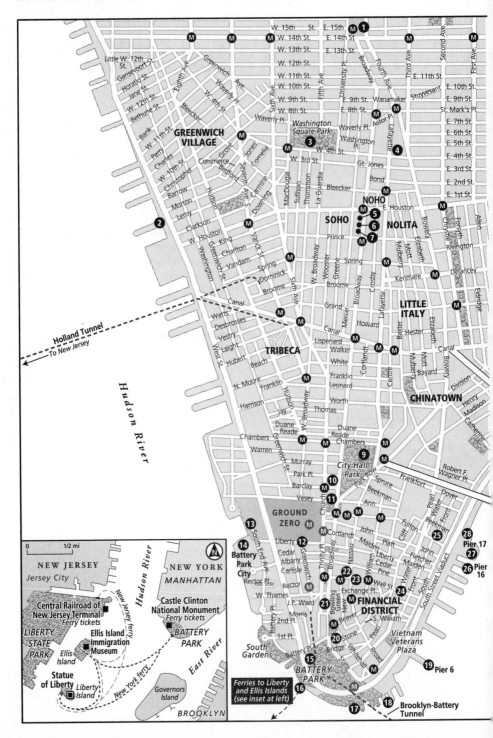

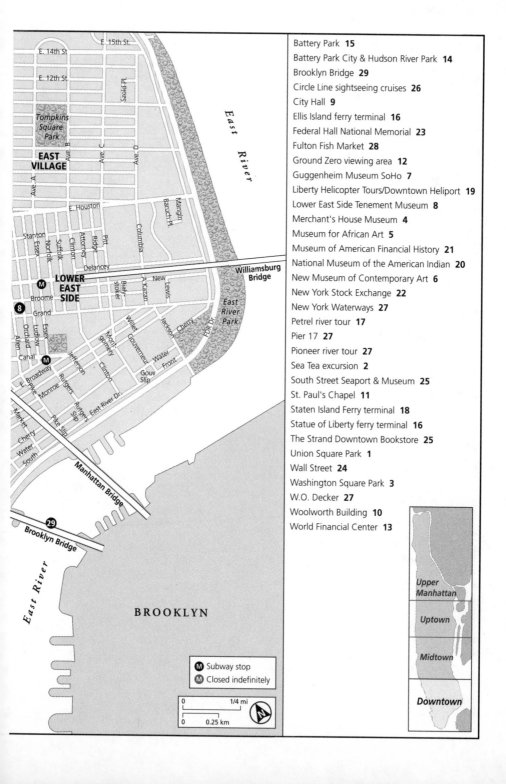

Midtown Attractions

Adirondak sailing cruise **15**
Bateaux New York **13**
Carnegie Hall **1**
Chelsea Piers Sports &
 Entertainment Complex **14**
Chrysler Building **24**
Circle Line Sightseeing Cruises **5**
Ed Sullivan Theater **2**
Empire State Building **18**
Flatiron Building & District **16**
Gramercy Park **17**
Grand Central Terminal **23**
Gray Line New York Tours **3**
Intrepid Sea-Air-Space Museum **4**
Liberty Helicopters/VIP Heliport **11**
Mets Clubhouse Store **22, 31**
MTV Studios **9**
Museum of Television & Radio **29**
New York Public Library &
 Bryant Park **21**
New York Waterways River Tours **7**
Pierpont Morgan Library **19**
Radio City Music Hall **28**
Rockefeller Center **27**
Sony Wonder Technology Lab **30**
Spirit Cruises **12**
St. Patrick's Cathedral **26**
Times Square **10**
United Nations **25**
World Yacht **6**
Yankees Clubhouse Store **8, 20, 32**

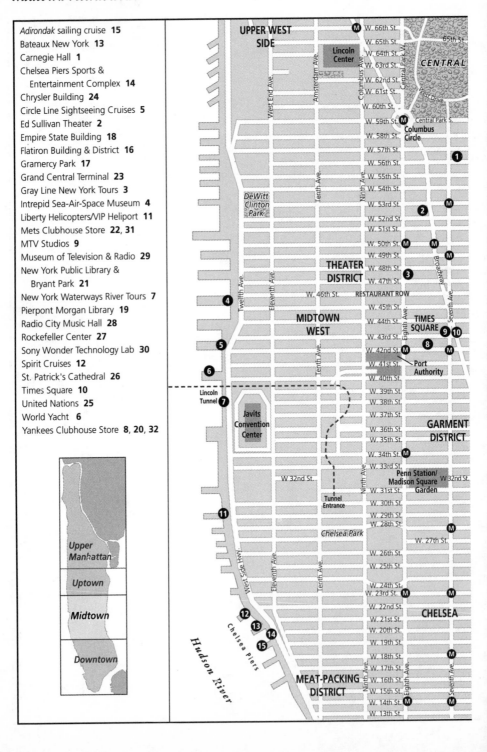

Uptown Attractions

American Museum of Natural History **2**

Asia Society **10**

Cathedral of St. John the Divine *(see inset)*

Central Park Zoo/Wildlife Conservation Center **12**

The Children's Museum of Manhattan **1**

Frick Collection **9**

Jewish Museum **5**

Lincoln Center **3**

Metropolitan Museum of Art **7**

Mount Vernon Hotel Museum (Formerly the Abigail Adams Smith Museum) **14**

Museum of the City of New York **4**

Roosevelt Island Tram **13**

Solomon R. Guggenheim Museum **6**

Walter Reade Theater **3**

Whitney Museum of American Art **8**

Wollman Rink **11**

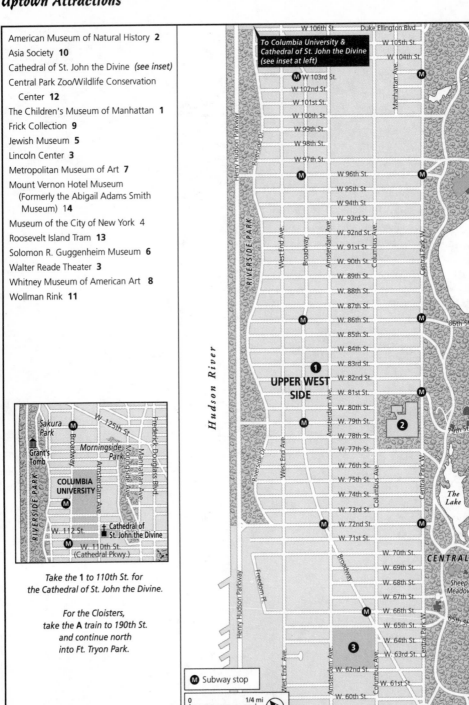

Take the **1** to 110th St. for the Cathedral of St. John the Divine.

For the Cloisters, take the **A** train to 190th St. and continue north into Ft. Tryon Park.

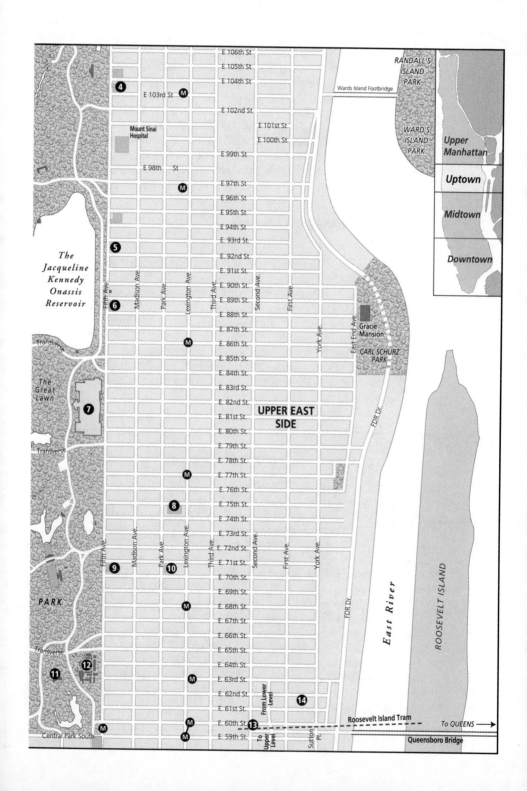

Central Park West between 77th and 81st streets. ☎ *212-769-5100. Internet:* www.amnh.org. *Subway: B/C train to 81st Street/Museum of Natural History stop, and then walk south along the front to the entrance. Bus: M10 (north/south bus running on Central Park West, Eighth Avenue uptown, and Seventh Avenue downtown) and M79 (crosstown bus running on 79th Street) are very convenient and stop right at the museum. Open: Daily 10:00 a.m.–5:45 p.m.; Fri closes at 8:45 p.m. Suggested admission: $10 adults, $6 children 2–12 (free under 2), $7.50 seniors and students. Museum admission plus Space Show: $19 adults, $11.50 children, $14 seniors and students; Rose Center audio tour $4; for the IMAX show or special exhibit, add $6 adults, $3.50 children, $4.50 seniors and students. You can purchase and make reservations on the museum's Web site; for show reservations, call* ☎ *212-769-5200. The museum is fully accessible to wheelchairs and the hearing impaired.*

Brooklyn Bridge and Promenade
Downtown

A walk across this historic stone-and-steel bridge yields a sweeping view of lower Manhattan, Brooklyn, and the New York Harbor. Crossing takes between 20 and 40 minutes each way, depending on how long you linger to enjoy the views. At the Brooklyn end of the bridge, a half-mile promenade lined with beautiful homes affords a gorgeous view of the skyline and the harbor. To reach the promenade, walk to the Brooklyn end of the bridge, go down the stairs, make a right when you reach the bottom, walk through the park to Henry Street, take Henry to Montague Street, turn right, and walk until the street runs out. The entrance to the promenade will be right in front of you.

The CityPass

The New York CityPass (☎ **888-330-5008**; Internet: www.citypass.net) gives you admission to seven major attractions in the city: the American Museum of Natural History, Circle Line Harbor Cruise, Empire State Building Observatory, Intrepid Sea-Air-Space Museum, Guggenheim Museum, Whitney Museum, and Museum of Modern Art (MOMA). The pass costs $38 ($21 for youths aged 12 to 17), more than 50% less than the $85 you would pay if you purchased each ticket separately. You can buy the CityPass online, at the first attraction you want to visit, or at one of the Ticket Axis electronic kiosks maintained by NYC & Company (at the Visitor Information Center at 810 Seventh Ave. between 52nd and 53rd streets, NY Skyride on the second floor of the Empire State Building, Intrepid Sea-Air-Space Museum, Circle Line, Museum of American Financial History, Museum of the City of New York, Brooklyn Museum of Art, New York Hall of Science in Queens, and New York Botanical Gardens in the Bronx). Note that the CityPass is good for only nine days and that the pass does not include admission to the NY Skyride show on the second floor of the Empire State building or the Space Show at the Hayden Planetarium.

Sidewalk entrance to the Manhattan end of the bridge is on Park Row just across from City Hall, south of Chambers Street. Subway: 4/5/6 train to Brooklyn Bridge/City Hall; exit across the street from the entrance. Bus: M1 (north/south bus running down Broadway and up Center Street/Lafayette/Park and Madison avenues), although traffic congestion makes the subway a better choice.

Cathedral of St. John the Divine
Upper West Side

Towering over Amsterdam Avenue near the edge of Harlem is an unlikely sight: the largest Gothic cathedral in the world. The cathedral, begun in 1892, is still only two-thirds complete; the towers, transcepts, choir roof, and other aspects remain unfinished. The architects and builders have employed Gothic engineering, stone-cutting, and carving techniques. Numerous chapels throughout the cathedral commemorate various ethnic groups and traditions. A fire in December 2001 damaged the north transcept, destroying two of the 12 Roman Baroque tapestries from the 17th century and the top of one of the stained-glass windows. A tour ($3) is offered at 11 a.m. on Tuesday through Saturday and at 1 p.m. on Sunday. You can visit the towers on the first and third Saturdays of the month. Three services per day are held during the week (7:15 a.m., 12:15 p.m., and 5:30 p.m.), and four are held on Sunday (8 a.m., 9 a.m., 11 a.m., and 7 p.m.).

The cathedral hosts numerous concerts, including dance, choir, and classical music performances. But by far the most unforgettable special event is the **Blessing of the Animals,** held in early October as part of the Feast of St. Francis of Assisi. A procession of critters — everything from dogs and cats to camels and elephants — parades through the church; each is blessed in honor of St. Francis, the patron saint of animals. Call **212-316-7540** for tickets; advance reservations are necessary for this popular event.

1047 Amsterdam Ave. between 110th and 113th streets. ☎ 212-316-7540. Subway: 1/9 train to Cathedral Parkway (110th Street) stop, and then walk 1 block east to Amsterdam Avenue. Bus: M11 (running up Tenth/Amsterdam Avenue and down Columbus/Ninth Avenue). Open: Mon–Sat 7 a.m.–6 p.m., Sun 7 a.m.–7 p.m. Suggested admission: $2 adults, $1 children under 18 and seniors.

Central Park
Upper West Side, Upper East Side

At the heart of New York City lies Central Park, a refuge of green for all New Yorkers (see the map "Central Park Attractions"). People from all over the city gather in the park to take a break from the fast pace of city life, get some fresh air, and enjoy the scenery. Here you can spend hours strolling (or biking) miles of paths that wind through acres of landscaped fields and rolling hills. The park offers pleasures for kids of all ages — you and your children might enjoy taking a boat ride on the lake (call Loeb Boathouse,

☎ **212-517-2233,** for rental information), skating around Wollman Rink just north of the pond (☎ **212-396-1010**), or visiting the polar bears and other animals in Central Park Zoo (see Chapter 17). In the summer, the park plays host to Shakespeare in the Park (see Chapter 21) and SummerStage (see Chapter 22), a series of free concerts. For information about escorted tours of the park — by bike or on foot — see "Discovering Special-Interest Tours" and "Free Walking Tours" in Chapter 18.

From 59th to 110th streets, between Fifth Avenue and Central Park West (the con-tinuation north of Eighth Avenue). Information Center ☎ 212-794-6564. Subway: A/B/C/D/1/2 train to 59th Street/Columbus Circle stop for the southwest main entrance, N/R/W train to Fifth Avenue/59th Street stop for the southeast main entrance. Buses run along both sides of Central Park and make several stops; the M10 runs up and down Central Park West, and the M1, M2, M3, and M4 run south down Fifth Avenue on the east side of the park (they go north on Madison Avenue). Open: 24 hours.

Chinatown
Downtown

Ever restless and expanding, Chinatown is one of New York's largest and most famous ethnic neighborhoods. From the brash, bustling market-place that is Canal Street, activity radiates in all directions. Mulberry Street, East Broadway, and the smaller cross-streets are lined with Chinese shops, groceries, herbalists, and restaurants. Whether you want dim sum or acupuncture, Chinatown is the place. (For more on shopping in Chinatown, see Chapter 19.)

South of Canal Street between Broadway and East Broadway. Subway: J/M/N/Q/R/W/Z/6 train to Canal Street stop, and you'll be right in the center of the action. Bus: Forget it; it gets too crowded. If you insist on taking the bus, take the M1 (running down Fifth/Park Avenue/Broadway and up Center Street/Park/Madison Avenue).

Chrysler Building
Midtown East

Number 405 Lexington Avenue is one of the most stunning buildings in New York or any other city. Topped by a shiny steel needle, with trian-gular windows that are illuminated at night, it looks like something out of Oz. Strange steel sculptures are poised on its battlements like gargoyles. The building was designed by William Van Alen, was finished in 1930, and enjoyed the title of world's tallest until 1931, when the Empire State Building was completed. The observation deck is no longer open to the public, but be sure to visit the lobby — an Art Deco tour de force in chrome, wood, and marble.

Central Park Attractions

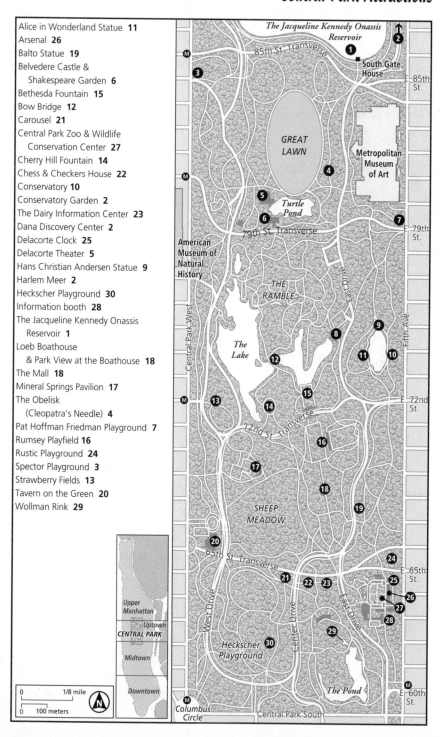

405 Lexington Ave. at 42nd Street. Subway: 4/5/6/7/S train to 42nd Street/Grand Central stop, follow the exit signs for Lexington Avenue, pass the barrier, and take the passage in front of you toward the right; it brings you right inside the Chrysler at the lower level. If you miss this exit, go up to street level, cross the street walking east, and there it is. Bus: M104 from the Upper West Side (runs down Broadway and crosses town at 42nd Street) and M42 across town on 42nd Street; both stop right in front of the building. On the east side and from downtown, take the M101, M102, or M103 (running up Third Avenue and down Lexington Avenue). Open: Weekdays 8 a.m.–6 p.m.

The Cloisters
Upper West Side

At the north end of Manhattan in Fort Tryon Park, this museum is constructed from portions of medieval and early Renaissance European cloisters that were shipped across the Atlantic. The Cloisters houses an important collection of medieval art, including stained glass, metalwork, sculpture, and an impressive series of unicorn tapestries. The gardens that hug one side of the complex authentically reproduce the herbs, flowers, and other plants found in a typical medieval cloisters. Both the museum and the gardens have a commanding view of the Hudson River and the New Jersey Palisades. If you choose to get there by bus, consider that although the bus takes you right to the museum and offers a scenic, interesting ride, the ride will be a long one (up to an hour or more, depending on where you start). The subway is a good alternative; it brings you right to the entrance of Fort Tryon Park.

At the north end of Fort Tryon Park, 1 block north of West 190th Street. ☎ 212-923-3700. Internet: www.metmuseum.org. *Subway: A train to 190th Street stop, and then take the elevator to street level (don't walk up the long ramp — it takes you out of your way). Once outside, you'll see the park entrance; walk north along Fort Washington Avenue to the entrance of Fort Tryon Park and follow the signs along the path north to the Cloisters. Bus: The M4 (north/south bus running on Madison Avenue, 110th Street, Broadway, Fort Washington Avenue uptown, and Fifth Avenue downtown) is very convenient and stops right at the museum; if you're in a hurry, you can take the subway and then catch the bus for the last part of the run. Open: Tues–Sun 9:30 a.m.–5:15 p.m.; Nov–Feb closes at 4:45 p.m. Suggested admission: $10 adults, $5 seniors and students, children under 13 free when accompanied by an adult; fee includes admission to the Metropolitan Museum.*

Ellis Island
Downtown

From its opening in 1892 to its closing in 1954, more than 12 million immigrants entered America through the Registry Hall on Ellis Island. After a $160 million restoration in the 1980s, it reopened as a museum dedicated to the history of immigration. An enormous pile of luggage and other personal items (children's dolls, hairbrushes, clothing, and the like) remind visitors of the huddled masses who passed through here. Other

Harlem & Upper Manhattan

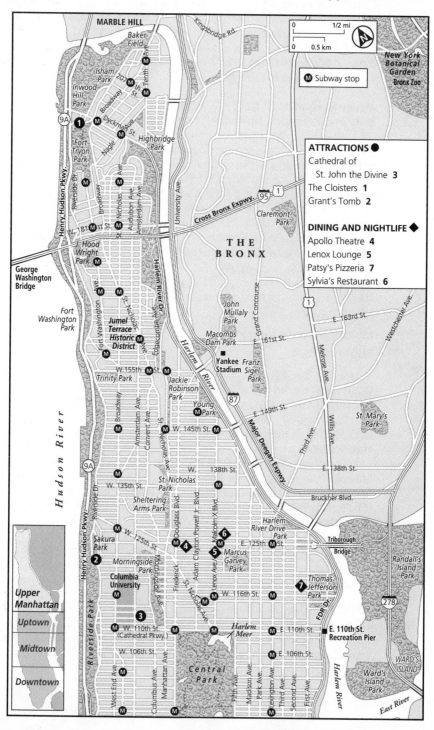

ATTRACTIONS ●
Cathedral of
  St. John the Divine **3**
The Cloisters **1**
Grant's Tomb **2**

DINING AND NIGHTLIFE ◆
Apollo Theatre **4**
Lenox Lounge **5**
Patsy's Pizzeria **7**
Sylvia's Restaurant **6**

Ⓜ Subway stop

exhibits illustrate how these immigrants changed the demography of the United States. And the American Immigrant Wall of Honor remembers more than half a million people who came to the U.S. in search of a better life. Ellis Island offers an optional audio tour (narrated by Tom Brokaw) and a documentary film called *Island of Hope, Island of Tears*. Note that a round-trip ferry ticket to Ellis Island includes a trip to Liberty Island, the site of the Statue of Liberty.

In New York Harbor. ☎ *212-363-7620 for general information, 212-269-5755 for ticket and ferry information. Internet:* www.statueoflibertyferry.com *or* www.nps.gov/elis. *Transport: Ferry from Battery Park. Subway to ticket booth: 4/5 train to Bowling Green stop, and then walk through the park heading south; the ticket booth is a little fortress at the edge of the trees by the promenade. Bus to ticket booth: M1 (running down Fifth/Park Avenue/Broadway), M6 (running down Broadway), or M15 (running down Second Avenue). Open: Daily 10:30 a.m.–5:00 p.m. (extended hours in summer). Ferries run from Manhattan about every 30 minutes, in winter 10:30 a.m.–3:30 p.m. and in summer 9:00 a.m.–4:30 p.m. Tickets are sold only until an hour before the last ferry departs. Admission: Ferry plus Statue of Liberty and Ellis Island $8 adults, $3 children 3–17 (free under 3), $6 seniors. Note that if you want to visit both Ellis Island and the Statue of Liberty, you can't take the last ferry; taking the last ferry enables you to visit only one of the two attractions. Due to security restrictions, no backpacks, luggage, or coolers are allowed.*

Empire State Building
Midtown East

You won't see King Kong dangling from the top of the Empire State Building as he did in the 1933 version of *King Kong*, but you will get one of the best views of Manhattan from this 1,472-foot Art Deco structure — that is, if visibility is good that day. You can find a visibility rating posted in the lobby of the building, and you should take the rating seriously — zero visibility means that you really won't see a thing, except clouds and fog. The observatory is on the 86th floor and has both an outdoor and an indoor viewing area. Huge lights glow in the top of the building and are lit up in different colors for various holidays. On the second floor is the **NY Skyride** (☎ 212-279-9777), a simulated aerial tour of New York, which is worth seeing if you can't go for the real thing (see Chapter 18).

Fifth Avenue at 34th Street. ☎ *212-736-3100. Internet:* www.esbnyc.com. *Subway: B/D/F/N/Q/R/V/W train to 34th Street/Herald Square, walk east on 34th Street, and turn right on Fifth Avenue to the entrance. Bus: M2/M3/M4/M5 run down Fifth Avenue and stop right in front of the entrance. Admission to observation deck: $9 adults, $7 seniors, $4 children under 12, children under 5 free (you can buy tickets online with a surcharge at the Web site). Open: Mon–Thurs 10:00 a.m.–12:00 a.m., Sat–Sun 9:30–12:00 a.m. For security reasons, no backpacks or large parcels are allowed, and visitors are required to present a photo ID.*

Grand Central Terminal
Midtown East

Finished in 1913, this Beaux Arts masterpiece features a 12-story vibrant blue ceiling on which the stars of the zodiac are traced in 24-karat gold. Aside from the gorgeous ceiling, the revitalized and restored Grand Central offers tons of shopping and dining opportunities. You can enjoy a free guided tour of the terminal given by the Municipal Art Society (12:30 p.m. Wednesdays; ☎ 212-935-3960).

Main entrance on 42nd Street at Park Avenue. Subway: S/4/5/6/7 train to 42nd Street/Grand Central stop. Bus: M1/M2/M3/M4 running up Madison Avenue and M101/M102/M103 running down Lexington Avenue take you right there. Open: 24 hours.

Greenwich Village
Downtown

The Village is the city's prime wandering area, with crooked tree-lined streets and architecture ranging from 1850s brownstones to low-rises from the 1920s and 1930s. The largest open space in the Village is Washington Square Park at the base of Fifth Avenue, where various street artists often perform. One of the area's architectural gems is the Jefferson Market Courthouse, a melange of Gothic, Victorian, and Venetian styles that occupies the triangular site where Sixth Avenue, Greenwich Avenue, and West 10th Street meet. The Village has been home to Edgar Allan Poe, Mark Twain, Edith Wharton, Jackson Pollock, and many others. Today, traces of its bohemian past remain, peppered as it is with cafes, restaurants, small theaters, used record shops, and a few jazz clubs.

From Houston Street north to 14th Street and from the Hudson River east to Broadway. Subway: A/C/E/F/V/S train to West 4th Street to reach the center of it all. Bus: M2/M3/M5 run downtown on Fifth Avenue and bring you steps from Washington Square.

Intrepid Sea-Air-Space Museum
Midtown West

The *Intrepid,* an aircraft carrier that saw active duty in World War II, is the focal point of this large naval museum. On deck, you find 40 aircraft from various periods on display. Some of the other vessels moored here are the submarine *Growler* and the lightship *Nantucket.* Memorabilia and naval displays are housed below decks.

Pier 86, Hudson River at 46th Street, west of Twelfth Avenue. ☎ 212-245-0072. Internet: www.intrepidmuseum.org. Subway: A/C/E train to 42nd Street/Port Authority Bus Terminal stop, and then continue west on 42nd Street for 4 blocks, *or change to the bus. Bus: M42 crosstown bus running on 42nd Street or, even better, the M50 crosstown bus running west on 49th Street and east on 50th Street. Admission: $13 adults; $9 seniors, students, youth under 18, and veterans; $6 children under 11; $2 children under 6; children under 2 free. Open: Daily 10 a.m.–5 p.m., summer Sat–Sun 10 a.m.–7 p.m., winter closed Mon. Last admission is 1 hour before closing time.*

Metropolitan Museum of Art
Upper East Side

As the largest museum in the Western Hemisphere, the Met has something for everyone, from its world-famous Egyptian collection to its massive holdings of European and American masterpieces to its beautiful sculpture garden. Highlights also include the Asian collection, the collection of musical instruments, and the armor collection. Kids in particular rave about the costume displays on the lower level. The Met is the city's top tourist destination, with 5 million visitors per year. Tours of various parts of the collection are conducted several times an hour; you also can take a self-guided audio tour or a "highlights" tour. For schedules, check at the tour bureau in the Great Hall or call ☎ 212-570-3930.

On the edge of Central Park at Fifth Avenue and 82nd Street. ☎ 212-879-5500 or 212-535-7710. Internet: www.metmuseum.org. *Subway: 4/5/6 train to 86th Street stop, walk 3 blocks west to Fifth Avenue, turn left, and walk along the park to the entrance. Bus: M1/M2/M3/M4 up Madison and down Fifth Avenue. Suggested admission: $10 adult, $5 seniors and students, children under 13 free when accompanied by an adult; fee includes admission to the Cloisters. Open: Tues–Sun 9:30 a.m.–5:30 p.m., Fri–Sat until 9:00 p.m. No strollers allowed on Sun.*

Museum of Modern Art (MOMA)

Queens (formerly Midtown West)

This mecca of modern art houses a world-reknowned permanent collection, which includes works of Fauvism, Cubism, Futurism, Surrealism, German Expressionism, and Abstract Expressionism, among other schools. Other attractions include a popular sculpture garden and special exhibits and programs, including films shown in an on-site theater. But MOMA is on the move; the 53rd Street location is currently closed for a major renovation and is scheduled to re-open in 2005. Exhibitions and programs are being held at a futuristic new location, MOMA QNS, in Long Island City, Queens, in a building that was once a Swingline staple factory.

MOMA QNS, 45–20 33rd St. at Queens Boulevard. ☎ 212-708-9480. Internet: www.moma.org. *Subway: 7 train to 33rd Street stop. Admission: $12 adults, $8.50 seniors and students, children under 16 free when accompanied by an adult; Fri 4:30 p.m.–8:15 p.m., pay what you wish. You can purchase tickets on the Web site. Open: Sat–Tues and Thurs 10:30 a.m.–5:45 p.m., Fri 10:30 a.m.–8:15 p.m.; closed Wed.*

Rockefeller Center
Midtown West

This complex of 18 buildings includes the GE building, a 70-story Art Deco tower. The entertainment ranges from the outdoor skating rink to Radio City Music Hall, where the Rockettes perform (call ☎ 212-632-4041 for backstage tours, and see Chapter 22 for more info), to the NBC Studios, which you can tour (call ☎ 212-664-4000). This is also where NBC's "Today" show tapes, so you can show up with your "We [heart] You, Matt!" sign and possibly get on TV. Under the center's concourse, you find a multitude of stores and restaurants. For a self-directed tour of the complex, pick up a map at 30 Rockefeller Center; if you prefer a guided tour, call ☎ 212-664-3700.

Rockefeller Center is popular during the holidays because of the huge Christmas tree and the outdoor skating rink (expect long lines on weekends to enjoy the latter). The rink, located at Rockefeller Plaza (☎ 212-332-7654), is very romantic, especially in winter, but it's *much* tinier in person that it appears on TV. Admission is $7.50–$9 adults and $6–$6.75 children; skate rental is $4. The rink is open from mid-October to mid-March.

Between Fifth and Sixth avenues and from 48th to 51st streets; Promenade main entrance between 49th and 50th streets on Fifth Avenue. ☎ 212-632-3975. Subway: B/D/F/V train to 47–50 streets/Rockefeller Center lets you out on the Sixth Avenue side of the complex. Bus: M1/M2/M3/M4/M5 down Fifth Avenue or M5/M6/M7 up Sixth Avenue.

Solomon R. Guggenheim Museum
Upper East Side

Frank Lloyd Wright designed this famous museum, whose shape resembles a shell or a beehive. Inside, the exhibition space curves in a spiral; you can take an elevator to the top and work your way down if you don't want to hike up. Exhibits are constantly changing. The museum's addition, the Tower Galleries, holds the permanent collection of 19th- and 20th-century art, which includes works by the Impressionists and founding modernists such as Picasso. Free tours of the museum are available; check the Web site for special events like films, concerts, and lectures that may be on the schedule.

The Guggenheim has a branch museum in SoHo, at 575 Broadway at Prince Street (☎ 212-423-3500). The SoHo branch houses continually changing exhibits of postmodern art, with an emphasis on multimedia works.

1071 Fifth Ave. at 89th Street. ☎ 212-423-3500. Internet: www.guggenheim.org. *Subway: 4/5/6 train to 86th Street stop, walk 3 blocks west to Fifth Avenue, turn right, and walk 2 blocks north to the entrance. Bus: The bus is a good idea because* *it brings you closer: Take the M1/M2/M3/M4 up Madison and walk 1 block west (it goes south on Fifth), or take the M86 crosstown on 86th Street. Admission: $12 adults, $8 seniors and students, children under 12 free when accompanied by an adult; Friday 6–8 p.m., pay what you wish. Open: Sun–Wed 9 a.m.–6 p.m.; Fri–Sat 9 a.m.–8 p.m. Closed Thurs.*

St. Patrick's Cathedral
Midtown East

St. Patrick's, the largest Catholic cathedral in the United States, features Gothic spires, beautiful stained-glass windows, and an impressive white marble facade. Mass is held eight times a day Sunday through Friday and five times a day on Saturday. It's a calm island in a busy thoroughfare, located as it is across from Rockefeller Center and next door to Saks Fifth Avenue.

Fifth Avenue between 50th and 51st streets. ☎ *212-753-2261. Subway: B/D/F/V train to 47–50 streets/Rockefeller Center, and then walk west to Fifth Avenue. Bus: M1/M2/M3/M4/M5 down Fifth Avenue or M1/M2/M3/M4 up Madison Avenue. Open: Daily 7:00 a.m.–8:30 p.m., Sat opens at 8:00 a.m.*

South Street Seaport and Museum
Downtown

The whole neighborhood of the Seaport is an important historical landmark that has been progressively restored, in part by the South Street Seaport Museum and in part by private businesses. This attraction offers a look at commerce in the past and in the present. The Seaport's cobbled streets and restored brick buildings house many interesting shops and pubs, while two of the huge warehouses from the days when sailing ships ruled trade now contain indoor shopping complexes and fine restaurants. The museum is planning to finish the restoration of another strip on Fulton by the end of 2003, which will house the permanent exhibition "World Port New York." On the waterside, the museum has completed the restoration of a number of historical ships that you can visit, including the *Peking,* an enormous four-master built of steel; the *Ambrose,* a lightship; and the fishing schooner *Lettie G. Howard.* Still under restoration are the *Ellen McAllister,* a large tugboat, and the *Marion M.,* a wooden-hulled chandlery lighter. Two of the restored ships take people out for tours of the harbor from May through October: the schooner *Pioneer* and the *W. O. Decker,* a cute wooden tugboat.

Also an historical landmark of the Seaport — but not part of the Seaport Museum — is the Fulton Fish Market (at South Street and Fulton Street ☎ 212-669-9416), still operating daily from 12 a.m. to 9 p.m. If you'd like something fishy, you can schedule a guided tour (first and third Thursdays of every month at 6 a.m.; $10) by calling to make a reservation; it's quite impressive. Otherwise, just go for the morning outdoor fish market across the street.

At Pier 17 of the Seaport, on the third floor of the building there, two rows of deck chairs line the south terrace, overlooking the water. It's a great place to relax and take in the view of Brooklyn, the bridges, and New York Harbor. On weekends, though, the seats fill up fast.

From Pearl Street to the East River; the heart of the Seaport being between John Street and Peck Slip. ☎ *212-SEAPORT. Internet:* www.southstreetseaport. com. *Museum: 12 Fulton St. between Water and South streets.* ☎ *212-748-8725. Internet:* www.southstseaport.org. *Subway: 1/2/4/5/A/C/J/M/Z train to Fulton Street/Broadway Nassau stop; walk east on Fulton and you'll be right in the middle of it all. Bus: M15 (down Second Avenue and up First) stops at Fulton and Water streets. Museum admission: $5. Open: Wed–Mon 10 a.m.–5 p.m.; April–Sept closes at 6 p.m.*

Statue of Liberty
Downtown

Lady Liberty is one of New York's most popular sights, although a lot of her appeal has faded since the interior of the statue was closed to the public. The 305-foot statue, commissioned by the government of France as a gesture of friendship and solidarity, was dedicated on October 28, 1886. Frédéric-Auguste Bartholdi designed the statue, which was originally planned to be filled with sand to ensure stability.

The same ferry that stops at Ellis Island also travels to Liberty Island. At press time, the entire interior of the statue — crown, museum, and pedestal — was off-limits to visitors; only the grounds and outdoor exhibits were open to the public. The policy is not said to be permanent, so call ahead or check the Web site to find out whether the lady is receiving visitors. (If you'd rather not pay for the 20-minute ferry to Liberty Island, the free Staten Island Ferry offers a wonderful view of the statue on its round-trip circuit through the harbor.)

On Liberty Island in New York Harbor. ☎ *212-363-7620 for general information; 212-269-5755 for ticket and ferry information. Internet:* www.statueofliberty ferry.com. *Transport: Ferry from Battery Park. Subway to ticket booth: 4/5 train to Bowling Green stop, and then walk through the park heading south; the ticket booth is a little fortress at the edge of the trees by the promenade. Bus to ticket booth: M1 (running down Fifth/Park Avenue/Broadway), M6 (running down Broadway), or M15 (running down Second Avenue). Admission: Ferry plus Statue of Liberty and Ellis Island $8 adults, $3 children 3–17 (free under 3), $6 seniors. Open: Daily 10:30 a.m.–5:00 p.m. (extended hours in summer). Ferries from Manhattan run about every 30 minutes in winter 10:30 a.m.–3:30 p.m., in summer 9:00 a.m.–4:30 p.m. Tickets are sold only until an hour before the last ferry. Note that if you want to visit both Ellis Island and the Statue of Liberty, you can't take the last ferry; taking the last ferry enables you to visit only one of the two attractions. Due to security restrictions, no backpacks, luggage, or coolers are allowed.*

Times Square
Midtown West

The corner of Seventh Avenue and 42nd Street is one of the most heavily trafficked spots in the city, and there's no mystery as to why: Times Square has undergone a renaissance. Sleaze is down, family-friendly attractions are up, and Disney is in. It's like an amusement park without rides. The neon signs are bigger and more astounding than ever — even the police department has a glowing sign with blinking letters. Times Square is also the gateway to the Theater District (see Chapter 21). Other attractions include the New York version of Madame Tussaud's Wax Museum (see Chapter 17), two 20-plus-screen multiplex cinemas, and theme restaurants like Mars 2112 (1633 Broadway at 51st Street; ☎ 212-582-2112), the newly opened WWE — for World Wrestling Entertainment (1501 Broadway between 43rd and 44th streets; ☎ 212-398-2563) — and ESPN Zone (1472 Broadway at 42nd Street; ☎ 212-921-3776).

At the intersection of Broadway and Seventh Avenue between 42nd and 44th streets. Subway: 1/2/3/7/N/Q/R/S/W train to Times Square/42nd Street stop. Bus: M6/M7 down Seventh Avenue or M104/M10 down Broadway offer a perfect view of Times Square.

United Nations
Midtown East

A guided one-hour tour of the United Nations headquarters examines the history and purpose of the U.N. and takes you through the General Assembly Hall and the Security Council Chamber. You also can walk through the grounds and a beautiful garden (the rose garden is fantastic) that offers a view of the East River, Roosevelt Island, and Brooklyn, plus the many sculptures that member states have given the U.N., like the symbolic pistol with a knot in the barrel.

United Nations Plaza, on First Avenue between 42nd and 48th streets; visitor entrance at 46th Street. ☎ 212-963-7539. Subway: 4/5/6/7/S train to Grand Central/42nd Street stop, walk east on 42nd Street to First Avenue, turn left, and walk to the visitor entrance at 46th Street. Bus: Much more convenient than the subway; take the M15 down Second Avenue and up First Avenue, the M104 down Broadway and 42nd Street, or the M42 crosstown on 42nd Street. Admission: Free to the park and lobby; guided tour $8.50 adults, $5 children, $6 students, $7 seniors. Children under 5 are not allowed on the guided tours. Open: 9:30 a.m.–4:45 p.m.; tours every 30 minutes 9:15 a.m.–4:15 p.m.; no tours on weekends in Jan and Feb. Reservations required only for non-English tours (French, Spanish, Russian, or Chinese).

Wall Street and the Stock Exchange
Downtown/Wall Street

On weekdays, Wall Street offers a glimpse into the teeming world of finance that characterizes lower Manhattan. This is where it all started;

it's the historical heart of the city and its financial center today. See the skyscrapers — many among the first ever built — and throngs of people who inhabit this world. While you're here, pass by St. Paul Chapel — the oldest church in New York, completed in 1766 (Broadway just north of Fulton Street; ☎ **212-602-0800**), have a look at Federal Hall National Memorial and its exhibit (26 Wall St.; ☎ **212-825-6888;** open Monday through Friday 9 a.m. to 5 p.m.; admission free), and visit the Stock Exchange and its interactive information center (☎ **212-656-5165**) and the Museum of American Financial History (26 Broadway at Wall Street). The Stock Exchange building, which dates from 1903, is a classical temple for dollar worship; from the observation gallery, you can watch the world's largest stock frenzy in action. Closed to the public for security reasons, it is scheduled to reopen in the future, but no date has been set. Call the information center to find out if tourist visits to the exchange have resumed. If they have, get there early if you want to avoid a long wait in line; admission is free, but you need admission tickets, which are given out starting at 9 a.m.

Wall Street runs between Broadway and South Street. New York Stock Exchange: 20 Broad Street at Wall Street. ☎ 212-656-5168. Subway: 4/5 train to Wall Street stop, or N/R to Rector Street, and then walk east across Broadway to Wall Street. Bus: M1/M6 down Broadway and up Trinity Place. Admission: Free. Open: Call for information. Federal Hall National Memorial: 26 Wall St. at Nassau Street. ☎ 212-825-6888. Admission: Free. Open: Mon–Fri 9 a.m.–5 p.m.

A Solemn Site

Ground Zero
Downtown

The World Trade Center occupied 16 acres in lower Manhattan, a sprawling office complex of more than 12 million square feet, including the two spectacular 110-story Twin Towers. At 8:45 a.m. on September 11, 2001, the first plane hit the north tower. A second plane crashed into the south tower at 9:03 a.m. Less than 90 minutes later, the towers had collapsed, and the search began for the nearly 3,000 victims of this terrorist attack. Where the World Trade Center once stood is now a vast, empty crater.

To accommodate the large number of visitors to Ground Zero, the city of New York erected a special viewing platform. Originally scheduled to remain in place until after the first anniversary of the attacks, it was dismantled in June 2002 after the removal of the rubble was completed. The visitor information center now advises the public to view the site from Liberty Street, which has reopened, between the hours of 9 a.m. and 9 p.m. You won't see many New Yorkers there, except those working at the site: For most, the memories are still too painful and vivid.

Several projects regarding the future of the site are currently under discussion. Check with NYC & Company, New York City's official tourism office, at ☎ **888-805-4040** or 212-484-1222, Internet: www.nycvisit.com, or with the City of New York at www.nyc.gov.

Broadway at Fulton Street. Subway: 1/2/4/5/A/C/J/M/Z train to Fulton Street/Broadway Nassau stop, and then walk west on Fulton. Bus: M1 and M6 run down Broadway, letting you off at the entrance to the platform. Admission: Free, but tickets are required. Open: Daily 9 a.m.–8 p.m.

Index of Top Attractions by Neighborhood

If you plan to spend an afternoon or a day in a particular neighborhood, this list tells you the most interesting places to visit in each area. Turn to the section "The Top Sights from A to Z," earlier in this chapter, for a full description of each attraction listed here.

Upper West Side

American Museum of Natural History
Cathedral of St. John the Divine
Central Park
The Cloisters

Upper East Side

Central Park
Metropolitan Museum of Art
Solomon R. Guggenheim Museum

Midtown West

Intrepid Sea-Air-Space Museum
Rockefeller Center
Times Square

Midtown East

Chrysler Building
Empire State Building

Grand Central Terminal
St. Patrick's Cathedral
United Nations

Downtown

Brooklyn Bridge and Promenade
Chinatown
Ellis Island
Greenwich Village
South Street Seaport and Museum
Statue of Liberty
Wall Street and the New York Stock
    Exchange

Queens

Museum of Modern Art

Index of Top Attractions by Type

Museums

American Museum of Natural History
The Cloisters
Ellis Island
Intrepid Sea-Air-Space Museum

Metropolitan Museum of Art
Museum of Modern Art
Solomon R. Guggenheim Museum
South Street Seaport Museum

Parks

Central Park
United Nations

Historic Buildings and Architecture

Brooklyn Bridge and Promenade
Chrysler Building
Empire State Building
Grand Central Terminal
Rockefeller Center
Solomon R. Guggenheim Museum
Statue of Liberty
United Nations

Neighborhoods

Chinatown
Greenwich Village
South Street Seaport
Times Square
Wall Street

Churches

Cathedral of St. John the Divine
St. Patrick's Cathedral

Chapter 17

More Cool Things to See and Do

In This Chapter

▶ Visiting more museums

▶ Touring more historic sights and buildings

▶ Getting audience tickets for your favorite TV shows

▶ Discovering more activities for kids, sports fans, and others

*I*n this chapter, we talk about attractions that appeal especially to those with specific interests — to fans of history, books, or architecture, for example. We also give you the scoop on getting tickets to sporting events, TV tapings, and movies. In addition to special interests, you may have special needs — like where should you take your kids when they get bored with museums? We tell you about those options, too.

To locate the places mentioned in this chapter, see the maps in Chapter 16.

Especially for Kids

New York has plenty of attractions that you can enjoy with your children. If the art museums get to be too much, you can find museums with hands-on, interactive exhibits that appeal to the inner child in everyone. (The Bronx Zoo and the Sony Wonder Technology Lab, discussed in the following section, are great for kids as well.)

Central Park Zoo/Wildlife Conservation Center
Upper West Side

Conveniently located in the heart of the city, the park's zoo is home to hundreds of animals that your kids will love to see — swimming polar bears, fish-catching seals, and scores of waddling penguins. Make sure to swing by the rainforest house, where you can mingle with tropical wildlife, including fruit bats. Allow two to three hours for your visit.

Fifth Avenue and 64th Street. ☎ *212-861-6030. Internet:* www.wcs.org. *Subway: F train to Lexington Avenue/63rd Street stop, and then walk 2 blocks west; N/R/W train to Fifth Avenue/59th Street stop, and then walk 5 blocks north; 6 train to 68th Street/Hunter College stop, walk west to Fifth Avenue, turn left, and walk 2 blocks south. Open: Mon–Fri 10:00 a.m.–4:30 p.m. Admission: $3.50 adults, $1.25 seniors, 50¢ children 3–12 (under 3 free).*

The Children's Museum of Manhattan
Upper West Side

You and your kids can look forward to five floors of interactive exhibits geared mostly toward the 10-and-under set. Along with a media center where you can produce your own TV show, an early-childhood center especially for children 4 and under, and a reading center for quiet time, the museum features special exhibits, such as an interactive tour of the human body. Allot at least two hours.

212 W. 83rd St. between Broadway and Amsterdam avenues. ☎ *212-721-1234. Internet:* www.cmom.org. *Subway: 1/9 train to 79th Street stop, walk north on Broadway to 83rd, and turn right. Open: During the school year, Mon, Wed, Thurs 1:30–5:50 p.m., Fri–Sun 10 a.m.–5 p.m.; in the summer, Wed–Sun 10 a.m.–5 p.m. Admission: $5 adults and children, $3 seniors, children under 2 free.*

New York Aquarium/Wildlife Conservation Park
Brooklyn

The oldest aquarium in operation in the United States (since 1896), the New York Aquarium is huge, extending over 14 acres by the sea at Coney Island. It houses more than 350 species and 8,000 specimens, including beluga (white) whales and sharks. The top attraction is always the dolphin show, at the Aquatheater from May through October.

Surf Avenue and West 8th Street, Brooklyn. ☎ *718-265-FISH. Internet:* www.wcs.org. *Subway: F/Q train to West 8th Street/NY Aquarium stop, and then take the pedestrian bridge directly to the aquarium. Open: Mon–Fri 10:00 a.m.–5:00 p.m., Sat–Sun 10:00 a.m.–5:30 p.m. Admission: $11 adults, $7 seniors and children under 12, children under 2 free.*

Especially for Teenagers

In this section, we talk about some of the sights you *and* your teenager are likely to approve of (the New York Aquarium in the preceding section is great for teenagers as well). A huge hit with teens is scoring tickets to MTV's *Total Request Live* — or at least standing below the studio's picture window and screaming in recognition whenever a pop star shows up. See "Especially for TV Fans," later in this chapter.

Battery Park and Hudson River Park
Downtown

With a great view of New York Harbor (and its most famous resident, Miss Liberty), open green spaces, and plenty of shops and cafes, this area offers lots of opportunities to see and be seen, kick the soccer ball around a little, and hang out. It stretches all the way from Battery Park to Chelsea Piers between 18th and 23rd streets, passing by the World Financial Center with its beautiful waterfront plaza, where concerts are held in the summer months, and its spectacular Winter Garden (scheduled to reopen in September 2002). The promenade includes a pedestrian path by the water and a parallel bicycle and inline skating route, divided by grassy areas and benches for sitting. On the way, you'll even find miniature golf. The huge **Chelsea Piers Sports and Entertainement Complex** (☎ **212-336-6666;** Internet: www.chelseapiers.com) includes, among other things, an ice-skating rink, a golf range, a harbor with pubs and restaurants, and inline skate rental.

On the Hudson River between Battery Park and 23rd Street. Battery Park: Subway: 4/5 train to Bowling Green stop, and then walk west toward the river. Bus: M1 and M6 running down Broadway and up Trinity Place. Hudson River Park: Subway 1/2 train to Chambers Street stop. Bus: M20 running down Seventh Avenue and Varick Street and up Hudson Street and Eighth Avenue, and M22 and M9 running east-west on Barkley and Chambers streets. Chelsea Piers: Subway: C/E train to 23rd Street stop, and then walk west to the river. Bus: M11 running up Tenth Avenue and down Ninth Avenue, M14 running east-west on 14th Street, or M23 running east-west on 23rd Street.

The Bronx Zoo/Wildlife Conservation Park
Bronx

The Bronx Zoo's reputation as one of the world's best is certainly deserved: It features thousands of animals roaming in naturalistic habitats, including JungleWorld (an indoor rainforest), the Himalayan Highlands with its snow leopards, and the Baboon Reserve. Check out the World of Darkness, home to nocturnal creatures, including bats, and the world's largest rat, the cloud rat. You'll need at least three hours to even sample the zoo and park.

Fordham Road and Bronx River Parkway. ☎ 718-367-1010. Internet: www.wcs.org. Subway: 2/5 train to Pelham Parkway stop, and then walk west to the entrance. Bus: Take the Liberty Line BxM11 bus, which stops on Madison Avenue and runs express to the zoo ($4; Liberty schedule: ☎ 718-652-8400). Open: Mon–Fri 10:00 a.m.–5:00 p.m., Sat–Sun 10:00 a.m.–5:30 p.m. Admission: $11 adults, $7 seniors, $6 children under 12, children under 2 free; Wed suggested donation. Discounted admission in winter.

Madame Tussaud's Wax Museum
Times Square/Midtown West

The New York branch of Madame Tussaud's is a centerpiece of the new, ultraneon, family-friendly Times Square. Princess Diana, the Dalai Lama, Frank Sinatra, and Abraham Lincoln are just a few of the luminaries memorialized in wax. The kids are sure to be entertained, but for such a steep admission price, the number of figures on display (especially for a five-floor museum) seems skimpy.

234 W. 42nd St. between Seventh and Eighth avenues. ☎ *800-246-8872 or 212-512-9600. Internet:* www.madame-tussauds.com. *Subway: 1/2/3/7/A/C/E/N/Q/R/S/W train to 42nd Street/Times Square stop, and then walk ½ block west to the entrance. Open: Daily 10 a.m.–8 p.m. Admission: $22 adult, $19 seniors, $17 children 4–12, free for children under 4.*

Staten Island Ferry
Downtown

Few things capture the spirit of New York like a ride on the Staten Island Ferry. Wait for one of the older-model ferries, which offer lots of open-air deck space, and then take the half-hour free ride that gives you a great view of downtown, the Statue of Liberty, and the harbor (one hour round-trip). The ferries run frequently, especially at peak times: every 20 to 30 minutes during rush hours, but less frequently (every half-hour, then every hour) later at night. You can stay on the same ferry for the return trip a few minutes after getting to the Staten Island side.

Staten Island Ferry Terminal, Peter Minuit Plaza, at the end of South Street and State Street (the southern continuation of Broadway). ☎ *212-487-8403. Subway: 4/5 to Bowling Green or N/R to Whitehall St., and then walk south to the big rounded terminal. Open: 24 hours. Fare: Free.*

Especially for Art Lovers

The Met and MOMA (see Chapter 16) are probably New York's best-known art museums, but many, many others are there for the exploring. Each has a specific strength and a unique collection. And don't forget that the museums of ethnic heritage include artworks in their collections.

The Frick Collection
Upper East Side

This museum features the splendid collection of tycoon Henry Clay Frick and is housed in his Gilded Age mansion, more or less as he organized it. The painting collection includes works by old masters of the 16th and 17th centuries such as Tiziano (also known as Titian), Vermeer,

Rembrandt, and El Greco, as well as 19th-century artists, including Turner and Whistler. The furnishings and ceramic collections are also worth seeing. Enjoy some fantastic art and see how the cultured aristocracy of Old New York lived. Allow at least two hours.

1 E. 70th St. at Fifth Avenue. ☎ *212-288-0700. Internet:* www.frick.org. *Subway: 6 train to Hunter College/68th Street stop, walk west to Fifth Avenue, and then walk 2 blocks north. Open: Tues–Sat 10 a.m.–6 p.m., Sun 1–6 p.m. Admission: $10 adults, $5 seniors and students (children under 10 not admitted, children under 16 admitted only with an adult); admission includes audio guide.*

Brooklyn Museum of Art
Brooklyn

New York's second largest museum after the Met, the Brooklyn Museum of Art is housed in a beautiful Beaux Arts building and has a wonderful collection that includes major Egyptian and African art — the largest collection of Egyptian artifacts in the world after London and Cairo. The museum also contains important 19th-century American and European paintings; 28 period rooms, some of them rescued from now-demolished historic buildings; and an important sculpture collection, including a rich Rodin gallery. The museum has built a reputation for dynamic temporary exhibitions. Recent ones have included a stunning watercolor retrospective, an exhibit of the Romanov treasures, and the controversial, Giuliani-boycotted show "Sensation," which presented cutting-edge artwork from Britain. You will have no trouble getting here, since the museum has its own subway stop. Allot at least three hours.

200 Eastern Parkway at Washington Avenue. ☎ *718-638-5000. Internet:* www.brooklynart.org. *Subway: 1/2 train to Eastern Parkway/Brooklyn Museum stop. Open: Wed–Fri 10 a.m.–5 p.m., Sat–Sun 11 a.m.–6 p.m.; first Sat of each month 11 a.m.–11 p.m. Suggested admission: $6 adults, $3 students and seniors, children under 12 free.*

New Museum of Contemporary Art
SoHo

This museum is famous for its exhibitions of contemporary art, stressing innovative art and artists. The permanent collection includes work by artists from around the world, ranging from installations to video, painting, and sculpture. On the ground floor is the Zenith Media Lounge, dedicated to digital art and interactive art projects; the whole floor is open to the public free of charge.

583 Broadway between Houston and Prince streets. ☎ *212-219-1222. Internet:* www.newmuseum.org. *Subway: N/R train to Prince Street stop, F/V/S train to Broadway-Lafayette Street stop, or 6 train to Bleecker Street stop, and then walk west to Broadway. Open: Tues–Sun 12–6 p.m., Thurs until 8 p.m. Admission: $6 adults, $3 seniors and students, youth under 18 free; free Thurs 6–8 p.m.*

Whitney Museum of American Art
Upper East Side

The big show here is the Whitney Biennial (in even-numbered years), which highlights the good, the bad, and the ugly in contemporary art. The Whitney also has a spectacular permanent collection of modern American art, including works by Hopper, O'Keefe, and others. Allow at least three hours.

945 Madison Ave. at 75th Street. ☎ *212-570-3676. Internet:* www.whitney.org. *Subway: 6 train to 77th Street stop. Open: Tues–Sun 11 a.m.–6 p.m.; Fri until 9 p.m. Admission: $10 adults, $8 students and seniors, children under 12 free; pay what you wish Fri 6–9 p.m.*

Especially for Culture Lovers

Asia Society
Upper East Side

This museum was founded in 1956 by John D. Rockefeller, who donated 285 masterpieces of Asian art that form the core of the society's permanent collection. Its exhibits have expanded to include art, films, and performances. Allow at least two hours.

725 Park Ave. at 70th Street. ☎ *212-517-ASIA. Internet:* www.asiasociety.org. *Subway: 6 train to 68th Street/Hunter College stop, walk 2 blocks north, turn left, and walk 1 block west to Park Avenue. Open: Tues–Sun 11 a.m.–6 p.m., Fri until 9 p.m. Admission: $7 adults, $4 seniors, children under 16 free.*

Jewish Museum
Upper East Side

The Jewish Museum, located in a renovated mansion, houses an exhaustive collection of Judaica. Its state-of-the-art modern exhibition spaces have seen shows of paintings by Whistler and artworks from Berlin in recent years. Allot at least two hours.

1109 Fifth Ave. at 92nd Street. ☎ *212-423-3271. Internet:* www.thejewish museum.org. *Subway: 6 train to 96th Street stop, walk west to Fifth Avenue, and then walk 4 blocks south. Open: Sun–Wed 11 a.m.–5:45 p.m., Thurs 11 a.m.–8 p.m., Fri 11 a.m.–3 p.m. Admission: $8 adults, $5.50 seniors and students, children under 12 free; pay what you wish Thurs 5–8 p.m.*

Museum for African Art
SoHo

This museum has temporary exhibitions but no permanent exhibits. It is, however, an ever-changing look into the rich and diverse cultural traditions of the African continent and its peoples. Both contemporary and traditional art have been featured in exhibitions. Allow at least an hour.

593 Broadway between Prince and Houston streets. ☎ *212-966-1313. Internet:* www.africanart.org. *Subway: N/R train to Prince Street stop. Open: Wed–Fri 10:30 a.m.–5:30 p.m., Sat–Sun noon–6:00 p.m. Admission: $5 adults, $2.50 seniors and children; Sunday free.*

National Museum of the American Indian, George Gustav Heye Center
Downtown

Covering 10,000 years of Native American heritage, this branch of the Smithsonian Institution is located in the elegant Beaux Arts building of the former U.S. Customs House (built in 1907). The core of the collection is thousands of objects collected by Heye, a wealthy New Yorker. The largest such collection in the world, it organizes important special exhibits.

1 Bowling Green between State and Whitehall streets. ☎ *212-668-6624. Internet:* www.si.edu/nmai. *Subway: 4/5 train to Bowling Green stop. Open: Daily 10 a.m.–5 p.m., Thurs until 8 p.m. Admission: Free.*

Especially for Sports Fans

New York is a sports town bar none, and New Yorkers support their teams through thick and thin. Baseball is the easiest sport to get tickets for when you're in town. In this section, you find out which spectator sports are worth checking out and how to get tickets.

Baseball

During the regular season, tickets are easy to obtain for **New York Mets** and **New York Yankees** home games (the series that sell out most often are Yankees–Red Sox and Yankees–Mets interleague play).

The Yankees play at Yankee Stadium in the Bronx; to get there, take the B/D/4 train to the 161st Street–Yankee Stadium stop. You can purchase tickets at the stadium ticket office (☎ **718-293-6000**), at the team's Web site (www.yankees.com), through Ticketmaster (☎ **212-307-1212**; Internet: www.ticketmaster.com), or at one of the Yankees clubhouse stores in Manhattan: 393 Fifth Ave. between 36th and 37th streets (☎ **212-685-4693**; call for other locations).

The Mets play at Shea Stadium in Queens; to get there, take the 7 train (which stops in Manhattan at Times Square, Fifth Avenue and 42nd Street, and Grand Central Station) to the Willets Point–Shea Stadium stop. You can purchase tickets at the team's Web site (www.mets.com), at the stadium ticket office (☎ 718-507-TIXX), or at one of the two New York Mets clubhouse stores in Manhattan: 143 E. 54th St. between Lexington and Third avenues and 11 W. 42nd St. between Fifth and Sixth avenues.

Basketball

The **New York Knicks** play at Madison Square Garden, on 33rd Street between Seventh and Eighth avenues. Tickets are usually impossible to come by, but given the team's poor showing of late, you may get lucky. Tickets are available through Ticketmaster (☎ 212-307-7171; Internet: www.ticketmaster.com). Also playing at the Garden are the **New York Liberty** of the WNBA; for ticket information, contact ☎ 212-564-WNBA or try the Web site www.wnba.com/liberty.

Ice hockey

The **New York Rangers** play at Madison Square Garden, on 33rd Street between Seventh and Eighth avenues. Tickets can be difficult to get; for information and availability, check the team's Web site (www.newyorkrangers.com) or try Ticketmaster (☎ 212-307-7171; Internet: www.ticketmaster.com).

Tennis

The Monday before Labor Day weekend marks the start of the **U.S. Open,** the final Grand Slam tournament of the calendar year. The tournament is waged at the USTA's National Tennis Center in Flushing, Queens (across the subway tracks from Shea Stadium), a delightful, sprawling state-of-the-art facility. To get there, take the 7 train to the Willets Point–Shea Stadium stop.

A ticket to Arthur Ashe Stadium, the main court, guarantees admission to every other court on the grounds. Ashe Stadium is impressive but dissatisfying; fans grumble loudly because the best seats are reserved for corporate sponsors, relegating "true" fans to the nosebleed seats. Indeed, the best thing about this tournament is the chance to wander over to a small outer court early in the tournament and get a *very* up-close-and-personal look at the superstars of tomorrow.

Tickets go on sale every year in late May or early June. The tournament sells out quickly — especially for matches closer to the finals. Tickets are sold for day and night sessions. You also can line up at the Tennis Center on the morning of the day you want to attend to purchase a grounds pass, which admits you to all matches except those played at Ashe Stadium. For information about tickets, write to US Open Ticket Department, USTA National Tennis Center, Flushing Meadow–Corona

Park, Flushing, NY 11358 (☎ 718-760-6200; Internet: www.usopen.org). You also can purchase tickets through Tele-charge (☎ 212-239-6200; Internet: www.telecharge.com).

Especially for TV Fans

New York has much to offer fans of TV past (see the Museum of Television and Radio review at the end of this section) and present. In this section, we give you the information you need to get tickets to the local tapings of some popular TV shows.

One TV taping you won't need a ticket for is *The Today Show*. All you have to do to see Matt, Katie, and Al is get up early and join the crowd outside the Rockefeller Center studio, on 49th Street between Fifth and Sixth avenues. (The show schedules more out-of-doors segments in warmer weather, including the Friday Summer Concert Series.) The three most likely scenarios for you getting on TV are 1) you're holding up a creative sign; 2) you want to propose to your significant other on the air; or 3) you show up and stick around during some *really bad* weather.

For the shows listed here, it's a good idea to arrange for tickets as far in advance of your trip as possible — we're talking six months or more. Tickets are always free. For more information about getting tickets to TV tapings, contact NYC & Company at ☎ 212-484-1222 (Internet: www.nycvisit.com).

✔ **The Daily Show with Jon Stewart:** Comedy Central's half-hour humor and news show tapes Monday through Thursday at 5:45 p.m.; the studio is at 513 W. 54th St. Request tickets in advance by phone (☎ 212-586-2477), or call Monday through Thursday between 11 a.m. and 4 p.m. for last-minute cancellations.

✔ **Late Night with Conan O'Brien:** Conan tapes Tuesday through Friday at 5:30 p.m. (ticket holders should arrive an hour early). No one under 16 is admitted. Send a postcard with your request to NBC Studios/*Late Night,* 30 Rockefeller Plaza, New York, NY 10112, or call ☎ 212-664-3056 Monday through Friday between 9 a.m. and 5 p.m. Standby tickets are distributed on the day of show starting at 9 a.m. on the 49th Street side of 30 Rockefeller Plaza; get there early if you want to get a seat.

✔ **The Late Show with David Letterman:** Dave's is the hardest TV ticket in town to score. Write *at least* nine months in advance with your ticket request; each person is allowed only two tickets, and multiple requests are discarded. Send a postcard with your name, address, and day and evening phone numbers to *Late Show* Tickets, Ed Sullivan Theater, 1697 Broadway, New York, NY 10019 (☎ 212-975-5853). You must be 18 years or older to attend. You also can fill out a form on the Web site (www.cbs.com/latenight/lateshow/) to be put on a list for last-minute cancellation tickets (last-minute in this case being three months or sooner). Standby tickets are available *only* by phone starting at 11:00 a.m. on taping day; call ☎ 212-247-6497. The line is answered until the tickets are gone. Tapings are Monday through Thursday at 5:30 p.m. (arrive by 4:15 p.m.), with an additional show taped Thursday evening at 8:00 p.m. (arrive by 6:45 p.m.).

✔ MTV's *Total Request Live:* Carson Daly has been called the 21st-century Dick Clark, and this show is his *American Bandstand*. An endless parade of music stars drops by the second-floor glassed-in studio to chat, sing songs, and wave to the adoring throngs that jam the sidewalk below. For tickets to the studio audience, call ☎ 212-398-8549 or e-mail TRLcasting@mtvstaff.com. You must be between 16 and 24 to attend. If you want to take your chances on the day of the show, join the crowd on the traffic island across from 1515 Broadway at 44th Street in Times Square, weekdays at 3:30 p.m. Sometimes staff members roam the crowd asking trivia questions, and correct answers land you a standby ticket.

✔ *Saturday Night Live*: *SNL* has enjoyed a resurgence, making tickets harder than usual to obtain. Tapings are Saturday at 11:30 p.m. (arrive by 10:00 p.m.), with a dress rehearsal at 8:00 p.m. (arrive by 7:00 p.m.). No one under 16 is admitted. Tickets requests are processed only during the month of August; send a postcard with your request (to arrive during August *only*) to NBC Studios/*Saturday Night Live,* 30 Rockefeller Plaza, New York, NY 10112 (☎ 212-664-4000 for information). Tickets are awarded by lottery, and you'll be given one to two weeks' notice if you win. For standby tickets, arrive *no later than* 7:00 a.m. on taping day, under the NBC Studios marquee at the 49th street entrance of 30 Rockefeller Plaza. You may choose a standby ticket for the 8:00 p.m. dress rehearsal or for the 11:30 p.m. live show. Only one ticket is issued per person.

Museum of Television & Radio
Midtown West

Have you ever wanted to travel back in time and "be there" during an unforgettable TV or radio moment — to watch the first moon landing, hear Orson Welles's *War of the Worlds* radio broadcast, or see the first ever *Sesame Street* program? Now you can. The Museum of Television & Radio has more than 100,000 radio and television programs in its permanent collection, almost all of which are available for viewing or listening. The museum is actually more like a library; instead of wandering from one exhibit to the next, you "check out" recordings or videotapes and view them in audiovisual cubicles — anything from Sid Caesar to vintage cartoons to your favorite commercials from childhood. Several theaters and listening rooms can accommodate large groups for special screenings. "Exhibits" are thematic documenatries available for viewing. It's best to go during the day, during the week; on evenings and weekends, the crowds make it hard to get a viewing booth.

25 W. 52nd St. between Fifth and Sixth avenues. ☎ *212-621-6800, 212-621-6600. Internet:* www.mtr.org. *Subway: E/V train to 53rd Street/Fifth Avenue stop. Open: Tues–Sun 12:30–6:00 p.m., Thurs until 8:00 p.m. Admission $6 adults, $4 seniors and students, $3 children under 13.*

Especially for Movie Buffs

New York is home to independent and art-house movie screens — one reason why the New York Film Festival is such a popular annual event (see the Calendar of Events in Chapter 2 for more information). The two major "alternative" cinemas are

✔ **Film Forum,** 209 W. Houston St. between Sixth and Seventh avenues (☎ 212-727-8110; Internet: www.filmforum.com), which organizes film festivals built around themes (the Great American Comedy, for example, or the Films of Pam Grier)

✔ **The Walter Reade Theater,** 165 W. 65th St. at Broadway (☎ 212-875-5600; Internet: www.filmlinc.com), part of the Lincoln Center complex, which sponsors the New York Film Festival and screens a broad range of international films as well

One of the most enjoyable movie nights in New York takes place on Mondays during the summer, when HBO sponsors free outdoor screenings in Bryant Park, at 42nd Street between Fifth and Sixth avenues. Hundreds bring a picnic supper and stake out spots on the grass; after sundown, the movie begins — a different crowd-pleasing favorite every week (think *The Sound of Music, Shaft, Grease*). For a schedule of what's playing, consult the weekly *Time Out New York* or try www.newyork.citysearch.com.

Especially for Architecture Buffs

New York is chock-full of interesting architectural monuments, some that date from the turn of the 20th century and some, like the Cathedral of St. John the Divine (see Chapter 16), that evoke a much earlier time. The city's most famous buildings are the Empire State Building and the Chrysler (see Chapter 16), but that's only scratching the architectural surface of the city that invented the skyscraper.

Flatiron Building
Flatiron District

The Flatiron Building (its original name was the Fuller Building) takes its name from its unusual triangular shape. Built in 1902, it was one of the first skyscrapers in Manhattan. Although only 20 stories tall, it's one of the most recognized, and unique, buildings in the city. The area surrounding the building features beautiful architecture, boutiques, restaurants, and nightlife.

175 Fifth Ave. where Fifth Avenue and Broadway cross at 23rd Street. Subway: N/R train to 23rd Street stop. Bus: M6 and M7 down Broadway or M2/M3/M5 down Fifth Avenue for a magnificent view of the building; the buses stop right there, too.

Woolworth Building
Downtown

Completed in 1913, the Woolworth was the tallest building in the world for a time. Designed by famous architect Cass Gilbert, the Gothic tower is known for its beautifully decorated interior and exterior: Mr. Woolworth paid $15.5 million cash for the structure and it shows. Besides the stunning exterior, this building — once known as "The Cathedral of Commerce" — has gorgeous mosaic ceilings, a marble staircase, and statues of people involved in the building's construction.

233 Broadway at Park Place. Subway: 1/2 train to Park Place stop or 4/5/6 train to Brooklyn Bridge/City Hall stop, and then walk west across the park. Open: Daily 9 a.m.–5 p.m. Admission: Free.

Especially for History Buffs

New York was the nation's first capital, and a lot of this country's culture was fashioned here. Its historical heritage is preserved in numerous places.

Lower East Side Tenement Museum
Lower East Side

This fascinating, accurate, and sobering reconstruction of a New York tenement portrays the kind of home in which most of the people who arrived at Ellis Island lived. The visitor's center is at 90 Orchard St., where you enter and sign up for a group tour (tours meet every 30 minutes); the guides are very informative. Reservations are strongly recommended.

97 Orchard St. at Broome Street. ☎ 212-431-0233. Internet: www.tenement.org. Subway: F train to Delancey Street stop, walk 2 blocks east to Orchard, and turn left 1 block. Open: Tues–Fri 1:00–4:00 p.m.; Sat–Sun 11:00 a.m.–4:30 p.m. Admission: $8 adults, $6 seniors and students, children under 5 free.

Merchant's House Museum
East Village

This house is a unique example of a wealthy Manhattan merchant's home, which has remained intact only because the descendants of the merchant — Seabury Treadwell — continued to live in the house until 1934. The 1832 building, a Greek Revival townhouse, and the 19th-century furnishings inside are worth a visit. Unscheduled tours are given on Sundays.

28 E. 4th St. between Lafayette Street and the Bowery. ☎ *212-777-1089. Subway: 6 train to Astor Place, walk south 1 block on Lafayette, and then turn left on East 4th Street. Open: Sun–Thurs 1–4 p.m. Admission: $5 adults, $3 seniors and students.*

Mount Vernon Hotel Museum
Upper East Side

This building was actually the carriage house belonging to Abigail Adams Smith, daughter of President John Adams. It was restored by the Colonial Dames of America and has nine period rooms with furnishings dating from 1800 to 1830. In the early 19th century, this building was a hotel in the countryside surrounding New York! The museum is closed in August.

421 E. 61st St. between First and York avenues. ☎ *212-838-6878. Bus: M31 running east-west on 57th Street and up York Avenue, or M15 running up First Avenue and down Second Avenue. Open: Tue–Sun 11 a.m.–4 p.m.; in June and July open Tues until 9 p.m.; closed in Aug. Admission: $4 adults, $3 seniors and students, children under 12 free.*

Museum of the City of New York
Upper East Side

Learn about this city's rich history through inventive displays packed with information. A number of decorative objects related to New York are on display here, including a collection of Tiffany glassware. Allow at least an hour for your visit. The museum is scheduled to move from its present site and reopen in its new location at the Tweed Court House (downtown behind City Hall) in fall 2003; be sure to check for updated information if you're planning a visit around that time or later.

1220 Fifth Ave. at 103rd and 104th streets. ☎ *212-534-1672. Internet:* www.mcny.org. *Subway: 6 train to 103rd Street stop, and then walk west toward Central Park. Open: Wed–Sat 10 a.m.–5 p.m., Sun noon–5 p.m. Suggested admission: $7 adults; $4 seniors, students, and children; $12 for families.*

Especially for Book Lovers

New York is a great city for people who love books. Perhaps because of the prominence of the publishing industry here, there's always a buzz surrounding the printed word. Whether you're here to buy or browse, New York offers an incredible ticket to the Gutenberg revolution.

New York Public Library and Bryant Park
Midtown East

A tour of this massive Beaux Arts structure includes a stop in the Main Reading Room, the largest uncolumned hall in New York. See the library's famous guardian lions and take in one of the changing exhibitions of manuscripts, prints, and documents. Afterward, stroll in Bryant Park, located behind the library, which has plenty of paths and chairs for relaxing. The park features free films and outdoor performances in the summer (see "Especially for Movie Buffs," earlier in this chapter). Plan to spend at least an hour here.

Fifth Avenue between 42nd and 41st streets. ☎ *212-869-8089. Subway: B/D/F/V train to 42nd Street stop, walk east along Bryant Park to Fifth Avenue, and turn right to the main entrance. Bus: M1/M2/M3/M4/M5 down Fifth Avenue or M5/M6/M7 up Sixth Avenue. Open: Main Reading Room Mon, Thurs–Sat 10 a.m.–6 p.m.; Tues–Wed 11 a.m.–6 p.m.; closed Sun. Admission: Free.*

Pierpont Morgan Library
Midtown East

This often-overlooked cultural attraction is also one of the city's great buildings: J. P. Morgan's fabulous collection of medieval and Renaissance manuscripts, rare books, and drawings is housed in an Italian *palazzo*–style mansion built in 1906. Take a break in the indoor atrium/ cafe, a great place to sit with a book and a cup of coffee or tea. Allow at least an hour for your visit.

29 E. 36th St. at Madison Avenue. ☎ *212-685-0610. Internet:* www.morgan library.org. *Subway: 6 train to 33rd Street stop, walk one block west, turn right, and walk three blocks north. Open: Tues–Thurs 10:30 a.m.–5:00 p.m., Fri 10:30 a.m.– 8 p.m., Sat 10:30 a.m.–6:00 p.m., Sun noon–6:00 p.m. Suggested admission: $8 adults, $6 seniors and students, children under 12 free if accompanied by an adult.*

Chapter 18

Seeing New York by Guided Tour

· ·

In This Chapter

▶ Orienting yourself with a sightseeing tour

▶ Sailing smoothly on a river cruise

▶ Enjoying architectural, historical, and other special-interest tours

· ·

*I*f you have limited time, have special needs, or just want an overview of the city's highlights, a guided tour can be a great way to go. We tell you about a few of the best tours in this chapter.

Some companies give you a discount on your tour if you book in advance. Seniors may be eligible for additional discounts.

Seeing the City with Orientation Tours

Several companies offer very general city sightseeing tours, many on double-decker buses. These tours are fine for seeing the sights and orienting yourself to the city, but don't expect too much from the running commentary.

Gray Line New York Tours (☎ 800-669-0051 or 212-397-2600; Internet: www.graylinenewyork.com) offers daily escorted bus tours ($75 adults, $55 children; total time 8½ hours), including lunch, a one-hour harbor cruise, and admission to the Empire State Building. Gray Line also offers daily hop-on–hop-off tours on double-decker buses organized around three loops: uptown, downtown, and a night loop, including about 50 stops ($49 adults, $39 children; total time 3 hours per loop, but tickets for the uptown and downtown loops are valid for 48 hours). You also can try out a number of mini-packages, such as helicopter and harbor tours. The daily "Essential New York" tour includes the three loops on the double-decker bus tour plus a harbor cruise, admission to the Empire

State Building, and a one-day FunPass MetroCard ($69 adults, $48 children; total time 3 hours per loop plus 1 hour for the cruise). You can buy tickets at the visitor center at 777 Eighth Ave. between 47th and 48th streets.

New York Double-Decker Tours (☎ 877-693-3253 or 718-361-6079; Internet: www.nydecker.com) also offers daily hop-on–hop-off tours on double-decker buses. The complete tour costs $40 for adults and $25 for children (tickets are valid for 48 hours). It is cheaper than the Gray Line tour but has fewer possibilities: The circuit is organized in only two loops, uptown and downtown, for a total of about 40 stops; no nighttime loop is available. You can purchase tickets from the dispatcher at any of the tour's stops or from the driver and guide on the bus.

Although they aren't tour buses, the **public buses** crisscross the city. If having a tour guide isn't essential, consider taking advantage of the $1.50 tour that the buses afford. Try the M1 all the way down Fifth Avenue from Museum Mile to 42nd Street; then change to the M104 and go across to Times Square, up Broadway through the Theater District, past Lincoln Center, and on to the Upper West Side. Or stay on the M1 all the way to City Hall and Battery Park.

Cruising Around the Island

You can see Manhattan from the water — a truly privileged view — in many ways, some more romantic than others. You can take advantage of a regular sightseeing cruise with narration, a dinner cruise, a sailing cruise, or a special-interest cruise. In this section, we list the best choices in each category.

Circle Line (☎ 212-563-3200; Internet: www.circleline.com) offers the famous "Full Island Cruise," which sails around Manhattan in three hours (daily March to December; $25 adults, $12 children, $20 seniors) from Pier 83 at West 42nd Street and Twelfth Avenue. You see Manhattan from both sides, go under the George Washington Bridge, and pass down through Hell Gate, the murky, swirling spot where the East River and the Harlem River meet. Departing from the same location, Circle Line also offers a shorter semicircle cruise, which goes back and forth around the lower half of Manhattan and lasts only two hours (daily March to December; $20 adults, $10 children, $17 seniors) — and a Harbor Lights cruise, also a two-hour cruise (at dusk; call for precise schedule; $20 adults, $10 children, $17 seniors). From Pier 16 at the South Street Seaport, Circle Line has a one-hour Liberty cruise to see the Lady and the harbor (daily March to December; $13 adults, $7 children, $11 seniors). Allow up to 45 minutes for ticketing and boarding.

To get to Pier 83 via the subway, take the A/C/E train to Port Authority or the N/Q/R/S/1/2/3/7 to Times Square, and then take the M42 bus westbound on 42nd Street or walk west to Twelfth Avenue. To reach

Pier 16, take the 1/2/4/5/A/C/J/M/Z train to the Fulton Street/Broadway Nassau stop and then walk east to the Seaport.

New York Waterways (☎ 800-533-3779; Internet: www.nywaterway. com) offers cruises around Manhattan and New York Harbor with similar features to the Circle Line, except that it sails on faster catamaran boats, which some people prefer; offers a free shuttle service from various locations in Manhattan and major hotels; and operates year-round. The two-hour Manhattan cruise goes around the island from Pier 78 at West 38th Street and Twelfth Avenue and from Pier 17 at the South Street Seaport (daily May to November from Pier 38, weekends May to September from Pier 17; $24 adults, $12 children, $19 seniors). The 90-minute harbor cruise departs from Pier 78 only and circles around the lower part of Manhattan and up the East River (daily year-round, but on a reduced schedule in January and February, so call for info; $19 adults, $9 children, $16 seniors).

To reach Pier 78, take the free shuttle (blue, red, and white; it stops at regular city bus stops and you hail it as a cab) that runs along 57th, 49th, 42nd, and 34th streets and up and down Twelfth Avenue; or take the hotel bus that runs twice a day (call for route and schedule). To get to Pier 17, take the 1/2/4/5/A/C/J/M/Z train to the Fulton Street/Broadway Nassau stop and then walk east to the Seaport.

Spirit Cruises (☎ 866-211-3805 or 212-727-2789; Internet: www.spirit cruises.com) runs year-round cabaret-style cruises, including a two-hour lunch cruise (with a narrated tour of the harbor and a buffet lunch; ranging from $29.95 weekdays January through March up to $43.95 weekends April through December) and a three-hour dinner sunset cruise (including live music and a buffet; from $52.95 weekdays January through March up to $83.95 Saturdays April through December). Prices include taxes and service. Cruises board 30 minutes before departure from Pier 61 at Chelsea Piers. To get there via the subway, take the A/C train to the 23rd Street stop and then take the westbound M23 bus on 23rd Street.

World Yacht (☎ 212-630-8100; Internet: www.worldyacht.com) offers more formal dinner and brunch cruises with live music and highly rated gourmet food. The three-hour dinner cruise includes a four-course sit-down dinner and dancing (daily April through December, weekends only January through March; $69.95 to $79). Prices do not include taxes or service. Board an hour before departure from Pier 81 at West 41st Street on the Hudson River. Jackets required for dinner, proper casual attire for brunch (no jeans, shorts, or sneakers). To get there via the subway, take the A/C/E train to the Port Authority or the N/Q/R/S/1/2/3/7 train to Times Square, and then take the M42 bus westbound on 42nd Street or walk west to Twelfth Avenue.

Even more upscale, **Bateaux New York** (☎ 212-352-1366 or 212-352-2022; Internet: www.bateauxnewyork.com) offers gourmet lunch and dinner cruises under a glass dome: The ship has a glass top with a special antifog system and is climate controlled, which makes the evening cruises quite romantic. The three-hour dinner cruise sails down the Hudson River and around to the East River and back, passing by the Statue of Liberty (daily; $102.87 weekdays, $116.89 weekends). Jackets and ties required. Board 30 minutes before departure from Pier 61 at Chelsea Piers. Via the subway, take the A/C train to the 23rd Street stop and then the westbound M23 bus on 23rd Street.

The *Petrel* (☎ **212-825-1976**), a 1938-vintage 70-foot Sparkman & Stephens wooden yacht, offers wonderfully exhilarating two-hour sailing cruises by Lady Liberty in New York Harbor (10:30 a.m. to 6:00 p.m. daily from May to September; call for the precise schedule; $20 adults, $13 seniors and children). No narration. Battery Park, just west of the Staten Island Ferry Terminal. Via the subway, take the 4/5 train to the Bowling Green stop.

The schooner *Adirondak* (☎ **917-447-SAIL** or 800-701-SAIL) also offers a sailing cruise down the Hudson River to the Statue of Liberty (10:30 a.m. to 9:00 p.m. daily May through September; $30 weekdays and $35 weekends; evening cruises with champagne $40 weekdays and $45 weekends adults, children $20 to $25). No narration, but drinks are included in all sails. From Chelsea Piers. To get there by subway, take the A/C train to the 23rd Street stop and then the westbound M23 bus on 23rd Street.

The *Pioneer,* a schooner, and the *W. O. Decker,* a wooden tugboat (☎ **212-748-8786** or 212-748-8725), offer two-hour cruises on New York Harbor to the Statue of Liberty. They are part of the South Street Seaport Museum and are fully restored historical ships. If you wish, you can help sail the boat (*Pioneer* daily, *W. O. Decker* Saturdays only, May through September; $20 adults, $15 seniors/students, $12 children). From Pier 17 at the South Street Seaport. Via the subway, take the 1/2/4/5/A/C/J/M/Z train to Fulton Street/Broadway Nassau stop and then walk east to the Seaport.

Billed as "America's only gay sailing tea dance," the "Sea Tea" excursion (☎ **212-675-HELP** for information and 212-242-3222 for reservations) departs from Pier 40 (two blocks south of Christopher Street on the Hudson River). The charge ($15 in advance, $20 at the gate) includes a buffet dinner. The boat boards at 6:00 p.m., departs at 7:30 p.m., and returns at 10:00 p.m. Sundays only June through October. You can purchase tickets in advance (or even through Ticketmaster, ☎ **212-307-7171**) or after 5:00 p.m. on Pier 40. Via the subway, take the 1/2 train to Christopher Street/Sheridan Square, walk west to the river, and turn left to Pier 40.

Flying High with Helicopter Tours

If you can afford it, a helicopter tour is something absolutely not to miss! For a breathtaking tour, try **Liberty Helicopters** (☎ 800-542-9933 or 212-967-6464; Internet: www.libertyhelicopters.com), which offers several packages from $56 up to $162. Liberty runs several tours every day, and reservations are necessary only for three people or more. The helicopters can hold up to six people. Note that tours are very short — from about ten minutes to about 25. The tours start from the VIP Heliport at West 30th Street and 12th Avenue and from the Downtown Manhattan Heliport at Pier 6 and the East River (four blocks south of Wall Street).

To get to the VIP Heliport by subway, take the A/C/E train to Penn Station, and then walk (or take the M34 crosstown bus) four blocks west on 34th Street, turn left on Twelfth Avenue, and walk two blocks south. To reach the Downtown Manhattan Heliport, take the 1/9 train to South Ferry, walk northeast on South Street for approximately four blocks to the Vietnam Veterans Memorial, and turn right toward the water.

Taking Architectural and Historical Tours

Most of the informative walking tours we tell you about in this section are available as both private and group tours.

If you decide to take a group tour, ask about group size when you call to reserve your spot. Generally, you want as small a group as possible to minimize the time required to get organized and move around.

Big Onion Walking Tours (☎ 212-439-1090; Internet: www.bigonion.com) has articulate guides for its tours of lower Manhattan. The "Eating Tour of the Lower East Side" lets you sample several types of ethnic cuisine. Big Onion also visits Ellis Island and Governors Island. Tours cost $12 to $18 for adults and $10 to $16 for seniors and students.

Joyce Gold History Tours of New York (☎ 212-242-5762; Internet: www.nyctours.com) features weekend walking tours of neighborhoods all over Manhattan, going everywhere from Harlem to Wall Street. Gold teaches New York City history at New York University and the New School. Tours are on weekends from March to December and cost $12.

Citywalks (☎ 212-989-2456) covers Midtown and downtown. We recommend this operator especially for tours of lower Manhattan. All tours cost $12.

Discover New York Walking Tours (☎ **212-439-1049** for information, 212-935-3960 for reservations; Internet: www.mas.org/events/tours. cfm) is sponsored by the Municipal Art Society. Historians conduct fascinating tours of Manhattan neighborhoods. The price ranges from $12 to $15.

The **Museum of the City of New York** runs tours on weekends, sometimes theme oriented and sometimes focused on neighborhoods. For information, call ☎ **212-534-1672,** extension 206.

Discovering Special-Interest Tours

Central Park Bicycle Tours (☎ **212-541-8759;** Internet: www.nyc tourist.com) offers just what the name declares: a guided tour of Central Park by bike ($35 adults, $25 children). The escort is usually knowledgeable and the pace leisurely, so you can really enjoy your ride and learn all about one of New York's main attractions. The company runs three two-hour tours per day at 10 a.m., 1 p.m., and 4 p.m., starting from the NY Visitors Bureau at Columbus Circle. Bicycle rental is, of course, included; by reserving in advance and mentioning the Web site, you can get up to 25% off. If you choose the 4 p.m. tour, you also get a 25% discount. Meet and book on Columbus Circle at the corner of West 59th Street and Broadway. To get there, take the A/B/C/D/1/2 train to the 59th Street/Columbus Circle stop.

The New York City Transit Museum offers a variety of tours dealing with the city's subways and their history. You can find information about upcoming tours by checking the Web site www.mta.info/ museum/outreach.htm; call ☎ **718-694-5139** to reserve a spot in advance. Prices vary by tour.

Radical Walking Tours (☎ **718-492-0069**) uncovers the subversive history of New York, from anarchism to the Civil Rights movement. The tour is $10.

Harlem Your Way! Tours Unlimited (☎ **212-690-1687;** E-mail: harlemyourway@compuserve.com) features jazz and soul-food tours during the week and gospel tours on Sundays, with a touch of brownstone history thrown in for good measure. Tours start at $32.

Harlem Spirituals Tours (☎ **212-391-0900;** Internet: www.harlem spirituals.com) offers a variety of tours of Harlem, including gospel tours, jazz tours, and soul-food tours. Tours leave from the office at 690 Eighth Ave. between 43rd and 44th streets. The Sunday Gospel tour costs $29 for adults and $27 for children ($70 for adults and $60 for children with brunch included); call or check the Web site for prices for other tours.

Free Walking Tours

You still *can* get something for nothing (like the Staten Island Ferry — see Chapter 17). Two groups in the Midtown area offer these free walking tours:

- ✔ **Big Apple Greeter** is a nonprofit organization with a staff of volunteer New Yorkers who take you around their beloved neighborhoods for three or four hours on a free tour. Call ☎ **212-669-8159** or 212-669-2896 (Fax: 212-669-3685) Monday through Friday from 9 a.m. to 5 p.m.; or check out the company's Web site at www.bigapple greeter.org. Make sure to book at least a week in advance.

- ✔ The handy *Guide to Lesbian & Gay New York Historical Landmarks,* published by the Organization of Lesbian and Gay Architects and Designers (☎ **212-475-7652**), includes a self-guided walking tour that highlights the contributions of the gay community.

Chapter 19

A Shopper's Guide to New York

. . . .

In This Chapter

▶ Getting a feel for the shopping scene

▶ Browsing through the big names in New York shopping

▶ Mapping the great shopping neighborhoods and their stores

▶ Knowing where to go for specific items

. . . .

*A*re you secretly thinking, "Forget about the Empire State Building and the Statue of Liberty; what I want to do in New York is shop!"? You're not alone; New York is a Mecca for both experienced and novice shoppers. Here you find every possible purveyor of goods — from fashion boutiques to art kiosks — and items in every possible price range. This chapter helps you sift through this sea of shopping possibilities. We explain a few of the reasons why shoppers dream about New York and tell you where to go to get quality merchandise at the best price.

Surveying the Shopping Scene

First, you need to know that "regular shopping hours" don't really exist in New York. Most department stores are open Monday through Saturday 10 a.m. to 6 p.m. and Sunday noon to 5 p.m. with a late-night Thursday (and often Monday) until 8 p.m. However, the open hours of other stores, shops, and boutiques vary widely, and the only way to know them for certain is to call the store you want to visit.

Sales tax in New York is 8.25% for most goods, although some luxury goods, such as cigars, are taxed at a higher rate. No sales tax is levied on clothes and shoes that cost less than $110, so feel free to stock up.

 If you're on the hunt for a specific item that we don't mention in this chapter, two excellent resources for shopping information are www.newyork.citysearch.com and the weekly magazine *Time Out New York* (available online at www.timeoutny.com).

Knowing the Big Names

For shoppers, no trip to New York is complete without a stop at some of the following department and specialty stores, which are famous the world over:

- ✔ **Barneys:** 660 Madison Ave. at 61st Street (☎ **212-826-8900;** Subway: N/R/W train to Fifth Avenue/59th Street stop). This is a great store for chic, stylish, upscale clothing for men and women.

- ✔ **Bergdorf Goodman** and **Bergdorf Goodman Men:** 754 Fifth Ave. at 57th Street (men's store) and 745 Fifth Ave. at 58th Street (main store ☎ **212-753-7300;** Subway: N/R/W train to Fifth Avenue/ 59th Street stop). Bergdorf's represents the pinnacle of exclusive shopping, with prices to match.

- ✔ **Bloomingdale's:** 1000 Third Ave. at 59th Street (☎ **212-355-5900;** Subway: 4/5/6 train to 59th Street stop or N/R/W train to Lexington Avenue/59th Street stop). The name is legendary — and the store is prized for its variety of goods and prices.

- ✔ **Brooks Brothers:** 346 Madison Ave. at 44th Street (☎ **212-682-8800;** Subway: 4/5/6/S/7 train to Grand Central stop). A traditional, classy men's clothier, with a selection for women and children, too.

- ✔ **The Disney Store:** The original store is at 711 Fifth Ave. at 55th Street (☎ **212-702-0702;** Subway: E/V train to Fifth Avenue/53rd Street stop), with branches at 210 W. 42nd St. at Seventh Avenue (☎ **212-221-0430**), 39 W. 34th St. between Fifth and Sixth avenues (☎ **212-279-9890**), and 141 Columbus Ave. at 66th Street (☎ **212-362-2386**). All things Disney for you and your kids.

- ✔ **FAO Schwarz:** 767 Fifth Ave. at 58th Street (☎ **212-644-9400;** Subway: N/R/W train to Fifth Avenue/59th street stop). This is more than a toy store — it's an institution. The giant stuffed animals and special attractions create a crazed atmosphere and lines around the block during the holidays.

- ✔ **Lord & Taylor:** 424 Fifth Ave. at 39th Street (☎ **212-391-3344;** Subway: B/D/F/V train to 42nd Street stop or 7 train to Fifth Avenue stop). Enjoy a wide selection of goods at moderate prices, plus great window displays during the holidays.

- ✔ **Macy's:** Herald Square, where West 34th Street, Sixth Avenue, and Broadway meet (☎ **212-695-4400;** Subway: B/D/F/N/Q/R/V/W train to 34th Street stop). Macy's has something for everyone and every price range. The annual floral show in its great hall is an unforgettable event. This store is where Natalie Wood got to know Santa in *Miracle on 34th Street.* The annual Thanksgiving Day parade ends here.

Downtown Shopping

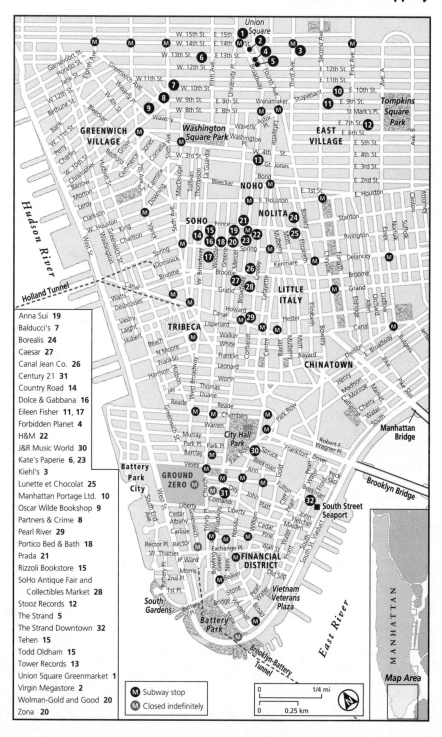

Anna Sui **19**
Balducci's **7**
Borealis **24**
Caesar **27**
Canal Jean Co. **26**
Century 21 **31**
Country Road **14**
Dolce & Gabbana **16**
Eileen Fisher **11, 17**
Forbidden Planet **4**
H&M **22**
J&R Music World **30**
Kate's Paperie **6, 23**
Kiehl's **3**
Lunette et Chocolat **25**
Manhattan Portage Ltd. **10**
Oscar Wilde Bookshop **9**
Partners & Crime **8**
Pearl River **29**
Portico Bed & Bath **18**
Prada **21**
Rizzoli Bookstore **15**
SoHo Antique Fair and
  Collectibles Market **28**
Stooz Records **12**
The Strand **5**
The Strand Downtown **32**
Tehen **15**
Todd Oldham **15**
Tower Records **13**
Union Square Greenmarket **1**
Virgin Megastore **2**
Wolman-Gold and Good **20**
Zona **20**

Ⓜ Subway stop
Ⓜ Closed indefinitely

0   1/4 mi
0   0.25 km

Map Area

Midtown Shopping

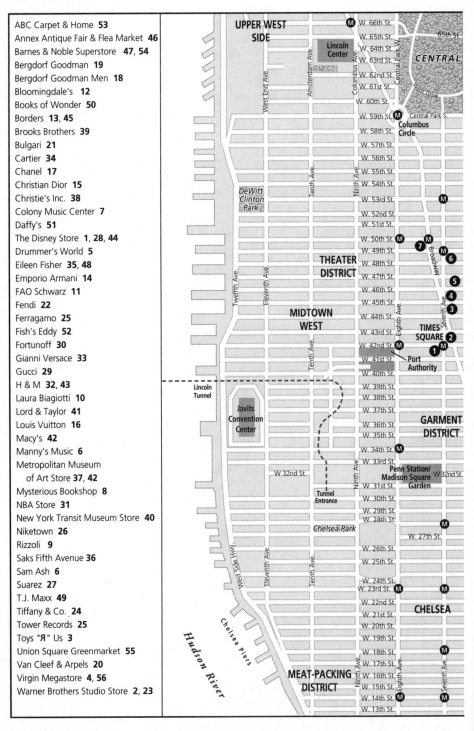

ABC Carpet & Home **53**
Annex Antique Fair & Flea Market **46**
Barnes & Noble Superstore **47, 54**
Bergdorf Goodman **19**
Bergdorf Goodman Men **18**
Bloomingdale's **12**
Books of Wonder **50**
Borders **13, 45**
Brooks Brothers **39**
Bulgari **21**
Cartier **34**
Chanel **17**
Christian Dior **15**
Christie's Inc. **38**
Colony Music Center **7**
Daffy's **51**
The Disney Store **1, 28, 44**
Drummer's World **5**
Eileen Fisher **35, 48**
Emporio Armani **14**
FAO Schwarz **11**
Fendi **22**
Ferragamo **25**
Fish's Eddy **52**
Fortunoff **30**
Gianni Versace **33**
Gucci **29**
H & M **32, 43**
Laura Biagiotti **10**
Lord & Taylor **41**
Louis Vuitton **16**
Macy's **42**
Manny's Music **6**
Metropolitan Museum
   of Art Store **37, 42**
Mysterious Bookshop **8**
NBA Store **31**
New York Transit Museum Store **40**
Niketown **26**
Rizzoli **9**
Saks Fifth Avenue **36**
Sam Ash **6**
Suarez **27**
T.J. Maxx **49**
Tiffany & Co. **24**
Tower Records **25**
Toys "Я" Us **3**
Union Square Greenmarket **55**
Van Cleef & Arpels **20**
Virgin Megastore **4, 56**
Warner Brothers Studio Store **2, 23**

Uptown Shopping

Barney's **7**
Bulgari **11**
Calvin Klein **6**
The Disney Store **5**
Dolce & Gabbana **13**
Filene's Basement **2**
Giorgio Armani **10**
Hermés **8**
I.S. 44 Flea Market **3**
Moschino **12**
Polo/Ralph Lauren **15**
Prada **14**
René Collections **16**
Sotheby's **17**
Tower Records **4**
Valentino **9**
Zabar's **1**

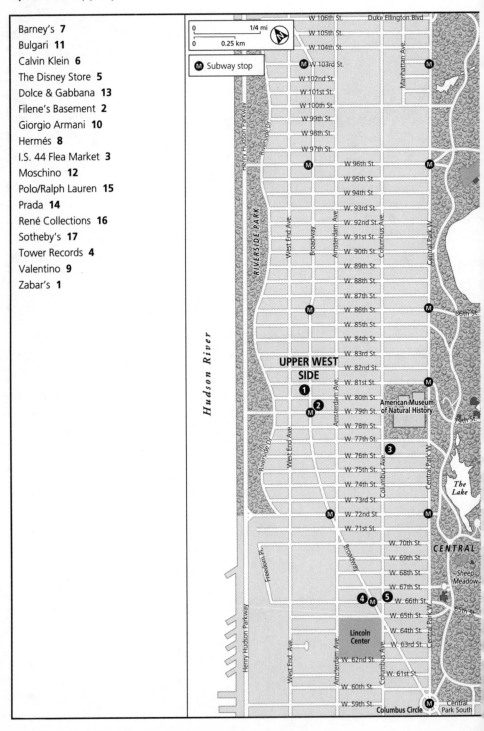

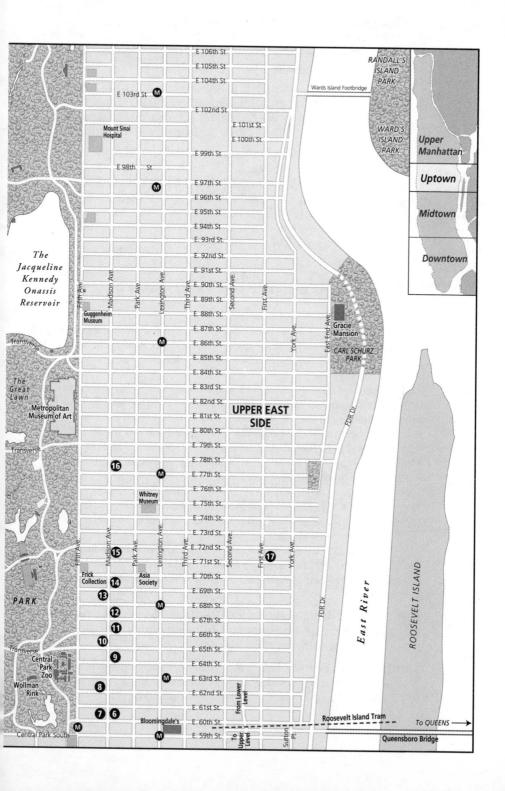

✔ **Saks Fifth Avenue:** 611 Fifth Ave. at 50th Street (☎ **212-753-4000;** Subway: E/V train to Fifth Avenue/53rd street stop). Smaller and more lavish than some of the other department stores, Saks has a name that has maximum cachet with shoppers.

✔ **Tiffany & Co.:** 727 Fifth Ave. at 57th Street (☎ **212-755-8000;** Subway: N/R/W train to Fifth Avenue/59th Street stop). Tiffany's, as in *Breakfast at . . .* You can ogle the jewels, housewares, and other shoppers just like Audrey Hepburn did in the movie.

✔ **Warner Brothers Studio Store:** 1 E. 57th St. at Fifth Avenue (☎ **212-754-0300;** Subway: N/R/W train to Fifth Avenue/ 59th Street stop. This shopping shrine honors funny little characters like that "wascally wabbit" with the New York accent (Bugs Bunny). A branch recently opened in Times Square at 1 Times Square at the intersection of 42nd Street, Seventh Avenue, and Broadway (☎ **212-840-4040**).

Shopping in Open-Air Markets

Besides a few regular specialized indoor fairs (see the calendar of events in Chapter 2), New York hosts some great outdoor farmers' markets, flea markets, and street fairs — weather permitting. Most are suspended during the coldest months of the year.

The **Union Square Greenmarket** is the liveliest and most colorful, with farmers and vendors coming from all around the tri-state area and selling homemade cheeses, cider, fresh fruit, home-baked pies and cookies, and other rural treasures. The Greenmarket is set up on the west and north sides of the square, between 14th and 17th streets, every Monday, Wednesday, Friday, and Saturday year-round from 6 a.m. to 6 p.m. Go early for the best selection.

Antiques are a big thing in New York, and the locals love to browse and (sometimes) stumble upon real treasures in several markets:

✔ The **Annex Antique Fair and Flea Market,** on Sixth Avenue at 25th Street, is probably the most famous. It has furniture, but also a lot of bric-a-brac, and is open Saturday and Sunday 9 a.m. to 5 p.m.

✔ The **SoHo Antique Fair and Collectibles Market,** on Grand Street at Broadway, also has furniture and accessories. It's open Monday through Saturday 9 a.m. to 5 p.m.

✔ The **I.S. 44 Flea Market,** on Columbus Avenue between West 76th and 77th streets, specializes in secondhand clothes, antiques, and jewelry; it's open on Sundays from 10 a.m. to 6 p.m.

During summer weekends, a typical New York activity is to stroll through one of the crowded street fairs. Avenues are closed to traffic (usually for about 10 to 20 blocks), and vendors selling clothes, crafts, and food open their stalls to the public from early morning to dusk. These fairs are great places to find summer clothing items for a few dollars each. You can find at least one fair each Saturday or Sunday. Look for listings in *Time Out New York, New York* magazine, or another of the magazines or newspapers listed in Chapter 9.

New York's sidewalks are also home to a plethora of (usually illegal) street vendors. They don't succumb to bad weather (indeed, at the first sign of rain the "umbrella men" magically appear on almost every corner!), and they operate year-round, cluttering the streets and subway stations of the most popular neighborhoods. These vendors sell everything from socks to "pre-owned" Rolex watches. Sometimes there are bargains to be had, but it's best to approach these enterprises with extreme skepticism. The thousands of street vendors who offer gold jewelry and watches at cheap prices are selling fake goods, of course — with the exception of the occasional vendor of stolen merchandise. You can find fake Rolexes and other phony big-name watches for as little as $25 if you bargain, even less for smaller models or if you buy more than one. They usually keep good time, but even if they don't, you obviously won't be getting a warranty with your purchase. Another hotbed for imitation (or knock-off) designer goods is the stall shops along Canal Street in Chinatown — see the following section for more information.

Identifying the Great Shopping Neighborhoods

New York has four prime shopping areas: the Upper East Side stretch of Madison Avenue for the classic and elegant; the NoHo/NoLiTa/SoHo area for the trendy and chic; Midtown/Fifth Avenue, home to many famous stores and boutiques; and Chinatown for Asian imports and a comprehensive selection of designer knockoffs.

Madison Avenue

High fashion (and high prices) is what you find in the stores on Madison Avenue between 57th and 78th streets. To catch everything, start at one end and walk the length of this swanky strip. Take the 6 train to the 77th Street stop and walk south, or take the 4/5/6 train to the 59th Street stop or the N/R train to Lexington Avenue stop and walk north. We've mentioned only a few of our favorite stores along this strip; you're sure to find others along the way.

Keep in mind that Madison Avenue is *not* the place to come if you're looking for a bargain. The stores in this neighborhood are some of the most expensive in town. But even if you won't be buying, it's still a charming strip for window-shopping.

Along Madison Avenue, you find top European fashion designers' shops, such as the ultra-elegant **Giorgio Armani,** 760 Madison Ave. at 65th Street (☎ **212-988-9191**), and his younger and less expensive line, **Emporio Armani,** 601 Madison Ave. at 60th Street (☎ **212-317-0800**); the sometimes-outrageous **Moschino,** 803 Madison Ave. at 68th Street (☎ **212-639-9600**); the trendy Italian designer **Dolce & Gabbana,** 825 Madison Ave. at 69th Street (☎ **212-249-4100**); and the famous **Valentino,** 747 Madison Ave. at 65th Street (☎ **212-772-6969**).

American designers are represented, too: **Calvin Klein,** 654 Madison Ave. at 60th Street (☎ **212-292-9000**); **Eileen Fisher,** 521 Madison Ave. at 53rd Street (☎ **212-759-9888**); and **Polo/Ralph Lauren** and **Polo Sport,** 867 Madison Ave. at 72nd Street (☎ **212-606-2100**), among others.

If you're in search of fine Italian shoes and leather, visit **Prada,** 841 Madison Ave. between 69th and 70th streets (☎ **212-327-4200**). Don't forget to stop by **Bulgari,** 783 Madison Ave. at 67th Street (☎ **212-717-2300**), the big name in Italian jewelry, to see what the ladies in Monte Carlo are wearing around their necks this year.

Fifth Avenue and 57th Street

Elegant shopping is the order of the day in this area, centered on Fifth Avenue south of 59th Street and East 57th Street up to Lexington Avenue. To get here, take the subway to one of the nearby stops: the E/V train to the Fifth Avenue/53rd Street stop, the N/R/W train to the Fifth Avenue/59th Street stop, or the 4/5/6 train to the 59th Street stop. From any of these starting points, you can explore north and south on Fifth Avenue and east and west on 57th Street.

You find some top European haute couture designers, such as **Christian Dior,** 21 E. 57th St. between Fifth and Madison avenues (☎ **212-931-2950**); **Chanel,** 15 E. 57th St. between Fifth and Madison avenues (☎ **212-355-5050**); **Gianni Versace,** 647 Fifth Ave. at 54th Street (☎ **212-317-0224**); and **Laura Biagiotti,** 4 W. 57th St. at Fifth Avenue (☎ **212-399-2533**). The high-end names for accessories and shoes are here also, including **Ferragamo,** 725 Fifth Ave. at 56th Street (☎ **212-759-3822**); **Gucci,** 685 Fifth Ave. between 53rd and 54th streets (☎ **212-826-2600**); **Hermés,** 11 E. 57th St. between Fifth and Madison avenues (☎ **212-751-3181**); **Louis Vuitton,** 19 E. 57th St. between Fifth and Madison avenues (☎ **212-371-6111**); and **Fendi,** 720 Fifth Ave. at 56th Street (☎ **212-767-0100**).

Among the other big names you find in this area are **Niketown,** 6 E. 57th St. at Fifth Avenue (☎ **212-891-6453**), the five-floor shoe and clothing emporium that appears to be one giant "Just Do It" commercial. As you enter, check out the five-story screen that unfurls periodically to show a video montage of Nike's ultra-famous pitchmen and -women. A few blocks down on Fifth Avenue is **The NBA Store,** 666 Fifth Ave. at 52nd Street (☎ 212-515-NBA1), where, in addition to all sorts of NBA and WNBA merchandise, you might catch a player appearing for an in-store signing.

And for super-affordable hip fashions for men, women, and children, you can't go wrong at **H&M,** 640 Fifth Ave. at 51st Street (☎ **212-489-0390**). The three-floor store is always crowded (it's a favorite with teens), and the wait for a fitting room can get *long.* But the fashions are of-the-moment trendy, and the prices can't be beat. Other branches are at 1328 Broadway at 34th Street, just across from Macy's (☎ **212-564-9922**), and in SoHo at 558 Broadway between Prince and Spring streets (☎ **212-343-8313**).

Also in this neighborhood are some of the world's most famous shops: FAO Schwarz, Tiffany & Co., and Saks Fifth Avenue, just to name a few. We covered those already in "Knowing the Big Names," earlier in this chapter.

SoHo, NoHo, and NoLiTa

This trendy area is where you're most likely to see an off-duty supermodel doing some personal shopping. SoHo is the stylish neighborhood where most big names of the international fashion scene have opened their boutiques, whereas NoHo and NoLiTa are the bohemian quarters of new and emerging stylists and fashion designers. Most shops here don't put out the welcome mat before 11 a.m.

Scoring at the sample sales

A bargain-hunter's dream, sample sales are events at which New York fashion designers sell — at *deep* discounts — discontinued styles, overstocks, and the sample outfits they create to show to store buyers (hence the name "sample sales"). How great are the deals? It's entirely possible to get a $300 dress from a big-name designer for $45 or less. Because the sales aren't widely publicized and may last anywhere between two days and a week, you have to hunt around to get the inside scoop. The weekly magazines *Time Out New York* and *New York* publish lists of upcoming sales; you also can try the Web sites www.nysale.com and www.inshop.com for information.

Bring cash; credit cards are rarely accepted. You'll have more to choose from if you fit what designers call an "average" size — a U.S. 8 or 10 for women, a 40 for men. Items are sold as-is, so try on before you buy.

SoHo is loosely bordered by Grand Street to the south, Avenue of the Americas (Sixth Avenue) to the west, Broadway to the east, and Houston to the north, forming a quadrangle. Here's our suggested plan of attack: Enter the quadrangle at one of the four corners and walk up and down or left and right (pretend that you're hoeing a field). Take the A/C/E train to the Canal Street stop, the C/E to the Spring Street stop, the N/R train to the Canal or Prince Street stop, the 6 train to the Bleecker or Spring Street stop, or the F/V/S train to the Broadway/ Lafayette Street stop.

Designer boutiques include American **Anna Sui,** 113 Greene St. (☎ 212-941-8406), and **Todd Oldham,** 123 Wooster St. (☎ 212-226-4668); French **Tehen,** 91 Greene St. (☎ 212-925-4788); Australian **Country Road,** 411 W. Broadway (☎ 212-343-9544); and Italian **Dolce & Gabbana,** 434 W. Broadway between Prince and Spring streets (☎ 212-965-8000). But the most interesting is the new art boutique opened by **Prada** at 575 Broadway on the corner of Prince Street (☎ 212-334-8888).

Caesar, 487 Broadway (☎ 212-941-6672), offers SoHo fashion at prices that won't blow your budget. **Canal Jean Co.,** 504 Broadway between Spring and Broome streets (☎ 212-226-1130), has casual wear for a sane price. Along Broadway from Houston to Canal streets, you find wall-to-wall trendy clothing and shoe stores for the budget-minded.

Portico Bed & Bath, 139 Spring St. (☎ 212-941-7722), offers fine linens and soaps (and the occasional good sale). **Wolman-Gold and Good,** 117 Mercer St. (☎ 212-431-1888), features outside-the-norm tabletop wares. **Zona,** 97 Greene St. (☎ 212-925-6750), sells can't-get-these-at-home home furnishings. **Rizzoli,** 454 W. Broadway (☎ 212-674-1616), a bookstore synonymous with elegance, is also in the area; shop here for unusual editions and extravagant art books.

NoLiTa and NoHo are on the east side of Broadway and Lafayette from SoHo. You find smaller buildings, smaller shops, and a less hyped atmosphere. Interesting boutiques dot these tree-lined streets; the best streets to start exploring are Elizabeth and Prince. **Borealis,** 229 Elizabeth St. between Prince and East Houston streets (☎ 917-237-0152), sells beautiful designer jewelry. **Lunette Et Chocolat,** 25 Prince St. between Elizabeth and Mott streets (☎ 212-925-8800), offers an interesting mix of chocolates and eyewear — the kind of place where you can ponder your choice of frames while having a chocolate crepe at the garden cafe in the rear.

Chinatown

Chinatown is a sprawling downtown neighborhood (see Chapter 10 for information about the neighborhood and its parameters), but the heart of its commercial zone is along Canal Street, from West Broadway to the Bowery. Here, interspersed with fruit, vegetable, and fish markets, you pass store after store — most merely hallway-sized stalls — selling "designer" sunglasses, watches, and handbags (think Gucci, Coach, Louis Vuitton, and kate spade, for example), as well as just about any kind of trinket or souvenir you can imagine. Frankly, a good bit of the counterfeit merchandise looks pretty cheap, but with persistence you can often unearth a few amazing finds. Do the watches keep time? For a while, at least. But what more do you expect from a $15 Rolex? Once you scope out a few shops and get a sense of the prices, you'll be in a position to haggle.

Existing alongside this fakes extravaganza is the "other" Chinatown, where you can find quirky, one-of-a-kind Asian-inspired gifts at bargain-basement prices. **Mott Street,** south of Canal Street, has a long stretch of knickknack and housewares shops that sell everything from lacquered jewelry boxes and toys to embroidered silk pajamas and gorgeous pottery dinnerware. If you prefer one-stop shopping, try **Pearl River,** 277 Canal St. at Broadway (☎ **212-431-4770**), a three-floor department store specializing in all things Chinatown — food, music, movies, clothing, and more.

Other specialized shopping areas

A host of other shopping "zones" exist all around Manhattan. If you're looking for something specific, chances are there's a part of town that sells nothing but. The most famous is probably the **Diamond District,** a conglomeration of jewelry and gem stores along West 47th Street between Fifth and Sixth avenues (Internet: www.47th-street.com). If it's **beads, crafts, and notions** you're after, the area between 35th and 39th streets between Fifth and Sixth avenues is the place to go. In the Village, Bleecker Street between Sixth and Seventh avenues is home to a number of **used CD stores** (check out St. Mark's Place between Second and Third avenues as well). As we mention in the section "Musical Instruments," later in this chapter, the area around Broadway between 46th and 48th streets is the place to go for **sheet music and musical instruments** of all kinds.

Teenagers and those striving for a younger look will love the **shoes, clothing, and leather shops** that populate 8th Street from Second to Sixth avenues (east of Broadway, 8th Street becomes known as St. Mark's Place). St. Mark's is also the place to go if you're in the market for a piercing or tattoo — the crowd you encounter along this strip is like a walking catalog of available tattoo styles and piercing options. Clothes and accessories for trendsters are also to be found on Seventh and Ninth streets.

New York Shopping A to Z

Whatever you want, you can find it in New York. More important, you can find some specialized items, often hard to find elsewhere, at bargain prices. In this section, we tell you where to get the goodies you desire.

Accessories

You want it, but you just can't afford it? Maybe you can. A few shops specialize in quality copies of famous designers' accessories, such as handbags and jewelry (and we're not talking about illegal knockoffs here). The quality is top-notch, so why not? The best are **Suarez,** 450 Park Ave. between 56th and 57th streets (☎ 212-753-3758), for designer handbags; and **René Collections,** 1007 Madison Ave. between

WORTH THE SEARCH

A shopping list of New York institutions

It's not so much that these stores are ultra-popular and beloved by all New Yorkers. We simply picked a few shops that best convey the flavor of living (and shopping) in this vibrant, eccentric, exciting city.

Two neighboring home-furnishing stores have a real treasures-found-in-Grandma's-attic feel. **ABC Carpet & Home,** 888 Broadway at 19th Street (☎ 212-473-3000; Subway: 4/5/6/L/N/R/Q/W train to 14th Street/Union Square stop), has ten floors of offbeat yet stylish furniture, linens, and gifts. **Fish's Eddy,** 889 Broadway at 19th Street (☎ 212-420-9020; Subway: 4/5/6/L/N/R/Q/W train to 14th Street/Union Square stop), is a quirky store that sells custom-printed china remainders and other whimsical designs (think baseball and city-skyline themes).

A legend among New York's bath-and-beauty stores is **Kiehl's,** 109 Third Ave. at 13th Street (☎ 212-677-3171; Subway: 4/5/6/L/N/R/Q/W train to 14th Street/Union Square stop), where the plain-Jane packaging conceals fabulous skin- and hair-care formulas beloved by supermodels and regular folks alike.

Two of the best museum gift shops are the **New York Transit Museum Store,** in Grand Central Terminal (☎ 212-876-0106; Subway: 4/5/6/S/7 train to Grand Central stop), where you can get subway-themed posters, T-shirts, and jewelry; and the **Metropolitan Museum of Art Store,** with locations inside Macy's (mezzanine level; ☎ 212-268-7266) and at Rockefeller Center (☎ 212-332-1360), as well as inside the museum itself (see Chapter 16 for information). The Met shops sell not only posters of the museum's famed works but also jewelry, note paper, and, during the holidays, Christmas ornaments. Speaking of high-quality paper goods, **Kate's Paperie,** 561 Broadway between Prince and Spring streets (☎ 212-941-9816; Subway: N/R train to Prince Street stop), has a delightful collection of handmade wrapping paper, stationery, and photo albums.

Have you ever wondered where those ultra-cool bike messengers and hipster-student types get their satchels and backpacks? Try **Manhattan Portage Ltd.,** 333 E. 9th St. between First and Second avenues (☎ 212-995-1949; Subway: 6 train to Astor Place stop; Internet: www.manhattanportageltd.com), which has a rainbow-colored assortment of waterproof nylon bags.

Rounding out our list are a number of stores we mention elsewhere in this chapter: **Pearl River** (see "Chinatown," earlier in this chapter), **J&R Music World** (see "Music," later in this chapter), **Century 21** (see "Discount Stores," later in this chapter), and **The Strand Bookstore** (see "Books," later in this chapter).

77th and 78th streets (☎ **212-327-3912**), particularly for evening bags and jewelry.

Antiques

New York is a great place to buy antiques, ranging from outrageously expensive, museum-quality pieces to affordable minor items.

You'll find antiques aplenty at the various antique shows (see the calendar of events in Chapter 2). Another good bet are auction houses, such as **Christie's Fine Art Auctioneers,** 502 Park Ave. at 59th Street (☎ **212-546-1000;** Subway: N/R train to Lexington Avenue/59th Street stop or 4/5/6 train to 59th Street stop); and **Sotheby's,** 1334 York Ave. at 72nd Street (☎ **212-606-7000;** Bus: M30 or M72 along 72nd Street).

You also find lots of antiques in the shops on East 60th Street between Second and Third avenues. Another major area for antiquing is south of Union Square on the blocks between University Place and Broadway — particularly East 12th Street (some shops are "to the trade" — that is, dealers only — but the window-shopping is good anyway).

If you're in town on a Sunday, be sure to check out the outdoor flea markets (see "Shopping in Open-Air Markets," earlier in this chapter). Grab a bagel and get there early — say around 8 a.m. — to get the best bargains.

Bookstores

New York is a great place for hard-to-find books and great bargain titles. **The Strand,** 828 Broadway at 12th Street (☎ **212-473-1452;** Subway: 4/5/6/N/R/L/Q/W train to 14th Street/Union Square stop), is a historical shop and an attraction in itself. It advertises "eight miles of books" on every subject conceivable, both new and used and mostly discounted (often half-price). **The Strand Downtown,** a second branch that's big but not as well organized, is near the South Street Seaport at 95 Fulton St. (☎ **212-732-6070;** Subway: 1/2/4/5/A/C/J/M/Z train to Fulton Street/Broadway Nassau stop).

The largest chain bookstore in New York is **Barnes & Noble.** Among its many branches are mammoth stores at 33 E. 17th St. at Union Square (☎ **212-253-0810;** Subway: 4/5/6/N/R/L/Q/W train to 14th Street/Union Square stop), 675 Sixth Ave. at 21st Street (☎ **212-727-1227;** Subway: F/V train to 23rd Street stop), and 2289 Broadway at 82nd Street (☎ **212-362-8835;** Subway: 1 train to 79th Street stop). **Borders,** another books-and-music chain, has branches at 461 Park Ave. at 57th Street (☎ **212-980-6785;** Subway: 4/5/6/F train to 59th Street stop) and 550 Second Ave. at 32nd Street (☎ **212-685-3938;** Subway: 6 train to 33rd Street stop).

In addition to these big names are dozens of charming specialty bookshops. **Mysterious Bookshop,** 129 W. 56th St. between Sixth and Seventh avenues (☎ 212-765-0900; Subway: F train to 57th Street stop), and **Partners & Crime,** 44 Greenwich Ave. between Sixth Avenue and 10th Street (☎ 212-243-0440; Subway: A/C/E/F/V/S train to West 4th Street stop), cater to mystery fans. **Rizzoli** specializes in art books and foreign literature, with branches at 31 W. 57th St. between Fifth and Sixth avenues (☎ 212-759-2424; Subway: F train to 57th Street stop) and at 454 W. Broadway, just below Houston (☎ 212-674-1616; Subway: N/R train to Prince Street stop). **Books of Wonder,** 16 W. 18th St. between Fifth and Sixth avenues (☎ 212-989-3270; Subway: 4/5/6/N/R/L/Q/W train to 14th Street/Union Square stop), is the place to go for children's books. **Forbidden Planet,** 840 Broadway at 13th Street (☎ 212-473-1576; Subway: 4/5/6/N/R/L/Q/W train to 14th Street/Union Square stop), is home to all things comic book and sci-fi, with a staff as enthusiastic and knowledgeable as you'll ever come across. And the **Oscar Wilde Bookshop,** 15 Christopher St. between Sixth and Seventh avenues (☎ 212-255-8097; Subway: 1, 2 train to Christopher Street stop), bills itself as the world's oldest gay and lesbian bookstore.

Discount stores

Getting quality designer duds for dirt cheap is like a professional sport for New York shoppers. The first place on most people's lists is **Century 21,** 22 Cortland St. between Broadway and Church Street (☎ 212-227-9092; 4/5/A/C train to Fulton Street/Broadway Nassau stop), with a huge selection of designer and quality items, from apparel to housewares, discounted up to 70%. It just reopened after a major restoration due to the damage it suffered after the collapse of the nearby Twin Towers.

Of the other discount chains in town, the best are **Daffy's,** 111 Fifth Ave. at 18th Street (☎ 212-529-4477; Subway: 4/5/6/L/N/R/Q/W train to 14th Street/Union Square stop; call for other locations), which has especially nice children's wear; and **Filene's Basement,** 2222 Broadway at 79th Street (☎ 212-873-8000; Subway: 1/2 train to 79th Street stop).

Food

In a city of foodies, specialty food stores are a given. Two of the largest that offer the best-quality gourmet foods (and great places to shop for gifts) are **Balducci's,** 424 Sixth Ave. at 9th Street (☎ 212-673-2600; Subway: F/V train to 14th Street stop or L train to Sixth Avenue stop), for gourmet food with an Italian flavor; and **Zabar's,** 2245 Broadway at 80th Street (☎ 212-787-2000; Subway: 1/2 train to 79th Street stop), for gourmet foods with a Jewish deli heritage, plus a whole floor of cooking utensils and appliances. (We list other gourmet food shops in Chapter 15.)

Jewelry

As we mentioned in "Other Specialized Shopping Areas," earlier in this chapter, the prime area for wholesale jewelers is West 47th Street between Fifth and Sixth avenues, which is jam-packed with stores. Otherwise, many of the big names are located near **Tiffany** on Fifth Avenue (mentioned earlier in this chapter). **Cartier,** 2 E. 52nd St. (☎ 212-446-3459; Subway: E/V train to Fifth Avenue stop), is there, as are **Bulgari,** 730 Fifth Ave. at 57th Street (☎ 212-315-9000; Subway: N/R/W train to Fifth Avenue/59th Street stop), and **Van Cleef & Arpels,** 744 Fifth Ave. at 58th Street (☎ 212-644-9500; Subway: N/R/W train to Fifth Avenue/59th Street stop). Bulgari also has a branch at 783 Madison Ave. (☎ 212-717-2300). For classic styles in gold and silver at affordable prices, try **Fortunoff,** 681 Fifth Ave. between 53rd and 54th streets (☎ 212-758-6660; Internet: www.fortunoff.com; Subway: E/V train to Fifth Avenue/53rd Street stop).

Music

Audio and video

At first glance, New York seems to have more "discount" electronics stores than it has cab drivers. In the major tourist areas around Times Square and the Empire State Building, you see countless stores with signs that shout some variation of "Store Closing! Everything Must Go!" These too-good-to-be-true deals on computers, cell phones, and other electronic gadgets often *are.* Such stores often have no return policies (even though the "soon-to-close" stores have been in business for years), so it pays to stick with more reputable establishments. Your best bet for quality, selection, and prices is **J & R Music World, Computers, Electronics and Appliances,** 15–21 Park Row at City Hall Park (☎ 212-238-9100; Subway: 4/5/6 train to Brooklyn Bridge/City Hall stop or N/R train to City Hall stop). You find separate entrances for each section of the store all along the sidewalk.

CDs, records, and tapes

Of the countless music stores in New York, the two largest are **Tower Records** and **Virgin Megastore.** Tower Records, 692 Broadway at 4th Street (☎ 212-505-1500; Subway: 6 train to Astor Place stop), has a comprehensive selection of all types of music. Other branches are at 1961 Broadway at 66th Street (☎ 212-799-2500; Subway 1/2 train to 66th Street/Lincoln Center stop) and 725 Fifth Ave. at 57th Street, inside the Trump Tower (☎ 212-838-8110; Subway: N/R/W train to Fifth Avenue/59th Street stop). Virgin Megastore's selection is not as deep as Tower's, but it has a more extensive offering of import CDs. Virgin's flagship store is in Times Square at 1540 Broadway at 46th Street (☎ 212-921-1020; Subway: 1/2/3/7/N/Q/R/S/W train to Times Square/42nd Street stop). Another equally large branch is at 52 E. 14th

St. at Union Square (☎ 212-598-4666; Subway: 4/5/6/L/N/R/Q/W train to 14th Street/Union Square stop). Both Virgin and Tower are open late, especially on weekends.

If you're looking to save money, cruise the used CD stores on St. Mark's Place just west of Astor Place, between Second and Third avenues. The East Village is a great place for picking up CDs, especially contemporary rock and alternative music, at half price. Our favorite is hole-in-the-wall **Stooz Records** at 122 E. 7th St. between First Avenue and Avenue A (☎ 212-979-6294; take the 6 train to Astor Place, walk east three blocks, turn right on First Avenue, and then turn left on 7th Street).

Sheet music and musical instruments

People come from all over the world to make it big in the New York music world, so it stands to reason that the city is a great place to buy musical instruments and supplies. West 48th Street between Sixth and Seventh avenues is the place to go; take the N/R/W train to the West 49th Street stop. **Sam Ash,** 160 W. 48th St. between Sixth and Seventh avenues (☎ 212-719-2299), and **Manny's Music,** 156 W. 48th St. between Sixth and Seventh avenues (☎ 212-819-0576), are the two biggies on the block; you find several smaller dealers along this stretch as well. For drums and percussion instruments from around the world, the best place in town is **Drummer's World,** 151 W. 46th St. between Sixth and Seventh avenues (☎ 212-840-3057). It's on the third floor, but look for a sign at street level.

Once you're set up with equipment, pick up your sheet music at **Colony Music Center,** 1619 Broadway at 49th Street (☎ 212-265-2050), which sells a comprehensive selection of Broadway cast recordings and theater posters as well.

Toys

The mother of all toy stores is certainly **FAO Schwarz,** which is every child's fantasy come to life (see "Knowing the Big Names," earlier in this chapter). There are a number of cute small toy shops in town, especially in the Village and on the Upper West and Upper East Sides — where Manhattanites with kids live. The recently opened Toys 'R' Us store in Times Square (1514 Broadway between 44th and 55th streets; ☎ 212-869-7787) is a huge showplace as well as a retail store; to call it noisy is a serious understatement. Also well known are the Disney Store and the Warner Brothers Studio Store (see "Knowing the Big Names," earlier in this chapter).

Chapter 20

Five Great New York Itineraries

. . . .

In This Chapter

▶ Sightseeing plans for New York's hot spots

▶ Making your visit hassle free

. . . .

The itineraries in this chapter can help you focus your plans and avoid feeling overwhelmed by all that New York has to offer. For more information about each attraction, please refer to Chapters 16 and 17.

New York in Two Days

In town just for the weekend? This short itinerary enables you to see the most important attractions and get a true feel for the city. You can always come back for seconds — New York is a pleasure to visit again and again. Even those who live here can never get around to see all the sights!

Day one

Start the morning with a walk down Fifth Avenue to warm up your muscles. At Central Park South (59th Street) and Fifth Avenue, admire the Plaza Hotel, and then stroll downtown past shops like Bergdorf Goodman, FAO Schwarz, Saks Fifth Avenue, and Tiffany (see Chapter 19 for more on shopping). Continue south and take a look at Rockefeller Center. Across the avenue, you can visit St. Patrick's Cathedral. A little farther south, you'll reach the New York Public Library and Bryant Park. At this point, you may want to stop in the park for a lunch break at one of the restaurants or kiosks or have a picnic. In the summer, you may find free entertainment in the park.

After lunch, resume your path and head east on 42nd Street for a visit to the United Nations, admiring the Chrysler Building and Grand Central Terminal on your way. Alternatively, you may want to go west on 42nd Street for a visit to the Intrepid Sea-Air-Space museum, or downtown for a feel of Chinatown and Little Italy or even a quick ride on the Staten Island Ferry. If you decide to head downtown, take the subway on 42nd Street by Fifth Avenue (take the 7 train to the Grand Central stop, and then switch to the 4/5 or 6 train depending on where you want to go). You also could take the M2, M3, or M5 bus that goes down Fifth Avenue (the M1 goes all the way to the Staten Island Ferry at the southern tip of Manhattan) and do some sightseeing from the bus, but the ride can get *very* long if you run into traffic (which you almost always do).

Wherever you go, take time for a coffee break, or grab a more substantial snack to fortify yourself until later if you're planning to take in a Broadway show. Then catch the subway or a bus back to Times Square. If you're up for a show, line up at the TKTS booth for a same-night performance ticket (see Chapter 21 for information about getting last-minute tickets). If you aren't theater-bound, time your arrival for dusk to see the neon light up. This is a perfect occasion for simply having dinner at one of the many restaurants in the area (see Chapters 13, 14, and 15 for our dining recommendations).

Day two

No visit to New York is complete without a quick peek at Museum Mile. Start your day with a visit to the Met (Metropolitan Museum of Art), unless it's a Monday, when the museum is closed. After the Met, head uptown to see the Guggenheim — at least the lobby. Pick up something for lunch (see Chapters 13 and 15 for suggestions) and then wander through Central Park and have a picnic. Alternatively, have lunch at one of the well-known restaurants in the park: Tavern on the Green or Park View at the Boathouse (see Chapter 14).

After lunch, cross the park to the Museum of Natural History or the Children's Museum. For more art, you can head back down Fifth to 70th Street and stop in at the Frick Collection for a look at the elegant private home and art collection of industrialist Henry Clay Frick. A treat at the end of the day is to take a bus down Fifth Avenue to the Empire State Building and catch a spectacular view of the evening lights from the top. You'll still be able to see a show and have a great dinner at night — maybe something really special at one of New York's top restaurants (see Chapter 14, and remember to make a reservation) or a lively night at one of New York's famous clubs (see Chapter 23).

New York in One Week

A one-week vacation gives you the chance to enjoy New York and truly get to know the city. To make the most of your week, we recommend that you make reservations for a few key activities before leaving home: dining at a special restaurant or attending the theater, a concert, or any other performance for which you need to buy tickets in advance (see Chapter 9 for listings of ticket brokers and other resources for getting tickets ahead of time). We've factored travel time into this itinerary and assume that your one-week trip will allow for six full days of sightseeing.

Day one

Start day one as you do in the "New York in Two Days" itinerary, but save some of the morning attractions for the afternoon so that you have more time to visit each of them — for example, at Rockefeller Center, you may want to take the guided tour of Radio City Music Hall (see Chapter 16). In fact, the area around Rockefeller Center is a good place for lunch (consult Chapters 14 and 15 for suggestions). End the afternoon with a visit to the New York Public Library and Bryant Park — in the summertime, you often can watch a movie under the stars if you stay until sundown (see Chapter 17).

Otherwise, the rest of the day should unfold according to your evening plans: If you want to catch a show, you may want to have an early dinner; otherwise, you could schedule dinner and a nighttime stroll for a bit later and head back to your hotel for a rest after a full day. Plan on having dinner in the Times Square area, either on Restaurant Row or nearby (see Chapters 13 and 14 for suggestions), so that you can see the neon at night.

Day two

Start your day downtown. If you're staying in Midtown or uptown, you can take one of the Fifth Avenue buses (M1, M2, M3, or M5) and do some sightseeing from the bus on your way — but during rush hour, this may take a lot longer than you expect. Walk to Wall Street for a visit to the financial heart of the city; if you're interested, you may want to see the Stock Exchange in action (see Chapter 16). On your way, admire some of the earliest examples of skyscrapers in the world. If you'd like to pay your respects to those who lost their lives in the World Trade Center attacks, you need to get a free ticket to Ground Zero in advance (see Chapter 16). Then, if you want to take the ferry to the Statue of Liberty and Ellis Island, continue west to Battery Park (you may want to have lunch first because the round-trip and visit take at least three hours). Otherwise, head east and have lunch in the South Street Seaport area. After lunch, stroll the small streets of the Seaport, which bustled with maritime traffic a couple of centuries ago. You can visit the South Street Seaport Museum and the ships if you like, or you can take one of the harbor tours (see Chapter 18).

After that, head north to get a feel for nearby Chinatown (time yourself to arrive there with some daylight left to get the full experience of this busy commercial area) and Little Italy. Plan to have dinner at one of the many excellent restaurants in the area — see Chapters 13 and 14 for recommendations.

Day three

This is the day you tackle Museum Mile. Depending on your personal tastes, you may want to do the Met (Metropolitan Museum of Art) in the morning and the Guggenheim in the afternoon, taking a lunch break in Central Park. Or you may prefer to visit the Frick Collection or the Whitney Museum. Be careful not to push yourself so hard that you catch museum fatigue, a syndrome common to museum-goers in which you see *so* much that you won't remember what you've seen. Plan a romantic dinner at one of the well-known restaurants in the park, like Tavern on the Green (see Chapter 14), or have a drink at the Rainbow Grill for a nighttime view of Manhattan (see Chapter 23) and then head to dinner at the restaurant of your choice.

Day four

Begin with a visit to the United Nations and its gardens, admiring the Chrysler Building and Grand Central Terminal on your way. Have lunch in the area (maybe even at the Delegates Dining Room inside the UN) and then head west and visit the Intrepid Sea-Air-Space Museum. Alternatively, you can take the Circle Line for a view of Manhattan from the water if you didn't do so on day two. Have dinner on the west side (along Ninth Avenue, for example — see Chapters 13, 14, and 15 for suggestions) and then head to the terraces of the Empire State Building (see Chapter 16) for the unique experience of seeing New York by night.

Day five

Head to the Upper West Side for a visit to the Museum of Natural History and the Rose Center for Earth and Space. You'll see a unique collection and fascinating temporary exhibitions — and at least one IMAX movie will be playing as well. Alternatively, you can take the subway across the East River and pay a visit to the Museum of Modern Art's temporary home in Long Island City, Queens (the new complex has been christened MOMA QNS). In the afternoon, take time off to do some shopping (see Chapter 19 for recommended shopping neighborhoods), and then head to Greenwich Village (if you have the time, take a bus for some more sightseeing on the way). Stroll along the narrow streets for a feel of what New York looked like once upon a time; walk to the Hudson River and enjoy the newly completed riverside recreation area that stretches all the way from Chelsea Piers at 24th Street to Battery Park downtown (watch out for kamikaze cyclists and in-line skaters!). Have dinner at one of the charming restaurants in the Village or Chelsea (see Chapters 13, 14, and 15, and remember to make a reservation) and maybe plan a lively night at one of the famous New York nightspots or jazz clubs (see Chapter 23).

Day six

Start the day with a leisurely breakfast or brunch at one of the big hotels or some other nice restaurant (see Chapter 15) — you've earned it! On your last day, do what New Yorkers do and wander the city, soaking up its various pleasures. (Hint: Wear comfortable shoes!) After breakfast, head to SoHo for a walk among the famous cast-iron buildings and do some boutique shopping if you feel like it (or window-shopping if you don't). Next, turn north to Union Square (on Monday, Wednesday, Friday, or Saturday, wander through the Farmers Market) and the Flatiron District. Continue west to Chelsea, taking time to visit some of the area's many art galleries. Or you can make your way back south and east for a look at the East Village. After all that walking, you'll no doubt need to kick back at one of the many cafes or bars in the area. Plan to have dinner at one of the many highly regarded restaurants in this part of town — and do something special for the night to say a proper good-bye to the city that never sleeps!

New York for Museum Mavens

This one-day itinerary works on any day of the week except Monday, when the Met is closed.

After breakfast, start at the Metropolitan Museum of Art. Plan to arrive at the museum around opening time (9:30 a.m.) to avoid the crowds. Give yourself a minimum of two hours for your visit.

Then walk up Museum Mile to the Guggenheim Museum. If you feel up to it, go in and visit; if you're a little tired, just look at this unique building from the outside and from just within the entrance.

Have a bite to eat in the area or walk south along the park to the Whitney Museum and lunch at Sarabeth's Restaurant (inside the museum) before viewing the art (see Chapter 17). Allow a minimum of one hour to visit the museum.

End the day with a trip to the Frick Collection. Alternatively, pick another of the museums listed in Chapter 17 or check out some galleries on 57th Street to see what newer artists are doing. If you're truly dedicated, you can try to make it to west Chelsea in time to hit the galleries there and then eat at one of the innumerable restaurants nearby.

New York for Families with Kids

Start the morning at the Metropolitan Museum of Art; the Egyptian Wing and medieval weapons are often hits with kids. (Remember that the museum is closed on Mondays.) Plan to be at the Met for at least two hours.

Then take a leisurely stroll in Central Park to release pent-up fidgeting; your little ones will welcome the breath of fresh air. Head southwest, passing by the obelisk and the lake. Have a picnic lunch in the park — if you had time to get some sandwiches — or go to the Boathouse Cafe, right on the lake (see Chapter 14).

After lunch, head to the American Museum of Natural History. Almost directly across the park from the Met and within walking distance from wherever you had lunch, this very interesting museum is great for both adults and kids (toddlers may be too young to appreciate it). Plan to spend at least two hours for the visit. If you have toddlers, you might choose the Children's Museum instead. If you've tired of museums, take a cab, bus, or subway to Pier 83 on the Hudson River and catch a three-hour cruise on the Circle Line (see Chapter 18).

At dusk, head for Times Square and stay there until just after dark to get the full effect of the neon. You're now in a prime spot for a great dinner. For food, choose something on Restaurant Row (see Chapter 13) or one of the many other restaurants in the area (see Chapters 14 and 15). You're in the Theater District, which presents you with the perfect opportunity to see a show, depending on how tired you and your children are. "But what if we didn't plan ahead?" you ask. Well, you're close to the TKTS booth, where you can get last-minute discount tickets (see Chapter 21). Take your kids to see *The Lion King* or some other child-friendly show in the revamped Times Square.

New York for the Lazy

The idea of trying to see a mega-city like New York in just a few days may overwhelm you. Just flipping through the 100,000 baseball cards at the Metropolitan Museum of Art can take days! So here's a good way to spend your day.

Get up in the morning and catch a late breakfast special (see Chapter 15 for recommendations). After you eat, you'll need a walk to digest. How about strolling inside the Metropolitan Museum of Art for an hour or two? Afterward, walk through Central Park, and when you reach the upper west side, take a subway or bus (you'll see more from the bus) to Greenwich Village and have a late lunch. From there, walk due west until you reach the Hudson River; walk south along the riverside park toward Battery Park (in nice weather, you can even stop at one of the many benches or patches of grass and read for a while). Even at a lazy pace, you should make it to the Staten Island ferry in time to see the harbor and the Statue of Liberty at sunset.

Later, you can think about getting same-day tickets for a Broadway show or have a leisurely dinner downtown and then catch the 10 p.m. set at a jazz club in the Village.

Organizing Your Time

Budgeting your time is the key to any successful trip, but it's often difficult to do: Things always take longer than you expect. Remember that an average sight takes two hours to visit. Some (Ellis Island/the Statue of Liberty) take more; others (the Chrysler Building, St. Patrick's Cathedral) take less. To that, you have to add commuting time as well as time to eat and rest. Therefore, you can do about three or four sights in a day if you're pushing yourself, and fewer if you're not.

Have a clear picture in your mind of which attractions you absolutely don't want to miss (use Chapters 16 and 17 to make a list if you want) and which ones you would like to see if you have time but are willing to skip if you must. Write down your top choices on the worksheet at the back of this book.

To make sure that you have reasonable expectations for your trip, count all the must-sees in your list and then divide by the number of full days in your trip. If the result is a number larger than four, your lineup is probably too ambitious. You'll have to choose one of two strategies: Cut down on your choices or opt for a more superficial visit — the touch-and-go (or bump-and-run) approach. The third option is to lengthen your stay, but doing so may be impossible for reasons of budget or time. Remember, you can always come back!

After you finalize your list of must-see attractions, use the maps in this book to locate them. You may discover that they are all in one area of town or are easy to reach from a specific neighborhood. If that's the case, choose a hotel in that area to cut down on commuting time.

When planning your day, try to find clusters of activities that naturally group together. Avoid the "Ricochet Rabbit" approach to sightseeing (United Nations — Intrepid Museum — Empire State Building, for example, which has you crisscrossing the city three times for three activities!). Don't let the city's layout trick you into thinking only vertically, either: You can see the Met in the morning and then visit Central Park on the way across to the Children's Museum on the upper west side.

Also, don't forget the season. It's always good to have a Plan B in case it rains. The weather also will partly determine how much walking you can do (or want to do).

Remember to take the sun into account when making plans, too: For example, Times Square's lights are best seen at night, but night comes at around 5 p.m. in the winter and at 9 p.m. in summer.

If you want to dine at specific places, allow yourself the time for a truly pleasurable experience. You don't want to go through the trouble of getting a reservation at one of the top restaurants in New York and then have to cram your meal into one hour because you have to run off to somewhere else.

If you want to enjoy the city's inexhaustible nightlife, you'll probably want a little downtime between the end of your sightseeing day and the beginning of your evening's activities. Try to head back to your hotel to curl up with a glass of wine or a novel for an hour, or maybe catch a quick snooze to recharge your batteries. This plan also enables you to think about your evening as a separate mini-itinerary rather than something tacked on to the day's activities. Plan a separate nighttime excursion from your hotel and hit the town refreshed and decked out in your evening best.

Part VI

Living It Up after the Sun Goes Down: New York Nightlife

The 5th Wave   By Rich Tennant

"It's a play in 2 Acts. The middle Act is about to start now."

In this part . . .

New York at night is like New York during the day — there are too many things to do to take it all in. No other city in the world can rival it for nightlife.

New York's most famous cultural attraction is Broadway. In Chapter 21, you can find specific information about Broadway and off-Broadway theater and how to get tickets at a discount. In Chapter 22, we describe the best venues for the performing arts, and in Chapter 23, you can find every kind (or most every kind) of club and bar.

Chapter 21

The Play's the Thing: The New York Theater Scene

*N*ew York City is perhaps the most famous theater town in the world. We strongly believe that taking in a show is an essential New York experience — whether you line up for a long-running Broadway favorite or stumble upon the Next Big Thing at a small, out-of-the-way theater. In this chapter, we tell you everything you need to know to make seeing a show the evening-to-remember that it should be.

Getting the Inside Scoop

Although we always refer to Broadway when talking about the theater, theaters technically are divided into three categories — Broadway, off-Broadway, and off-off-Broadway — and it has nothing to do with their location. An off-Broadway theater can be on Broadway, for example. It's true that the majority of theaters are clustered in the famous Theater District (see the map called "The Theater District") along Broadway just north of Times Square. However, the categories refer to a series of characteristics — such as size of the theater — that contribute to each theater's classification. Among other things, tickets to off- and off-off-Broadway theaters are less expensive. The quality of the performance, though, is not an issue, because you see many excellent performances in off-off-Broadway theaters (and, to be honest, a few stinkers on Broadway as well).

Shows that are still going strong

Broadway doesn't hold a monopoly on popular long-running shows. *The Fantasticks,* which opened in 1960 and is the longest-running musical in theater history, is still playing at the Sullivan Street Theater in the Village. *The Perfect Murder,* the longest-running off-Broadway play still around, is at the Duffy Theater, at Broadway and 53rd Street.

Broadway

Broadway is where you find the blockbuster shows that tend to run for quite a while, such as *The Lion King*, which is going strong and probably will be for a long time. Current popular shows are *Aida,* the pop version of an opera classic with music by Elton John; *The Producers,* a Mel Brooks musical comedy; and *Mamma Mia!,* with songs by Abba (if you can remember back that far). Long-standing favorites, such as *Phantom of the Opera, Les Misérables,* and *Rent,* may still be playing when you get here (and long after we're all dead, probably). On the other hand, *Cats* finally closed after a long, record-breaking run.

Broadway (nicknamed the Great White Way for the thousands of twinkling lights that line the marquees) is also home to big revivals; the past few years have seen the resurgence of *42nd Street, The Music Man,* and, currently, *Oklahoma!* For something in the "Where do they come up with this stuff?" category, there's the musical *Urinetown,* a half-serious spoof set in a future in which drought has led the government to infringe on the people's right "to go."

Off-Broadway and off-off-Broadway

The cost of producing a Broadway show has become astronomical. Off-Broadway and off-off-Broadway shows tend to be less glitzy than their Broadway counterparts — and therefore cheaper. Because of their lower costs, these shows can afford to be a little more experimental and cutting-edge with productions and themes.

Examples of off-Broadway and off-off-Broadway productions include one-man or one-woman shows and performance-art shows like *Blue Man Group: Tubes* (in which men covered in blue body paint pound percussion instruments and try to, er, wrap the audience in toilet paper). You also can see new twists on old themes, such as the shows put on by the New York Shakespeare Festival at the Public Theater.

The Theater District

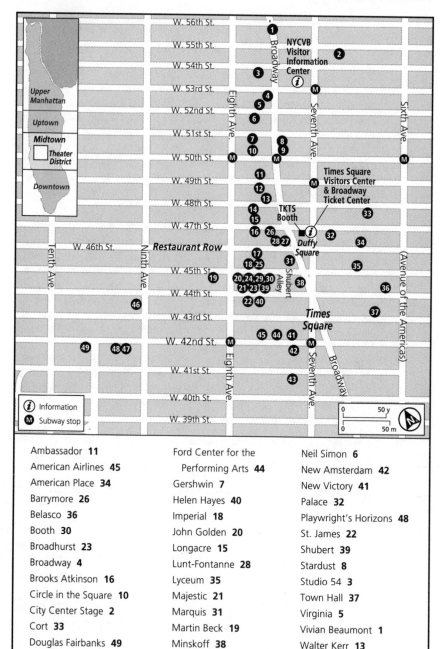

Ambassador **11**

American Airlines **45**

American Place **34**

Barrymore **26**

Belasco **36**

Booth **30**

Broadhurst **23**

Broadway **4**

Brooks Atkinson **16**

Circle in the Square **10**

City Center Stage **2**

Cort **33**

Douglas Fairbanks **49**

Duffy **27**

Ethel Barrymore **14**

Eugene O'Neill **12**

Ford Center for the
  Performing Arts **44**

Gershwin **7**

Helen Hayes **40**

Imperial **18**

John Golden **20**

Longacre **15**

Lunt-Fontanne **28**

Lyceum **35**

Majestic **21**

Marquis **31**

Martin Beck **19**

Minskoff **38**

Mitzi E. Newhouse **1**

Music Box **25**

Nederlander **43**

Neil Simon **6**

New Amsterdam **42**

New Victory **41**

Palace **32**

Playwright's Horizons **48**

St. James **22**

Shubert **39**

Stardust **8**

Studio 54 **3**

Town Hall **37**

Virginia **5**

Vivian Beaumont **1**

Walter Kerr **13**

WestSide **46**

Winter Garden **9**

Culture for free: Shakespeare in Central Park

Of all the things to love about summer in New York — baseball, Italian ices, street fairs, sidewalk cafes — few are as beloved and sought after as the Public Theater's annual free performances of Shakespeare in Central Park. Shakespeare in the Park began in 1957, when the late Joseph Papp, then director of the Public Theater, erected a portable stage in the park and invited people to watch the performances for free. He intended to conduct a "Shakespeare marathon," staging two plays every summer until he had completed every one of Shakespeare's plays. By 1962, the open-air Delacorte Theater had been constructed, and over the years Shakespeare in the Park became one of the most desirable tickets in town. (The performances are free, but tickets are handed out for admission.)

The company finished working its way through the Bard's plays years ago (Papp didn't live to see it; he died in 1991). These days, at least one of the summer's two plays is by Shakespeare, and the other is authored by another well-known dramatist. Each of the two productions runs for about four weeks and often boasts big-name stars, which makes tickets harder than usual to obtain. (In years past, Morgan Freeman and Tracey Ullman have starred in *Taming of the Shrew,* Raul Julia in *Othello,* and Patrick Stewart in *The Tempest,* which later graduated to a successful Broadway run.) The roughly 1,800 tickets are distributed at the theater on a first-come, first-served basis (only two per person), starting at 1 p.m. on the day of the performance. But keep in mind that people start lining up at least two or three hours in advance, so bring a book or some refreshments and be prepared to wait. Tickets are also available between 1 p.m. and 3 p.m. on the day of the performance at the Public Theater, 425 Lafayette St., between Astor Place and East 4th Street in the East Village (the lines get long here, too).

For more information about Shakespeare in the Park, contact the Public Theater (☎ 212-539-8750; Internet: www.publictheater.org), or call the Delacorte at ☎ 212-861-7277.

There's a huge market for these productions off the Great White Way; you see advertisements for them right next to those for Broadway shows in newspapers and magazines. You also can call the following theaters, known for their "off" productions, to check their offerings:

✔ **Actors Playhouse,** 100 Seventh Ave. South (☎ 212-463-0060)

✔ **Duffy Theater,** 1553 Broadway (☎ 212-695-3401)

✔ **LaMama E.T.C.,** 74A E. 4th St. (☎ 212-475-7710)

✔ **Manhattan Theatre Club,** at City Center, 131 W. 55th St. (☎ 212-581-1212)

  ✔ **Mitzi E. Newhouse Theatre,** in Lincoln Center, 150 W. 65th St.
    (☎ 212-239-6200)

  ✔ **New York Theatre Workshop,** 79 E. 4th St. (☎ 212-460-5475)

  ✔ **Orpheum Theatre,** Second Avenue at 8th Street (☎ 212-477-2477)

  ✔ **The Public Theater,** 425 Lafayette St. (☎ 212-260-2400)

Many of the theaters mentioned in this section are shown on the maps
in Chapter 23.

Finding Out What's On

A little research can get you an array of information and reviews of current shows. The *New York Times* is a good source for the scoop on big
theater shows; the *Village Voice* and *New York Press* are strong on alternative culture. The listings in *New York* magazine, the *New Yorker,* and
Time Out New York regularly offer information about both mainstream
shows and those that are off the beaten path. The following Web sites
also offer valuable theater information:

  ✔ **Applause:** www.applause-tickets.com

  ✔ **CitySearch New York:** www.newyork.citysearch.com

  ✔ **NYC & Company:** www.nycvisit.com

  ✔ **The Paperless Guide to New York City:** www.mediabridge.com

  ✔ **Ticketmaster:** www.ticketmaster.com

  ✔ **TKTS Sidewalk:** www.newyork.sidewalk.com

To get information by phone, call **Broadway Line** (☎ 888-BROADWAY
or 212-302-4111) and the **Off Broadway Theater Information Center**
(☎ 212-575-1423), the two official theater resources in New York. You
also can call **NYC/On Stage** (☎ 212-768-1818) or **NYC & Company**
(☎ 800-NYC-VISIT).

Kids like theater, too

Many long-running performances appeal especially to kids. These include off-
Broadway productions like **The Fantasticks,** at the Sullivan Street Theater (181
Sullivan St.; ☎ 212-674-3838) and **Blue Man Group: Tubes** at the Astor Place
Theater (434 Lafayette St.; ☎ 212-254-4370). And don't forget favorite seasonal
events like **Radio City Music Hall Holiday Shows** (1260 Sixth Ave.; ☎ 212-247-7777)
and **The Nutcracker** at the New York State Theater in Lincoln Center (Broadway
and 64th Street; ☎ 212-870-5570) if you're in town at that time of year.

Getting Tickets

If you've already decided on a show to see before you leave for your trip, just have your credit card in hand and contact any of the following telephone ticket agencies (they charge a small fee for their services):

- **Applause:** Internet: www.applause-tickets.com; also offers discounts

- **Manhattan Concierge:** ☎ 800-NY-SHOWS or 212-239-2591; Internet: www.manhattanconcierge.com

- **Showtix:** ☎ 800-677-1164 or 212-517-4306

- **Tele-charge:** ☎ 800-432-7250 or 212-239-6200; Internet: www.telecharge.com

- **Ticketmaster:** ☎ 212-307-4100; Internet: www.ticketmaster.com

- **Tickets and Travel/Tickets Up Front USA:** ☎ 800-876-8497 or 317-633-6406

If you didn't buy your tickets in advance, you can buy same-day tickets at the following outlets:

- **TKTS** sells discounted (up to 50%) tickets as they become available from theaters. It has a booth in the Theater District (Broadway at 47th Street, open daily from 3:00 p.m. to 8:00 p.m., 10:00 a.m. to 2:00 p.m. on Wednesday and Saturday for matinees, and Sunday from 11:00 a.m. to 6:30 p.m.). As this book went to press, the booth downtown had been temporarily relocated to Pier 17 at South Street Seaport (open Monday through Saturday 11:00 a.m. to 6:00 p.m. and Saturday 11:00 a.m. to 3:30 p.m.; at this location only, matinee tickets must be purchased the day before the show). A permanent downtown booth at the Seaport on the corner of John and Front streets should be open by the time you read this. For the most up-to-date information, consult www.tkts.com. Before you go there, keep in mind that long lines are the norm, and there is no guarantee that you'll be able to get tickets for a specific show. Also note that tickets for a popular show may be available because the cast for that day changed, which is not the best option if you have your heart set on seeing a particular production or actor.

- For same-day advance tickets at regular prices for most shows, visit the two official booths run by the League of American Theaters and Producers: the **Broadway Ticket Center** inside the Times Square Visitors Center (Broadway at 46th Street; ☎ 888-BROADWAY or 212-302-4111; open daily 8 a.m. to 8 p.m.) and the **Off-Broadway Theater Information Center** (251 W. 45th St., between Broadway and Eighth Avenue; ☎ 212-575-1423; open Tuesday through Thursday 12 p.m. to 8 p.m., Friday and Saturday 12 p.m. to 10 p.m., Sunday and Monday 12 p.m. to 6 p.m.).

You also can get tickets after you arrive by calling one of the telephone services listed earlier in this chapter, by asking the concierge at your hotel, or by using one of the numerous ticket brokers, whose listings you can find in newspapers and in the phone book. By law, these brokers are only supposed to charge a $5 fee or a 10% commission, whichever is less. Ask about the fee up front, and go elsewhere if a broker charges more than the legal fee.

Another option is to call the box office of the theater where the show is playing to ask whether they have any tickets available, because they often do. Some long-running shows run special promotions, so it pays to inquire when you call. And around showtime, reserved tickets that weren't picked up may be up for grabs at the theater. As a last option, remember that a cheap way to get a seat is not to have one: Standing room is available at some theaters for about $20.

Note that phone numbers for theater box offices are sometimes hard to track down, because so many list the Ticketmaster or Tele-charge number as their "box-office number." You may need to visit the theater in person to speak to a box office representative.

Pre-Theater Dining

If you decide to dine before an evening show, plan to start dinner by 6 p.m. — and make a reservation to minimize unexpected delays. When you order, tell the waiter that you're going to the theater and need to be out by X time. Remember to factor travel time to the theater into your dining schedule, and don't forget that traffic tends to snarl in the Theater District as curtain time approaches.

Many of the restaurants we list in Chapters 13 and 14 offer special fixed-price pre-theater menus, so ask when you arrive at the restaurant if such a menu is available. Although the Times Square area is chock full of nationally known chain restaurants (Olive Garden, Applebee's, and the like), we strongly recommend that, in a town like New York with such a sterling culinary reputation, you consult our recommendations to seek out a more unique dining experience.

Making the Most of Your Theater Experience

We've compiled a few tips that will help you enjoy your theatergoing experience.

Getting the best seats

Not all seats in a theater are created equal. Some seats are located behind columns, others are way off to the side where you get a skewed perspective of the stage, and still others, like those in the balcony, are too far away from the show for you to see anything well. Of course, these seats are less expensive than good seats, but any money you save will probably cost you in enjoyment of the show.

When you call for tickets, ask for the best seats available. Try to get seats that face the stage directly, either in the orchestra or in the first row of each balcony. Have a plan of the theater in hand and ask the salesperson to describe the view from any proposed seat. (You can find seating charts for many Broadway theaters at www.broadway.com.)

Dressing appropriately

If you plan to attend the first night of a show, dress to the nines. On any other night, you can wear just about whatever you want. To be on the safe side, men should wear jackets and ties (although a dress shirt and khakis are just fine in the summer), and women can don any nice outfit they've been wanting to show off. If you're especially concerned, take a stroll at showtime around the theater you plan to visit and see what other patrons are wearing.

Observing the curtain ritual

Shows almost always start right on time, so plan ahead. Allow yourself enough time to get seated (there may be a line) and check your coat, if necessary. If you arrive late, the ushers may ask you to wait until the conclusion of the scene to be seated. Arriving at the theater half an hour before showtime should ensure that you'll be sitting pretty when the curtain rises.

Sizing up your seat

Theaters make their money by packing in as many ticket holders as possible. For that reason, seats in theaters tend to be narrow and close together. To make your seat as comfortable as possible, avoid wearing bulky clothes and check large handbags and coats.

Tipping

You don't need to tip the ushers who show you to your seats. However, if you get a drink from the bar at intermission, tip the bartender 10% to 15% of your bill.

Chapter 22

The Performing Arts

- -

In This Chapter

▶ Getting the lowdown on what to see and where

▶ Buying tickets

- -

A world leader in music of all kinds, as well as dance and other performing arts, New York offers an endless variety of shows and performances to keep you more than entertained during your visit. Read on to discover the possibilities.

For information about dance, opera, and other performing arts, including information about getting tickets, consult Chapter 21.

Venues That Break the Mold

The following two venues offer such a diverse range of entertainment, including opera, dance, and film, that they are practically a tour of the world of culture by themselves.

The Lincoln Center for the Performing Arts

This celebrated complex, shown in the "Lincoln Center" map, extends over four blocks on the upper west side. It hosts an extraordinary range of productions, from opera to film to dance to classical music, in the following performance spaces:

 ✔ **Metropolitan Opera House** (☎ 212-362-6000; Internet: www.metopera.org) is home to the Metropolitan Opera Company (see the "Opera" section later in this chapter) and the American Ballet Theater (see "Dance"). It also showcases visiting ballet performers from around the world.

 ✔ **Avery Fisher Hall** (☎ 212-721-6500) is the seat of the New York Philharmonic (see "Symphony and Other Classical Music" later in this chapter), but it also hosts many important seasonal musical events organized by Lincoln Center, such as Mostly Mozart, and concerts by the famed Juilliard School. Parts of the JVC Jazz Festival (☎ 212-501-1390), a 35-concert extravaganza that takes place all over the city, and Jazz at Lincoln Center (Internet: www.jazzatlincolncenter.org), headed by Wynton Marsalis, also have events here.

✔ **New York State Theater** is home to the New York City Opera (see "Opera") and the New York City Ballet (see "Dance").

✔ **Alice Tully Hall** (☎ 212-875-5000) hosts the Chamber Music Society of Lincoln Center (☎ 212-875-5788; Internet: www.chamberlinc.org). Jazz at Lincoln Center also holds events there, and other groups perform concerts as well.

✔ **Walter Reade Theater** (☎ 212-875-5600) is home to the Film Society of Lincoln Center (Internet: www.lct.org), which sponsors the New York Film Festival and other events.

✔ The **Juilliard School** hosts many concerts — mostly classical but not only — as well as other performances. The quality is excellent and the prices are very attractive — many concerts are free. The maximum charge for a ticket is about $15. Check the bulletin board in the hall, or call ☎ 212-769-7406 (Internet: www.juilliard.org) for current productions. The school also sponsors many free outdoor concerts in summer.

✔ **Vivian Beaumont Theater** (☎ 212-362-7600) — the city's northernmost Broadway theater — shares a building with **Mitzi E. Newhouse Theater,** an important off-Broadway establishment. They host a variety of shows. Together they form the Lincoln Center Theater (Internet: www.lct.org).

The Center also has two outdoor spaces — a central plaza with a huge fountain and Damrosch Park toward the back. In summer, the outdoor spaces host some great series, such as Midsummer Night's Swing in July and Lincoln Center Out-of-Doors in August, as well as many free concerts. Summer is the season of special series indoors, too — such as the JVC Jazz Festival, Mostly Mozart, and the Lincoln Center Festival — because it is the resident companies' time off.

To get the Center's calendar, check its Web site at www.lincolncenter.org, which also has links to each of the companies and organizations that belong to the Center. You also can send a self-addressed stamped envelope (or a label and a stamp) to **Lincoln Center Calendar,** 70 Lincoln Center Plaza, New York, NY 10023-6583, or call ☎ 212-546-2656 for information about the current shows.

If you want to use public transportation to get to the Center, take the 1/2 train to the 66th Street/Lincoln Center stop, or take one of the following buses: M104 (running east/west on 42nd Street, north on Sixth Avenue, and south on Broadway), M5 and M7 (running up Sixth Avenue and Broadway), or M66 (across town running west on 67th Street).

Lincoln Center

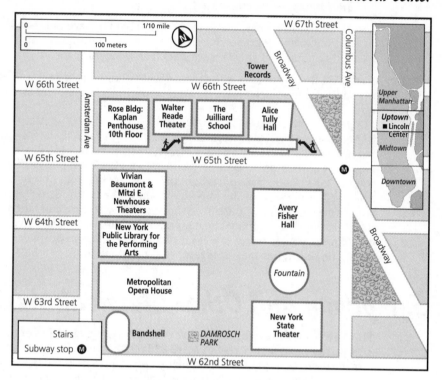

The Brooklyn Academy of Music (BAM)

Opened in 1859 as an opera house, the Brooklyn Academy of Music (known throughout the city simply as BAM) is the oldest still-operating performing arts center in the United States. Moved to its current location in 1907, BAM is the counterpart of Lincoln Center for contemporary performing arts. In its four main performance spaces, you can see some of the finest productions in the world, including opera, ballet, music, theater, and film.

Like Lincoln Center, BAM sponsors many special series, including the prestigious Next Wave Festival in the fall — a showcase for experimental American and international artists — and DanceAfrica in spring — a choice of productions with an African heritage, ranging from traditional to modern. BAM also sponsors three youth series during the year and free outdoor concerts in the summer throughout the city. Here are its venues:

✔ **BAM Café** presents live jazz and other innovative music on Fridays and Saturdays — with no cover charge!

✔ **BAM Majestic Theater** is the historical playhouse where theater performances are presented.

✔ **BAM Opera House,** home to the Brooklyn Philharmonic — more daring in its programs than its New York counterpart — also presents operas and special series such as DanceAfrica.

✔ **BAM Rose Cinemas** is the most recent addition; the four comfortable, large-screen movie theaters show independent and foreign films.

BAM (☎ 718-636-4100; Internet: www.bam.org) is at 30 Lafayette Ave. between Ashland Place and Felix Street; the BAM Majestic Theater is nearby at 651 Fulton St. between Ashland and Rockwell places. If you want to take public transportation, take the 2/4/5/Q train to the Atlantic Avenue stop or the M/N/R/W train to the Pacific Street stop. If you reserve tickets 24 hours in advance and pay $5, you can take the BAMbus from the Whitney Museum at Philip Morris, 120 Park Ave. at 42nd Street, which leaves one hour before scheduled performance time. The return bus makes several stops in Manhattan.

Symphony and Other Classical Music

The **New York Philharmonic** at Avery Fisher Hall in Lincoln Center, at Broadway and 64th Street (☎ 212-875-5030; Internet: www.ny philharmonic.org) offers what many consider to be the city's best concerts. Ticket prices range from less than $10 to $90.

With its reputation for hosting the crème-de-la-crème of visiting orchestras and soloists, plus its world-famous acoustics and the marvelous building itself, **Carnegie Hall,** at 57th Street and Seventh Avenue (☎ 212-247-7800; Internet: www.carnegiehall.org), is a gem in the crown of New York's music community. (You may recall the dusty old joke: Question: How do you get to Carnegie Hall? Answer: Practice, practice, practice . . . .) The price of a ticket depends on the performance; call or check the Web site for information.

The **Brooklyn Academy of Music** hosts performances of outstanding quality, some of them experimental or cutting edge. Don't let the location of this famed venue dissuade you from going to one of its shows — it's quite easy to reach. See the section "The Brooklyn Academy of Music (BAM)" earlier in this chapter for specifics.

The **World Music Institute** promotes the music of many cultures by sponsoring concerts at various venues throughout the city at least once a week. For a schedule of events, call ☎ 212-545-7536.

Opera

The **Metropolitan Opera Company,** housed at the Metropolitan Opera House at Lincoln Center, Broadway and 64th Street (☎ 212-362-6000; Internet: www.metopera.org), stages classic operas and is the world's premier opera company today. The sets are works of art, and the performers among the most famous in the world. Ticket prices range from $25 to $275.

The **New York City Opera,** in the New York State Theater at Lincoln Center, Broadway and 64th Street (☎ 212-870-5570; Internet: www.nycopera.com), stages less elaborate shows (but from the same classic repertoire) than the Metropolitan Opera Company, with lower ticket prices — seats range in price from $22 to $95.

Performances of the **Amato Opera Company,** 319 Bowery at 2nd Street (☎ 212-228-8200; Internet: www.amato.org), are likely to sell out quickly; the theater has only 100 seats, with an average ticket price of $20. Buy your tickets at least three weeks in advance to catch one of its performances of classic Italian and other opera.

Last but not least, **BAM Opera House** [home to the Brooklyn Philharmonic; see the section "The Brooklyn Academy of Music (BAM) for more information] presents innovative programs of the highest quality. Its specialty is contemporary opera.

Dance

The **New York City Ballet** (☎ 212-870-5570; Internet: www.nycballet.com) performs at the New York State Theater, sharing this space with the New York City Opera (see the preceding section). The leading dance company in the world, it presents wonderfully staged productions featuring world-class dancers. New works of choreography use both classical and modern music. *The Nutcracker* is a highlight of the Christmas season.

The **American Ballet Theater** (☎ 212-362-6000; Internet: www.abt.org) performs at the Metropolitan Opera House and shares its space with the Metropolitan Opera (see the preceding section). The guest companies and dancers are of international renown in the world of dance.

City Center, 131 W. 55th St. between Sixth and Seventh avenues (☎ 212-581-1212; Internet: www.citycenter.org), hosts premier companies such as the Alvin Ailey American Dance Theater, Twyla Tharp, and Martha Graham Company. Some of the world's leading choreographers have performed there.

The **Joyce Theater,** 175 Eighth Ave. at 19th Street (☎ 212-242-0800; Internet: www.joyce.org), boasts performances by the likes of the Erick Hawkins Dance Company and Meredith Monk.

Radio City Music Hall, 1260 Sixth Ave. at 50th Street (☎ 212-247-4777), is home to a longstanding tradition in New York that is popular with children of all ages and needs no introduction: the Rockettes. You can even take a Stage Door Tour guided by one of the famed leggy beauties!

Other Major Concert Spaces

For live music of a more contemporary variety, you have a choice of venues. (For information about other places to hear live music, see Chapter 23.)

- ✔ **Radio City Music Hall** (see the preceding section) has hosted artists from crooner Tony Bennett to crossover salsa star Mark Anthony to retro '80s act Culture Club.

- ✔ **Madison Square Garden,** Seventh Avenue at 32nd Street (☎ 212-465-6741; Internet: www.thegarden.com), is where the biggies perform. If you can get by using only one name in the pop-music world (Madonna, Janet, Bruce, Mick), this is where you'll end up. Adjacent to the Garden is The Theater at Madison Square Garden, a smaller space that usually features popular but not cover-of-*People*-magazine-famous musical acts.

- ✔ **Town Hall,** 123 W. 43rd St. between Sixth and Seventh avenues (☎ 212-840-2824; Internet: www.the-townhall-nyc.org), is a lovely medium-sized theater that hosts a wide range of events — everything from world music to modern dance to one-man shows to live ensemble performances of Garrison Keillor's *Lake Wobegon* program.

- ✔ Harlem's legendary **Apollo Theater,** 253 W. 125th St. between Adam Clayton Powell and Frederick Douglass boulevards (☎ 212-749-5838), saw the birth of such musical legends of Ella Fitzgerald, Dinah Washington, and the Jackson Five. These days, a steady stream of hip-hop and R&B acts perform at this beautifully restored theater; Wednesday night is the famous (and infamously unforgiving) Amateur Night.

In summer, **Central Park** hosts a wide variety of (often free) concerts. Open-air classical music and opera comes courtesy of the New York Philharmonic and the Metropolitan Opera (see the listings earlier in this chapter). A more ambitious, eclectic group of pop, blues, world music, and performance artists — anyone from punk songster and poet Patti Smith to legendary '70s funkmaster George Clinton — appear thanks to **SummerStage,** at Rumsey Playfield near 72nd Street (☎ 212-360-2777; Internet: www.summerstage.org). Some performances are free, but donations are always gladly accepted; call or check the Web site for an up-to-date schedule of events.

Chapter 23

Hitting the Clubs and Bars

. . . .

In This Chapter

▶ Discovering live music and dance venues

▶ Downing some drinks

▶ Enjoying the city into the wee hours

. . . .

*N*ew York's entertainment scene isn't limited to opera, ballet, and the theater, of course. You can pass many happy hours in any of the places we mention in this chapter, which serve all different sorts of musical and social tastes.

Listening to All That Jazz

Jazz may not have been invented here, but New York's many clubs have certainly raised jazz to high art. One of the city's most famous jazz emporiums, **Blue Note,** 131 W. Third St. (☎ 212-475-8592), pays homage to the best in jazz with big-name acts (and high cover prices to match). Equal in fame is **The Village Vanguard,** 178 Seventh Ave. South at 11th Street (☎ 212-255-4037), which has a more intimate feeling but still features the top names in jazz.

The sounds of jazz aren't to be heard only in the Village. In Midtown, you find not one but two great places to hear jazz — the revived **Birdland,** 315 W. 44th St. between Eighth and Ninth avenues (☎ 212-581-3080; Internet: www.birdlandjazz.com), which is a big space that has lots of seating and room at the bar for a cheaper cover, and the new **Iridium Jazz Club,** 1650 Broadway at 51st Street (☎ 212-582-2121; Internet: www.iridiumjazzclub.com).

Up in Harlem is the renovated, rejuvenated Art Deco gem **Lenox Lounge,** 288 Malcolm X Blvd. (Lenox Avenue between 124th and 125th streets; ☎ 212-427-0253). The club's history includes past perform-ances by such artists as Billie Holliday and Dinah Washington; these days, it's once again an unforgettable place to hear vocal and instru-mental jazz.

If you want to hear jazz on the cheap, go to **Small's,** 183 W. 10th St. at Seventh Avenue South (☎ 212-929-7565). The cover charge is $10, no liquor is served, and the club opens at 10:30 and goes all night. The musicians are lesser known and the playing more variable. Across town, **Detour,** 349 E. 13th St. at First Avenue (☎ 212-533-6212; Internet: www.jazzatdetour.com), has opened, offering free (no cover charge) jazz every night. **The Knitting Factory** (see "Hearing Cutting-Edge Sounds," later in this chapter) also books major and minor jazz artists in its ever-changing, ongoing exploration of music's frontiers.

Enjoying Rock and the Blues

Anyone can get the blues in Manhattan's venerable blues clubs. What better place to hear blues greats than the **B. B. King Blues Club & Grill,** 237 W. 42nd St. between Seventh and Eighth avenues (☎ 212-997-4144; Internet: www.bbkingblues.com)? The club showcases a diverse bunch of acts besides blues, too. The stage at **The Bottom Line,** 15 W. Fourth St. at Mercer Street (☎ 212-502-3471), hosts occasional blues acts as well as many other kinds of music, including established rock bands. **Mercury Lounge,** 217 E. Houston St. at Essex Street (☎ 212-260-4700), also features name rock shows in an intimate setting. **Irving Plaza,** 17 Irving Plaza at 15th Street (☎ 212-777-1224), books acts ranging from the world-famous to the emerging, with a specialty somewhere in between.

If nothing at these places floats your musical boat, a glance at a copy of *Time Out New York* or the free weeklies *Village Voice* and *New York Press* will net you a bunch of other options. For other, larger venues, see Chapter 22.

Hearing Cutting-Edge Sounds

The Knitting Factory, 74 Leonard St., four blocks below Canal between Broadway and Church streets (☎ 212-219-3055; Internet: www.knitting factory.com), is a temple for those who like to experiment with music. Here you can hear work from an array of brilliant minds — cutting-edge rock 'n' roll, seriously far-out jazz, and music that defies categorization. The Factory has several bars and places to hang out, including the dark and cozy subterranean taproom where happy hour drinks are incredibly cheap.

CBGB, 315 Bowery at Bleecker Street (☎ 212-982-4052; Internet: www.cbgb.com), is a punk institution that presided over the birth of bands like the Ramones, Talking Heads, and Blondie. Current acts are appropriately alternative. It's loud and not so big, so get there early if you don't want to be straining to listen from the entranceway. Next door is **CB's 313 Gallery** (☎ 212-677-0455), a mellower space where you can listen to the music but still hear your companions speak.

Downtown Arts & Nightlife

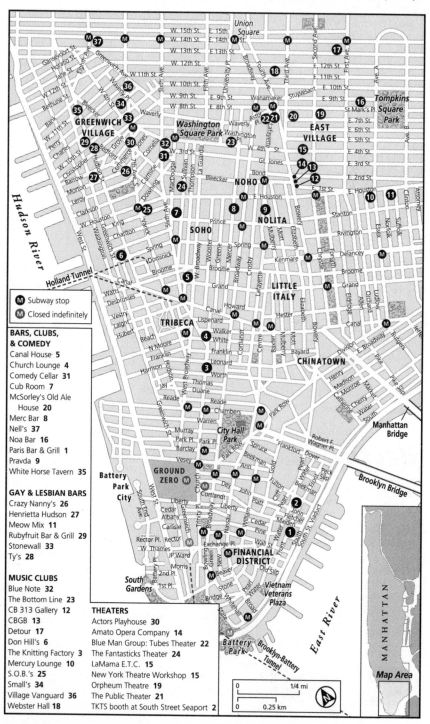

M Subway stop
M Closed indefinitely

BARS, CLUBS, & COMEDY
Canal House 5
Church Lounge 4
Comedy Cellar 31
Cub Room 7
McSorley's Old Ale House 20
Merc Bar 8
Nell's 37
Noa Bar 16
Paris Bar & Grill 1
Pravda 9
White Horse Tavern 35

GAY & LESBIAN BARS
Crazy Nanny's 26
Henrietta Hudson 27
Meow Mix 11
Rubyfruit Bar & Grill 29
Stonewall 33
Ty's 28

MUSIC CLUBS
Blue Note 32
The Bottom Line 23
CB 313 Gallery 12
CBGB 13
Detour 17
Don Hill's 6
The Knitting Factory 3
Mercury Lounge 10
S.O.B.'s 25
Small's 34
Village Vanguard 36
Webster Hall 18

THEATERS
Actors Playhouse 30
Amato Opera Company 14
Blue Man Group: Tubes Theater 22
The Fantasticks Theater 24
LaMama E.T.C. 15
New York Theatre Workshop 15
Orpheum Theatre 19
The Public Theater 21
TKTS booth at South Street Seaport 2

Midtown Arts & Nightlife

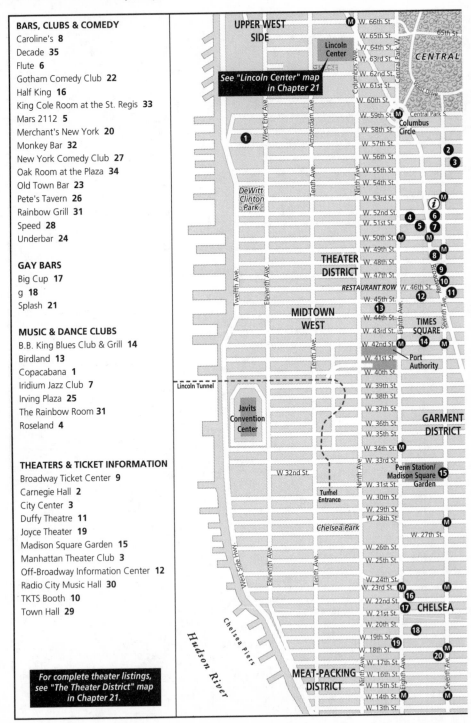

BARS, CLUBS & COMEDY
Caroline's **8**
Decade **35**
Flute **6**
Gotham Comedy Club **22**
Half King **16**
King Cole Room at the St. Regis **33**
Mars 2112 **5**
Merchant's New York **20**
Monkey Bar **32**
New York Comedy Club **27**
Oak Room at the Plaza **34**
Old Town Bar **23**
Pete's Tavern **26**
Rainbow Grill **31**
Speed **28**
Underbar **24**

GAY BARS
Big Cup **17**
g **18**
Splash **21**

MUSIC & DANCE CLUBS
B.B. King Blues Club & Grill **14**
Birdland **13**
Copacabana **1**
Iridium Jazz Club **7**
Irving Plaza **25**
The Rainbow Room **31**
Roseland **4**

THEATERS & TICKET INFORMATION
Broadway Ticket Center **9**
Carnegie Hall **2**
City Center **3**
Duffy Theatre **11**
Joyce Theater **19**
Madison Square Garden **15**
Manhattan Theater Club **3**
Off-Broadway Information Center **12**
Radio City Music Hall **30**
TKTS Booth **10**
Town Hall **29**

*For complete theater listings,
see "The Theater District" map
in Chapter 21.*

UPPER WEST SIDE

Lincoln Center

*See "Lincoln Center" map
in Chapter 21*

CENTRAL

Columbus Circle

THEATER DISTRICT

MIDTOWN WEST

RESTAURANT ROW

TIMES SQUARE

Port Authority

Lincoln Tunnel

Javits Convention Center

GARMENT DISTRICT

Penn Station/ Madison Square Garden

Tunnel Entrance

Chelsea Park

CHELSEA

Chelsea Piers

Hudson River

MEAT-PACKING DISTRICT

Uptown Arts & Nightlife

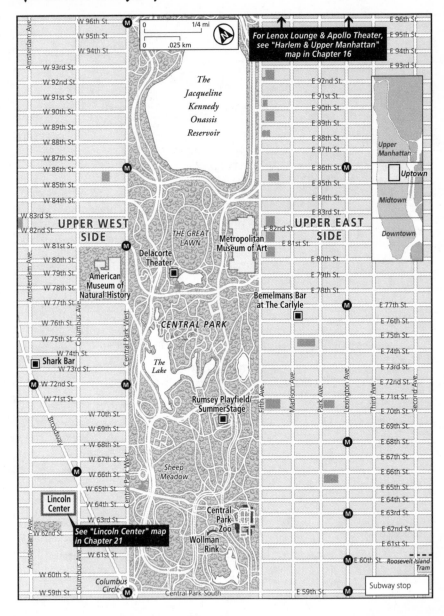

For Lenox Lounge & Apollo Theater, see "Harlem & Upper Manhattan" map in Chapter 16

See "Lincoln Center" map in Chapter 21

The East Village is the place for grinding chords and what may be tomorrow's hot young rock group. Look in the *Village Voice* or the *New York Press* for listings of clubs and bars featuring music.

Dancing the Night Away

If you're interested in the clubbing-all-night kind of dancing, see the "Hitting the Clubs and Getting Across the Velvet Rope" section later in this chapter.

Ballroom dancing is still alive in New York at **Roseland,** 239 W. 52nd St. (☎ **212-247-0200;** Internet: www.roselandballroom.com) — but just barely. Developers have eyed Roseland's enormous aged building for demolition/transformation for years, but for now, you can still ballroom dance there on Thursdays and Saturdays from 2:30 to 11 p.m. for the low cover charge of $11. But check in advance to see if dancing at Roseland is still alive and kicking when you get to New York.

Dancers will love this New York bargain: **Lincoln Center,** at Broadway and 64th Street (☎ **212-546-2656;** Internet: www.lincolncenter.org), offers free dance nights in July as part of its Midsummer Night's Swing series. A variety of dances and music are offered on different nights of the week, and if you need help getting started with the beat, you can go early for a free dance lesson.

If you're willing to shell out relatively big bucks, the **Rainbow Room** on the 65th Floor of Rockefeller Plaza, 49th Street between Fifth and Sixth avenues (☎ **212-632-5000**), offers the utmost in scenery and elegant dancing to a live band, which it sponsors only on selected nights. It's definitely a special occasion ($150 per person for a three-course dinner and all the dancing you want).

The swing craze may have died down, but many clubs still feature swing nights — check *Time Out New York,* the *Village Voice,* or the *New York Press* for listings. **Don Hill's,** 511 Greenwich St. at Spring Street (☎ **212-219-2850**), is an eclectic downtown nightspot that has been known to run a Wednesday night swing party with name bands.

Lovers of Latin dancing may want to check out **Copacabana,** 617 W. 57th St. between Eleventh and Twelfth avenues (☎ **212-582-2672**) — but call first because they may be holding their Latin nights off-site. **S.O.B's,** 204 Varick St. at West Houston Street (☎ **212-243-4940;** Internet: www.sobs.com), is a New York landmark. The name stands for Sounds of Brazil, and the club features musical from around the world, with a special emphasis on South American beats.

Pubbing from Place to Place

For a pint and a dose of Old World flavor, it doesn't get much better (or more crowded) than at **The Old Town Bar,** 45 E. 18th St. between Broadway and Park Avenue (☎ **212-529-6732**). The bar has been featured on film *(The Devil's Own)* and TV (the opening credits of Letterman in his NBC days); upstairs is a congenial space to eat that bans smoking. The ever-popular **Pete's Tavern,** 129 E. 18th St. at Irving Place (☎ 212-473-7676), opened during the Civil War and offers a cool, if often crowded, place to tip your glass. **McSorley's Old Ale House,** 15 E. 7th St. between Second and Third avenues (☎ 212-473-9148), has been in business since 1857, although women weren't allowed in the bar until 1970. McSorley's serves only two kinds of beer — light and dark — and the place vibrates with atmosphere. However, it's not the place to come on a weekend night, when it's overrun with loud, obnoxious college kids lined up halfway down the block for a chance to get in and get liquored up.

The **White Horse Tavern,** 567 Hudson St. at 11th Street (☎ 212-989-3856), is a famous ramshackle establishment whose wooden benches and tables were already well seasoned when the beat poets drank there. Its outdoor picnic tables are popular in summer. Downtown, you can go to **The Paris Bar & Grill,** 119 South St., along the East River one block north of Pier 17 (☎ 212-240-9899), for a true waterfront pub in the historical South Street Seaport.

A new entry in the pub crawl is **The Half King,** 505 W. 23rd St. (☎ 212-462-4300), a writerly hangout partly owned by Sebastian Junger, author of *The Perfect Storm.* It has an old pub atmosphere — the wood used inside came from a 200-year-old Pennsylvania barn — and typical pub food, as well as weekly evening readings by writers. The pub also features a gallery and a garden where you can sit in nice weather.

Savoring a Martini or Cocktail

Manhattan is home to so many other "watering holes" that it would be impossible to give even a complete sampling of these places, so here's a diverse list of suggestions.

For a young, sophisticated, and comfortable setting, try **Merchant's New York,** 112 Seventh Ave. at 17th Street (☎ 212-366-7267). If you just want a drink as an excuse to stare at other people, there's **Merc Bar,** 151 Mercer St. between Prince and Houston streets (☎ 212-966-2727; Internet: www.mercbar.com) in SoHo, where you can show off your looks, charm, and wardrobe. Also in SoHo is **Cub Room,** 131 Sullivan St. at Prince Street (☎ 212-677-4100). A beautifully designed and decorated space, the bar is often jammed with a hip and trendy crowd. If you want to head east, on the ever-changing St. Mark's Place is **Noa Bar,** 126 St. Mark's Place (☎ 212-979-6276), which has an interior like an East Village version of a Mexican hacienda. It's a wine-and-beer bar with inventive tapas to match.

A unique uptown joint is **Flute,** 205 W. 52nd St. between Seventh Avenue and Broadway (☎ 212-265-5169). The specialty is, you guessed it, champagne; the atmosphere is classy, and in the basement is a former speakeasy. **Shark Bar,** 307 Amsterdam Ave. between 74th and 75th streets (☎ 212-874-8500), has a reputation for hot music, good soul food, and a

A bar that's out of this world

Theme restaurants are usually considered mere burgers-and-memorabilia kinds of places. But for an otherworldly take on the concept, consider checking out **Mars 2112**, 1633 Broadway at 51st Street, lower level (☎ 212-582-2112). You take a simulated space ride before entering the restaurant (the idea being that you have to "travel" from Earth to Mars to get there), although there's a plain old door for the queasy or less adventurous. Don't plan to eat there (the food is typically mediocre sandwich-and-pasta fare), but the slice-of-Mars cocktail area (you have never *seen* so much red!) is cozy in a weird, kitschy way — the kind of place where you'd expect to see George Jetson stop in for a quick one on his way home from a hard day at Spacely Sprockets. Cozy up in a booth with the specialty drink of the house, called — no kidding — the Mars-tini.

"buppie" crowd. Another trendy bar scene is at **Monkey Bar** in the Hotel Elysée, 60 E. 54th St. between Madison and Park avenues (☎ 212-838-2600). Despite its name, the atmosphere is more glamorous than simian.

For a great view and a better cocktail, try **The Rainbow Grill,** 30 Rockefeller Plaza between 49th and 50th streets (☎ 212-632-5100) at Rockefeller Center. Dancing and dinner at the Rainbow Room next door (see the listing in the "Dancing the Night Away" section earlier in this chapter) is now a special event. Call for a schedule.

Don't forget to check out a few hotel bars for that intimate, insider, wood-paneled feeling. The **King Cole Room** at the Street Regis, 2 E. 55th St. at Fifth Avenue (☎ 212-339-6721), and the **Oak Room** at the Plaza, 768 Fifth Ave. at 59th Street (☎ 212-546-5330), are worth a visit just for the romantic setting. There are a few elegant new openings worth visiting as well, such as the **Bemelmans Bar** at the Carlyle, 35 E. 76th St. (☎ 212-744-1600); the **Underbar** at the W New York Union Square, 201 Park Ave. South (☎ 212-358-1560); the **Canal House** at the SoHo Grand, 310 W. Broadway (☎ 212-965-3000); and **Church Lounge,** the atrium bar and lounge at its sibling Tribeca Grand, 2 Avenue of the Americas (☎ 212-519-6600).

Searching Out Gay Clubs and Bars

Most gay nightspots are in the Village and Chelsea, but you can find others around town. The best places to find out about gay goings-on are the weeklies *Time Out New York* (www.timeoutny.com) and *Homo Xtra* (www.hx.com).

For men, **Stonewall**, 53 Christopher St. just east of Seventh Avenue South (☎ 212-463-0950), is a new place built on the site of the bar where the 1969 riots gave birth to the gay rights movement. **Ty's,** 114 Christopher St. at Bedford Street (☎ **212-741-9641**), is also legendary. In Chelsea, try **g,** 223 W. 19th St. between Seventh and Eighth avenues (☎ **212-929-1085**), a comfy, mellow lounge, or **Splash,** 50 W. 17th St. at Sixth Avenue (☎ **212-691-0073**), the place for drag queens, singalongs, and all-around campy fun. The coffeehouse **Big Cup,** 228 Eighth Ave. between 21st and 22nd streets (☎ **212-206-0059**), is a real neighborhood hangout populated with ultra-buff pretty boys.

For women, **Henrietta Hudson,** 438 Hudson St. at Morton Street (☎ **212-243-9079**), offers a good jukebox and a dance floor on which to enjoy it. **Crazy Nanny's,** 21 Seventh Ave. South at Leroy Street (☎ **212-366-6312**; Internet: www.crazynannys.com), is more footloose and very diverse. **Meow Mix,** 269 E. Houston St. at Suffolk Street (☎ **212-254-0688**), draws an alternative, bohemian crowd of ladies and often showcases live bands. For a more low-key evening, try **Rubyfruit Bar & Grill,** 531 Hudson St. between Charles and West 10th streets (☎ **212-929-3343**).

Some of the hottest "clubs" are actually traveling parties that alight in various spots depending on the day, making them hard for visitors to find. Gay publications — *Time Out New York, Homo Xtra,* and others we list in Chapter 4 — provide the best up-to-the-minute club information. Another good source is the Web; try the gay NYC site at www.gay center.org.

Hitting the Clubs and Getting Across the Velvet Rope

New York nightlife starts late and finishes *really* late. Things don't start happening until at least 11 p.m. Most places don't take credit cards, so bring cash. Cover charges can range from $5 to $30 and often increase in price as the night goes on. And as we mentioned in the gay and lesbian section earlier in this chapter, most of the most happening clubs and parties are "traveling" or "mobile" events that change venues from week to week. The best source for such information is the weekly *Time Out New York* magazine. It lists cover charges for the week's big events and gives sound advice on the type of music *and* the type of crowd each event attracts.

Some swanky, exclusive places actually put up a velvet rope to restrict access to those clubbers approved by a doorman. Don't drive yourself crazy trying to win over the bouncer. It helps to be polite, dress fashionably, and arrive early (think 9 p.m.), and then be willing to hang out at a mostly empty club until the action heats up. Ultimately, it's a crap shoot no matter how great you look (unless you happen to be with

Mick Jagger or Calvin Klein). Hence, even our friend who built the beautiful Soviet-era interior of **Pravda,** 281 Lafayette between Prince and Houston Streets (☎ 212-226-4696), might get turned away at the door.

Some places offer a good chance at getting in, including **Decade,** 1117 First Ave. at 61st Street (☎ 212-835-5979), an all-night dance and supper club for the 30-and-over set. **Nell's,** 246 W. 14th St. between Seventh and Eighth avenues (☎ 212-675-1567; Internet: www.nells. com), is famous for its lounging-around couches and a comfortable melting-pot atmosphere. **Speed,** 20 W. 39th St. between Fifth and Sixth avenues (☎ 212-719-9867), is an enormous space with one unusual item: a rooftop deck that's open in summer.

Your one-stop shopping for New York nightlife (with all the pluses and minuses implied in that phrase) is undoubtedly **Webster Hall,** 125 E. 11th St. between Third and Fourth avenues (☎ 212-353-1600; Internet: www.webster-hall.com). This cavernous club has six separate lounges (meaning music to satisfy myriad tastes), a pool hall, a tarot card reader, several different deejays, and the occasional live band.

Laughing It Up at Comedy Clubs

The big names in comedy tickle your funny bone at **Caroline's,** 1626 Broadway between 49th and 50th streets (☎ 212-757-4100; Internet: www.carolines.com). Make sure to ask about the cover charge when you call for reservations — it can vary greatly depending who's onstage that night. **Gotham Comedy Club,** 34 W. 22nd St. between Fifth and Sixth avenues (☎ 212-367-9000; Internet: www.gothamcomedy club.com), has a less frenetic and more thoughtful vibe; writers for talk-show host Conan O'Brien often come here to try out new material.

Two other comedy clubs offer great value for the money: **The Comedy Cellar,** 117 MacDougal St. between Bleecker and West Third streets (☎ 212-254-3480; Internet: www.comedycellar.com), often advertises free-drink coupons and other special offers on its Web site; the cover charge at **New York Comedy Club,** 241 E. 24th St. between Second and Third avenues (☎ 212-696-5233; Internet: www.newyorkcomedyclub. com), ranges from only $7 on weeknights to $10 on weekends. (Are you brave enough for Open Mike Night?)

Part VII
The Part of Tens

The 5th Wave
By Rich Tennant

"Unfortunately, on me, Giorgio Armani clothes take on a certain Lou Costello quality."

In this part . . .

These two chapters are *For Dummies* Top Ten lists, covering in brief paragraphs New York's bests, worsts, and lesser-known charms. From where to spend your Sunday (or holiday) to how to blend in with the locals, this indispensable information will help you make the most of what New York has to offer while avoiding its most noxious annoyances.

Chapter 24

The Top Ten New York Experiences

*N*ew Yorkers may complain about their city, but they remain incredibly fond and proud of it. In the wake of September 11, many residents have rediscovered ways to absorb the spirit of the city they love. This chapter talks about some of the experiences they explore time and again — the activities and pastimes that represent the city's essence.

Spending Sunday in Central Park

Central Park is the green heart of New York City, and many people come to enjoy their patch of nature on weekends. The park swarms with families barbecuing, children playing, businessmen inline skating, and people reading and even celebrating birthdays, weddings, and other special events. Amateur baseball leagues use the diamond here. Tennis players line up to use the courts. Spring and summer are the seasons of choice, of course, but people enjoy the park even in the dead of winter, when snow and ice transform it into a fairy world.

Going Out for Dinner

New Yorkers are crazy about gourmet and exotic food (as we explain in Chapter 13); dining out has become almost a sport. Sample the listings in Part IV, and try those restaurants recommended in the weekly reviews in the *New York Times, Time Out New York* magazine, or the two free papers distributed around the city: *New York Press* and *The Village Voice*. Any day of the week is good for the hunt; don't expect many quiet nights.

Shopping in Chinatown

Chinatown is the largest marketplace in New York, and the neighborhood teems with activity. Canal Street, from the Manhattan Bridge to Seventh Avenue, is lined with stall shops and sidewalk displays; vendors sell T-shirts, souvenirs, fresh fish, veggies, gold, Chinese pottery, and, it must be said, a good bit of counterfeit and fake merchandise (handbags, sunglasses, and watches, primarily). Prices are good ($15 for a "Roleks" watch), and you have the added thrill of the unexpected. For more on Chinatown, see Chapter 19.

On weekends, the crowds in Chinatown can be maddening — beware the pickpockets who thrive in those crowds.

Taking in a Play

Theater is serious fun. No other city in the United States offers the sheer variety that New York does — you'll come across everything from the latest musical smash to an off-Broadway revival of a classic musical or play to a bunch of guys in blue face paint who beat drums, splatter paint, and wrap the audience in toilet paper (we're not making this stuff up). Line up at TKTS for discount tickets, or follow some of the other tips we give you in Chapter 21 to score the best seats for the most interesting shows.

Exploring the Met

The Metropolitan Museum is a New York institution in more ways than one. The Met's collection is so huge that it's impossible to imagine ever seeing it all. That's why we keep going back. Stay for a couple of hours, see a section or a special exhibit, and then, if the weather is good, take a stroll in the park just behind the museum. Try going on a Friday or Saturday evening, when the museum's open until 9 p.m.

Riding the Staten Island Ferry

You can't get a free ride in many places in New York, but you can on the Staten Island Ferry. Join the hundreds commuting back home to Staten Island (just like Melanie Griffith in the 1988 movie *Working Girl*) and take the half-hour ferry trip that gives you an up-close-and-personal view of the Statue of Liberty and New York Harbor. If you can catch one of the older-model ferries, you'll get lots of open-air deck space and more sweeping views. When you get to the Staten Island side, stay on the boat for the ride back to Manhattan. The return trip is a chance to see just how radically the destruction of the Twin Towers has altered New York's skyline.

Seeing the Department-Store Windows at Christmastime

Shopping is a classic New York pastime, but at Christmastime it becomes a magical (if jam-packed) experience. Department stores spare no expense in decorating their display windows, and hundreds line up to take a gander at the fanciful holiday creations at Saks Fifth Avenue, Lord & Taylor, Macy's, Bergdorf Goodman, and Barney's New York, to name a few. The crowds tend to be heaviest at Saks, given its location opposite the Christmas tree at Rockefeller Center, and the windows at Barney's are generally the most stylistically eccentric.

Clubbing

Hip New York crowds love to see and be seen. Each group has its own meeting grounds — gay people in Chelsea and the West Village, film people in the Flatiron District and TriBeCa, fashion people around Union Square and SoHo, and artists in the Village. Meet and mingle at the clubs and cafes (see Chapter 23 for recommendations).

Enjoying Outdoor Entertainment

During the summer, New York offers outdoor shows of every kind (see Chapter 2 for the most important). You can join the locals at SummerStage in Central Park and at free concerts all around town. Or take dance lessons at the outdoor stage in Lincoln Center by the fountain. And every Monday night, Bryant Park turns into one big drive-in, but without the cars — people come bearing picnics to watch classic movies on a giant screen under the stars. For more information about outdoor nightlife, see Chapters 21 and 22.

Window-Shopping and People-Watching along Fifth Avenue

Fifth Avenue is busy and sometimes too much to take, thanks to the crowds that congregate at the Empire State Building and Rockefeller Center. But hey, what says New York more than a big crowd? Browse the windows of expensive shops (from 42nd to 59th streets), visit the top New York galleries (from 70th to 90th streets), and admire the people all along the avenue. You get a refreshing bath of sensations — artistic, fashionable, and surprising.

Chapter 25

Ten Ways to Start a Conversation with a New Yorker

. . . .

In This Chapter

▶ Soliciting opinions large and small

▶ Spotting celebrities and scrutinizing sports stars

▶ Getting the inside scoop on pizza and the perfect apartment

. . . .

*O*pinions — everybody's got 'em, and New Yorkers have 'em in spades. If you want to find out what makes this city tick, get the story straight from the mouths of those who make it happen. Ask one of these simple questions and open a window on life in this big, loud, crazy city that we all love.

What's the Best Way to Get to . . . ?

If you want to start a spirited dialogue that's sure to suck people in off the street, all you have to do is ask for directions. Everyone in this city is convinced that he knows the fastest way from Point A to Point B — and he can debate the issue until the cows come home. City folk are even fond of philosophical subway pronouncements like, "The V [train] is the new G [train]" — whatever that means. This is one of the easiest ways to start a conversation with a local, and despite New York's long-standing (and unfair) reputation as a hostile, unfriendly place, most people are more than happy to slip you some insider info and point you in the right direction. We're not unfriendly; we're just in a hurry.

Mets or Yankees?

Ah, the eternal baseball question. The legendary Babe Ruth, Joe DiMaggio, and Lou Gehrig or the scrappy, never-say-die Amazin's? These days, the question is more like, "Who's a better player, Mike Piazza or Jason Giambi? And just how big of a hunk *is* Derek Jeter, anyway?" (Yep, he sure is a cutie.) New Yorkers tend to be polarized about their favorite sports teams — you won't find many indifferent opinions in these parts. For more on seeing New York baseball (and other pro sports) in person, see Chapter 17.

Mayor Mike: How's He Doing?

Until September 10, 2001, former Mayor Rudolph Giuliani was a strangely schizophrenic figure; his administration was marked both by the city's return to stratospheric prosperity and by his own seemingly out-of-left-field crusades (boycotting controversial but utterly marginal art exhibits and publicly attacking ferret owners on his call-in radio show, for example). But in the aftermath of the World Trade Center attacks, Giuliani's grave yet calming presence at Ground Zero pulled the city, and the country, together. And he finished his term a hero.

On New Year's Day 2002, another man arrived at City Hall to follow in those giant footsteps — millionaire media mogul Michael Bloomberg, suddenly the city's most eligible bachelor (he's divorced). Not as charismatic or as brash as Rudy, "Mayor Mike" is developing a reputation as a consensus builder and a fast learner (for a guy who has never before held political office, that's probably a good thing). It's still early in his administration, but that doesn't stop local residents from chiming in with their two cents about his performance to date.

Ground Zero: Rebuild or Erect a Memorial?

Ground Zero is a painful subject, one that everyone in the city grapples with: How best to memorialize the thousands who lost their lives in the World Trade Center attacks? Rebuild the Twin Towers in defiance to terrorists everywhere or turn the site into a place of peace and remembrance? As this book went to press, the city was holding hearings to solicit ideas for the site. Whatever the plans, New Yorkers will never forget that bright, sunny Tuesday morning when the city's skyline changed forever.

What Was Your Best Celebrity Encounter?

New York seems to be home to more than its share of famous people, but even for us regular city folks, seeing a celebrity is still a thrill and a half. Sometimes it's on location at a movie shoot, and sometimes it's just waiting in line at the ATM. But it's always memorable, and we love to tell our brush-with-fame tales. *Hint:* Wait staff and hotel employees often have the best stories.

What's Your Best Apartment-Hunting War Story?

It's difficult to overstate how maddening it is to find an apartment in New York, especially in Manhattan. Every New Yorker dreams of scoring that perfect, cheap, charming apartment in a "quirky" (think seedy, but with potential) neighborhood that's on the verge of getting hot. Rumors of unimaginable rent bargains spread in the hushed whispers of a typical urban legend. Everyone has a rite-of-passage housing tale, from the guy who rented out his walk-in closet for $1,000 a month (happens all the time) to the woman whose "great find" turned out to be an apartment on the same floor as a transvestite brothel (we hope not so common). The stories never end.

Where Can I Get the Best Pizza in the City?

What does "best" mean to you? A thin, crispy crust? Oodles of cheese? Or a purity of ingredients that shouts "straight from the streets of Rome"? The competition is fierce for the title Best New York City Pizza — another subject hotly debated and never resolved. We review the three major contenders in Chapter 14: John's Pizza, in Greenwich Village, Times Square and other locations throughout the city; Lombardi's, in NoLita, regarded as the city's very first pizzeria; and Patsy's Pizza, which originated in Harlem and now has locations around the city. So take an informal poll, have a taste test or two, and you'll end your trip as a true pizza expert.

What's Your Favorite Tabloid Headline?

The *Daily News* and the *New York Post* wage a fierce circulation war for readers, and the battle lines are drawn every day with each paper's hokey, outrageous, funny, and sometimes tasteless front-page headlines. No politician, celebrity, mob figure, or sports star is beyond the reach of the tabloid papers. Even city residents who don't read the tabs can name a few favorite headlines. Two of the classics are the *Daily News* zinger that ran during the city's early 1970s financial crisis: "FORD TO CITY: DROP DEAD!"; and the front page so famous it spawned a T-shirt: the *New York Post* gem "HEADLESS BODY IN TOPLESS BAR."

Which Restaurant Is New York's Best-Kept Secret?

Every person in this city knows of a special, out-of-the-way place that's romantic, welcoming, affordable, and delicious — the place that's perfect for a first date, a birthday celebration, or a parent-sponsored splurge. The kind of place you could spend hours in, catching up with an old friend, knowing the staff would never hustle you out. We found some of our most favorite restaurants through shared tips and overheard conversations. So ask around, and savor the fruits of your quest.

How Do You Get to Carnegie Hall?

Hee hee — we couldn't resist. Just for kicks, see if anyone recognizes this older-than-dirt joke and responds with the correct punch line ("Practice, practice, practice . . .").

Appendix

Quick Concierge

● ●

Ambulance

Call ☎ 911.

American Express

Several locations, including Macy's in Herald Square (Sixth Avenue at 34th Street, ☎ 212-695-8075); for other New York branches, call ☎ 800-AXP-TRIP.

Area Codes

The area codes for Manhattan are 212 and 646. The area code for the Bronx, Brooklyn, Queens, and Staten Island is 718.

ATMs

ATMs are virtually everywhere in New York — even inside small shops, delis, supermarkets, and some restaurants. Banks are on almost every corner in commercial districts; finding one may be harder in less touristed or commerical areas. Most ATMs now accept cards on both the PLUS and Cirrus networks. For information about PLUS ATM locations, call ☎ 800-843-7587 or try www.visa.com. For Cirrus locations, call ☎ 800-424-7787 or try www.mastercard.com.

Baby-sitters

We discuss baby-sitting in Chapter 4. Try the Baby Sitters Guild (☎ 212-682-0227) or the Frances Stewart Agency (☎ 212-439-9222).

Doctors

For an emergency, go to a hospital emergency room (see the "Hospitals" listing later in this appendix). Walk-in clinics can handle minor ailments; one example is New York Healthcare Immediate Care, 55 E. 34th St. between Park and Madison avenues (☎ 212-252-6001), open Mon–Fri 8 a.m.–7 p.m. and Sat–Sun 9 a.m.–2 p.m. The charge is $100 for a visit. Doctors on Call (☎ 212-737-2333) connects you with doctors who make house calls and is available 24 hours a day.

Emergencies

For police, fire, and ambulance, call 911. For the Poison Control Center, call ☎ 212-764-7667 or 212-340-4494.

Hospitals

From south to north, here are the numbers of specific Manhattan hospitals: New York Downtown Hospital, 170 William St. at Beeckman Street, near City Hall (☎ 212-312-5000); St. Vincent's Hospital, Seventh Avenue at 11th Street (☎ 212-604-7000); Beth Israel Medical Center, First Avenue at 16th Street (☎ 212-420-2000); Bellevue Hospital Center, First Avenue at 27th Street (☎ 212-562-4141); New York University Medical Center, First Avenue at 33rd Street (☎ 212-263-7300); Roosevelt Hospital Center, Tenth Avenue at 58th Street (☎ 212-523-4000); New York Hospital Emergency Pavilion, York Avenue at 70th Street (☎ 212-746-5050); Lenox Hill Hospital, 77th Street between Park and Lexington avenues (☎ 212-434-2000); St. Luke's Hospital Center, Amsterdam Avenue at 113th Street (☎ 212-523-4000).

Hotlines

The 24-hour Crime Victim Hotline is ☎ 212-577-7777; the Sex Crime Report Line is ☎ 212-267-7273. For local police precinct numbers, call ☎ 212-374-5000; the Department of Consumer Affairs is at ☎ 212-487-4444.

Information

For tourist information, call NYC & Company (formerly the Convention and Visitors Bureau) at ☎ 212-484-1222 or 212-397-8222 (Internet: www.nycvisit.com). For telephone directory information, dial ☎ 411 or the area code you're calling plus 555-1212. These calls are free from Verizon public pay phones. Not all public pay phones in New York are affiliated with Verizon, and the ones owned by other companies charge for 411 calls. It's also worth noting that Verizon has dropped the price of a local call from 50¢ to 25¢ at its own pay phones. For more sources of information, consult "Where to Get More Information," later in this appendix.

Internet Access and Cyber Cafes

Some of the hotels we recommend now offer the option of checking your e-mail even if you didn't bring your laptop along; the alternative is one of the Internet cafes in town. EasyInternetCafé, 234 W. 42nd St. between Seventh and Eighth avenues (☎ 212-398-0724, 212-398-0775; Internet: www.easyinternetcafe.com; open 24 hours), has 800 computers and no minimum charge. The price per minute depends on the number of people using the facilities: The more demand, the higher the price, but it's always very reasonable. You get a pre-paid card from a machine for the amount of money you want, say $3; the card is valid for 30 days and enables you to log on as many times as you want at the going rate. Other choices are NY Computer Café, 247 E. 57th St. between Second and Third avenues (☎ 212-872-1704; Internet: www.nycomputercafe.com; open Mon–Fri 8 a.m.–11 p.m., Sat 10 a.m.–11 p.m., Sun 11 a.m.–11 p.m.), which charges $3 per 15 minutes; and CyberCafe, with two locations: one at 273 Lafayette St. at Prince Street (☎ 212-334-5140, open Mon–Fri 8:30 a.m.–10:00 p.m., Sat–Sun 10 a.m.–10 p.m.) and the other at 250 W. 49th St. between Broadway and Eighth Avenue (☎ 212-333-4109, open Mon–Fri 8:30 a.m.–11:00 p.m.,

Sat–Sun 11 a.m.–11 p.m.). Its Web site is www.cyber-cafe.com, and it charges $6.50 per 30 minutes minimum.

Liquor Laws

The minimum legal age to buy and consume alcoholic beverages in New York is 21. Liquor and wine are sold only at licensed stores, which are closed on Sundays, holidays, and election days while the polls are open. You can purchase beer at grocery stores, delis, and supermarkets 24 hours a day, except on Sundays before noon.

Maps

Transit maps for the subways and buses are available free at token booths inside subway stations and at public libraries; bus maps are also available on the buses. Free city maps are available at hotels inside the free city guides. To buy maps of all kinds, go to Hagstrom Map and Travel Center, 57 W. 43rd St. between Fifth and Sixth avenues (☎ 212-398-1222; open Mon–Fri 9:00 a.m.–5:30 p.m.), or Rand McNally Map & Travel Center, 150 E. 52nd St. between Lexington and Third avenues (☎ 212-758-7488; open Mon–Fri 9 a.m.–7 p.m., Sat 10 a.m.–6 p.m., Sun noon–5 p.m.). For simple New York City street maps, go to any of the bookstores in town.

Newspapers/Magazines

The three major daily newspapers are the *New York Times*, the *New York Daily News*, and the *New York Post*. Two weekly newspapers distributed free in the city are the *New York Press* and the *Village Voice* (Wednesdays). The *New Yorker* is a weekly magazine that publishes listings of local events, news features, criticism, and short stories. *New York* magazine, also weekly, publishes news and commentaries about the city, along with well-regarded restaurant, film, and theater reviews. *Time Out New York* is an indispensable weekly service-oriented magazine that offers dining, music, and entertainment reviews, shopping news, and insider advice about living in the city, as well as an exhaustive compilation of local events.

Pharmacies

Here are two 24-hour pharmacies, both members of the Duane Reade chain: One is at Broadway and 57th Street (☎ 212-541-9708); the other is at Third Avenue and 74th Street (☎ 212-744-2668). In addition, CVS and Rite Aid have branches throughout the city. For homeopathic cures and other natural medicines, try C.O. Bigelow Pharmacy, 414 Sixth Avenue between 8th and 9th streets (☎ 212-533-2700).

Police

Dial ☎ **911** for emergencies and ☎ **212-374-5000** for the phone number of the nearest police precinct.

Radio Stations

Find National Public Radio on WFUV-FM 90.7, WNYC-AM 820, and WNYC-FM 93.9. WBAI-FM 99.5 and the cluster of college radio stations at the lower end of the radio dial broadcast an interesting mix of music and talk. WQHT-FM 97.1 plays hip-hop and R&B. Find salsa and merengue on the mostly Spanish-language WSKQ-FM 97.9, classical on WNYC-FM 93.9, country on WYNY-FM 107.1, classic rock on WAXQ-FM 104.3, modern rock on WXRK-FM 92.3, light rock at WQCD 101.9, and top 40 and contemporary hits at WPLJ-FM 95.5 and WHTZ-FM 100.3. Yankees games are broadcast on WCBS-AM 880, and WINS-AM 1010 is an all-news station that provides traffic and weather reports every ten minutes. WFAN-AM 660 is an all-sports station.

Restrooms

There are public restroom facilities in all transportation terminals — Grand Central Terminal, Penn Station, and the Port Authority Bus Terminal; in Central Park and Bryant Park; and in the New York Public Library and some other branch libraries — but in some of these places, cleanliness may leave much to be desired. Department stores, museums, and large hotels have wonderful restrooms. If you see a sign in a restaurant that says, "Restrooms for customers only," you may have to buy a token snack or beverage in order to use the facilities.

Safety

New York is reasonably safe, much more so than it was even ten years ago. Still, it's a good idea to keep in mind a few basic tips. The number-one rule is to trust your instincts: If it feels unsafe, it probably is, so go elsewhere. Don't flash money or check your wallet in public; pickpockets sometimes loiter near ATM machines to fleece unsuspecting customers. Modesty pays; keep valuables out of sight. Don't leave a purse or jacket with a wallet inside hanging on your chair in a restaurant; someone could brush by and snag it while you're enjoying your meal. Although most hotel room doors lock automatically these days, it pays to double-check when you're coming and going. Subway stations have off-hours waiting areas, usually near the entrances, with camera surveillance; look for the signs overhead. In the unlikely and unfortunate event that you are mugged, don't be foolish enough to resist. Give the mugger what he or she wants, get to a safe place, and call the police.

Taxes

The tax on food and other goods is 8.25%. Since March 2000, purchases of clothes and shoes under $110 carry no sales tax. Hotel taxes are 13.25% plus a room charge of $2 per night.

Taxis

Authorized, legal taxis in Manhattan are yellow. Yellow cabs have city medallions posted inside the vehicles that have the driver's name and identification number, in case you need to lodge a complaint (or, heaven forbid, if you leave something in the cab and need to track down the driver). A taxi will cost you $2 just for stepping in the door, plus 30¢ per ⅕ mile or 20¢ a minute while you're stuck in traffic. The average fare within Manhattan is $5.25.

Transit Info

For ground transportation to and from all the area airports, call Air-Ride (☎ 800-247-7433). For all transit information, call the MTA (Metropolitan Transit Authority) Transit Information Center (☎ 718-330-1234; operators available daily 6 a.m.–9 p.m.).

Toll-Free Numbers and Web Sites

Airlines

For the latest on airline Web sites, check out www.air.findhere.com.

Aer Lingus
☎ 800-474-7424 in the U.S.
☎ 01-886-8888 in Ireland
www.aerlingus.com

Air Canada
☎ 888-247-2262
www.aircanada.ca

Air New Zealand
☎ 800-262-1234 or -2468 in the U.S.
☎ 800-663-5494 in Canada
☎ 0800-737-767 in New Zealand
www.airnewzealand.com

Airtran Airlines
☎ 800-247-8726
www.airtran.com

Alaska Airlines
☎ 800-426-0333
www.alaskaair.com

American Airlines
☎ 800-433-7300
www.aa.com

American Trans Air
☎ 800-225-2995
www.ata.com

America West Airlines
☎ 800-235-9292
www.americawest.com

British Airways
☎ 800-247-9297
☎ 0345-222-111 or 0845-77-333-77 in Britain
www.british-airways.com

Continental Airlines
☎ 800-525-0280
www.continental.com

Delta Air Lines
☎ 800-221-1212
www.delta.com

Frontier Airlines
☎ 800-432-1359
www.frontierairlines.com

Jet Blue Airlines
☎ 800-538-2583
www.jetblue.com

Midway Airlines
☎ 800-446-4392
www.midwayair.com

Midwest Express
☎ 800-452-2022
www.midwestexpress.com

National Airlines
☎ 888-757-5387
www.nationalairlines.com

Northwest Airlines
☎ 800-225-2525
www.nwa.com

Qantas
☎ 800-227-4500 in the U.S.
☎ 61-2-9691-3636 in Australia
www.qantas.com

Southwest Airlines
☎ 800-435-9792
www.southwest.com

United Airlines
☎ 800-241-6522
www.united.com

US Airways
☎ 800-428-4322
www.usairways.com

Virgin Atlantic Airways
☎ 800-862-8621 in the U.S.
☎ 0293-747-747 in Britain
www.virgin-atlantic.com

Major hotel and motel chains

Use the following information to help you get a hold of your favorite hotel or motel chain.

Best Western International
☎ 800-528-1234
www.bestwestern.com

Comfort Inns
☎ 800-228-5150
www.hotelchoice.com

Crowne Plaza Hotels
☎ 800-227-6963
www.crowneplaza.com

Doubletree Hotels
☎ 800-222-TREE
www.doubletreehotels.com

Hilton Hotels
☎ 800-HILTONS
www.hilton.com

Holiday Inn
☎ 800-HOLIDAY
www.holiday-inn.com

Hyatt Hotels & Resorts
☎ 800-228-9000
www.hyatt.com

Inter-Continental Hotels & Resorts
☎ 888-567-8725
www.interconti.com

ITT Sheraton
☎ 800-325-3535
www.sheraton.com

Marriott Hotels
☎ 800-228-9290
www.marriott.com

Quality Inns
☎ 800-228-5151
www.hotelchoice.com

Radisson Hotels International
☎ 800-333-3333
www.radisson.com

Super 8 Motels
☎ 800-800-8000
www.super8.com

Westin Hotels & Resorts
☎ 800-937-8461
www.westin.com

Wyndham Hotels & Resorts
☎ 800-996-3426 in the U.S. and Canada
www.wyndham.com

Where to Get More Information

We packed this book with information, but if you still haven't had enough, you can consult the following resources for additional info.

General interest information

NYC & Company (the former Convention and Visitors Bureau) offers a 24-hour telephone hotline (☎ 800-NYC-VISIT, 212-397-8222) that you can call to order a kit, which includes a 100-page Big Apple Visitor Guide plus a map and other materials; you pay only shipping, and you should receive it in seven days. The guide, which you can order separately (and for free), contains tons of information about hotels, restaurants, theaters, events, and so on and is updated quarterly. NYC & Co. also maintains a Visitor Information Center at 810 Seventh Ave. between 52nd and 53rd streets (☎ 212-484-1222; open Monday through Friday 8:30 a.m. to 6:00 p.m., weekends and holidays 9:00 a.m. to 5:00 p.m.; mailing address 810 Seventh Ave., New York, NY 10019).

You can get information about current theater productions over the phone through NYC/On Stage (☎ 212-768-1818) and the Broadway Line (☎ 888-BROADWAY, 212-563-2929, 212-302-4111).

For all transit information, call the MTA Transit Information Center (☎ 718-330-1234). Call ☎ 718-330-3322 for a copy of Token Trips Travel Guide, a brochure that gives you instructions on how to get to New York City's main attractions via mass transit.

Air-Ride (☎ 800-247-7433) is a service that provides recorded information about ground transportation from all the area airports.

Here are some of the more useful online sources:

- **Citysearch** (Internet: www.newyork.citysearch.com) is another comprehensive, user-friendly site that lists tons of entertainment and dining prospects. The listings are ample and the reviews quite useful. Citysearch is now associated with NYC & Company (later in this list).

- You can access bus and subway maps and information at the **MTA (Metropolitan Transit Authority)** Web site, www.mta.info.

- **New York City Reference** (Internet: www.panix.com/clay/nyc/) is an excellent index of links to other New York–related Web sites — a couple thousand of them — such as the Web sites of all the museums in New York.

- *The New York Times* (Internet: www.nytimes.com) is a prime site for gathering cultural information, reading reviews, and checking out the Sunday "Arts & Leisure" section. The only drawback is that you have to register and may have to pay for access to certain sections.

✔ **NYC & Company,** New York City's official tourism site (Internet: www.nycvisit.com), is the Web site of the former Convention and Visitors Bureau; it provides a wealth of information and links, and you can book hotels online.

✔ **NYC.gov** (Internet: www.nyc.gov) is the official site of the city of New York. It's very comprehensive and clear and has a bunch of useful links to sightseeing and entertainment information.

✔ www.nyctourist.com offers an excellent selection of very useful information, although it's a little more commercial than the other Web sites we list.

Some good, informative newspapers, magazines, and guides include the following:

✔ Excellent sources of information that you can find nationwide are the weekly *The New Yorker,* the daily *New York Times,* and the weekly *Time Out New York* (see the "Newspapers/Magazines" entry in the "Fast Facts" section for more information).

✔ If you want a more detailed guidebook, check out *Frommer's New York City* or *Frommer's New York City from $80 a Day.*

Additional information for travelers with children

If you're bringing your kids along on your trip to New York, you may want to get some of these printed materials before your trip:

✔ **Big Apple Parents' Paper:** 36 E. 12th St., New York, NY 10003. ☎ 212-533-2277. Fax: 212-475-6186. Internet: www.parentsknow.com. $29 per year.

✔ *Frommer's New York City with Kids:* A guidebook all about traveling to the Big Apple with children.

✔ **ParentGuide:** Parent Guide Network Corp., 419 Park Ave. S., New York, NY 10016. ☎ 212-213-8840. Fax: 212-447-7734. Internet: www.parentguidenews.com. $19.95 per year.

Additional information for senior travelers

The following resources may be helpful to seniors:

✔ *The Book of Deals,* published by GEM Publishing Group, is a collection of more than 1,000 senior discounts on airlines, lodging, tours, and attractions around the country; it's available for $9.95 by calling ☎ 800-460-6676.

- ✔ *The Mature Traveler,* a monthly 12-page newsletter on senior citizen travel, is a valuable resource that's available by subscription ($30 a year) from GEM Publishing Group, Box 50400, Reno, NV 89513-0400.

- ✔ *101 Tips for the Mature Traveler,* available from Grand Circle Travel, 347 Congress Street, Suite 3A, Boston, MA 02210 (☎ 800-221-2610 or 617-350-7500; Fax: 617-350-6206), is another useful publication.

Additional information for travelers with disabilities

The following resources may be helpful to travelers with disabilities:

- ✔ **MTA (Metropolitan Transit Authority)** gives information about public transportation in the city at the following numbers: Accessible Travel Information (☎ 718-596-8585), 6 a.m. to 9 p.m. eastern time; the 24-hour escalator and elevator hotline (☎ 800-734-6772, TTY 718-596-8273); and Customer Service (☎ 718-330-3322).

- ✔ **The Travel Information Service** (☎ 215-456-9603, TTY 215-456-9602) gives you more personal assistance in your travel needs.

- ✔ *A World of Options,* a 658-page book of resources for disabled travelers, covers everything from biking trips to scuba outfitters. It costs $30 plus $5 shipping and is available from Mobility International USA, P.O. Box 10767, Eugene, OR 97440 (☎ 541-343-1284, voice and TTY; Internet: www.miusa.org).

Making Dollars and Sense of It

Expense	Daily cost	x	Number of days	=	Total
Airfare					
Local transportation					
Car rental					
Lodging (with tax)					
Parking					
Breakfast					
Lunch					
Dinner					
Snacks					
Entertainment					
Babysitting					
Attractions					
Gifts & souvenirs					
Tips					
Other					
Grand Total					

Fare Game: Choosing an Airline

When looking for the best airfare, you should cover all your bases — 1) consult a trusted travel agent; 2) contact the airline directly, via the airline's toll-free number and/or Web site; 3) check out one of the travel-planning Web sites, such as www.frommers.com.

Travel Agency_____ Phone_____

    Agent's Name_____ Quoted fare_____

Airline 1_____ Quoted fare_____

    Toll-free number/Internet_____

Airline 2_____ Quoted fare_____

    Toll-free number/Internet_____

Web site 1_____ Quoted fare_____

Web site 2_____ Quoted fare_____

Departure Schedule & Flight Information

Airline_____ Flight #_____ Confirmation #_____

Departs_____ Date_____ Time_____ a.m./p.m.

Arrives_____ Date_____ Time_____ a.m./p.m.

Connecting Flight (if any)

Amount of time between flights_____ hours/mins

Airline_____ Flight #_____ Confirmation #_____

Departs_____ Date_____ Time_____ a.m./p.m.

Arrives_____ Date_____ Time_____ a.m./p.m.

Return Trip Schedule & Flight Information

Airline_____ Flight #_____ Confirmation #_____

Departs_____ Date_____ Time_____ a.m./p.m.

Arrives_____ Date_____ Time_____ a.m./p.m.

Connecting Flight (if any)

Amount of time between flights_____ hours/mins

Airline_____ Flight #_____ Confirmation #_____

Departs_____ Date_____ Time_____ a.m./p.m.

Arrives_____ Date_____ Time_____ a.m./p.m.

Sweet Dreams: Choosing Your Hotel

Make a list of all the hotels where you'd like to stay and then check online and call the local and toll-free numbers to get the best price. You should also check with a travel agent, who may be able to get you a better rate.

Hotel & page	Location	Internet	Tel. (local)	Tel. (Toll-free)	Quoted rate

Hotel Checklist

Here's a checklist of things to inquire about when booking your room, depending on your needs and preferences.

❏ Smoking/smoke-free room

❏ Noise (if you prefer a quiet room, ask about proximity to elevator, bar/restaurant, pool, meeting facilities, renovations, and street)

❏ View

❏ Facilities for children (crib, roll-away cot, babysitting services)

❏ Facilities for travelers with disabilities

❏ Number and size of bed(s) (king, queen, double/full-size)

❏ Is breakfast included? (buffet, continental, or sit-down?)

❏ In-room amenities (hair dryer, iron/board, minibar, etc.)

❏ Other_____

Places to Go, People to See, Things to Do

Enter the attractions you would most like to see and decide how they'll fit into your schedule. Next, use the "Going My Way" worksheets that follow to sketch out your itinerary.

Attraction/activity	Page	Amount of time you expect to spend there	Best day and time to go

Going "My" Way

Day 1

Hotel_____ Tel._____
Morning_____
_____

Lunch_____ Tel._____
Afternoon_____
_____

Dinner_____ Tel._____
Evening_____
_____

Day 2

Hotel_____ Tel._____
Morning_____
_____

Lunch_____ Tel._____
Afternoon_____
_____

Dinner_____ Tel._____
Evening_____
_____

Day 3

Hotel_____ Tel._____
Morning_____
_____

Lunch_____ Tel._____
Afternoon_____
_____

Dinner_____ Tel._____
Evening_____
_____

Going "My" Way

Day 4

Hotel_____ Tel._____

Morning_____

_____

Lunch_____ Tel._____

Afternoon_____

_____

Dinner_____ Tel._____

Evening_____

_____

Day 5

Hotel_____ Tel._____

Morning_____

_____

Lunch_____ Tel._____

Afternoon_____

_____

Dinner_____ Tel._____

Evening_____

_____

Day 6

Hotel_____ Tel._____

Morning_____

_____

Lunch_____ Tel._____

Afternoon_____

_____

Dinner_____ Tel._____

Evening_____

_____

Index

• D •

311

• *Restaurants* •